MOZART

Series edited by Stanley Sadie

THE MASTER MUSICIANS

Titles Available in Paperback

Berlioz • Hugh Macdonald   *Puccini* • Julian Budden

Brahms • Malcolm MacDonald   *Purcell* • J. A. Westrup

Britten • Michael Kennedy   *Rossini* • Richard Osborne

Chopin • Jim Samson   *Schumann* • Eric Frederick Jensen

Handel • Donald Burrows   *Richard Strauss* • Michael Kennedy

Liszt • Derek Watson   *Tchaikovsky* • Edward Garden

Mahler • Michael Kennedy   *Vaughan Williams* • James Day

Mendelssohn • Philip Radcliffe   *Vivaldi* • Michael Talbot

Monteverdi • Denis Arnold

Titles Available in Hardcover

J. S. Bach • Malcolm Boyd   *Musorgsky* • David Brown

Beethoven • Barry Cooper   *Schütz* • Basil Smallman

THE MASTER MUSICIANS

MOZART

Julian Rushton

OXFORD
UNIVERSITY PRESS

2 0 0 6

OXFORD
UNIVERSITY PRESS

Oxford University Press, Inc., publishes works that
further Oxford University's objective of excellence
in research, scholarship, and education.

Oxford   New York

Auckland   Cape Town   Dar es Salaam   Hong Kong   Karachi
Kuala Lumpur   Madrid   Melbourne   Mexico City   Nairobi
New Delhi   Shanghai   Taipei   Toronto

With offices in

Argentina   Austria   Brazil   Chile   Czech Republic   France   Greece
Guatemala   Hungary   Italy   Japan   Poland   Portugal   Singapore
South Korea   Switzerland   Thailand   Turkey   Ukraine   Vietnam

Published by Oxford University Press, Inc.
198 Madison Avenue, New York, NY 10016
www.oup.com

Oxford is a registered trademark of Oxford University Press

Library of Congress Cataloging-in-Publication Data
Rushton, Julian.
Mozart / Julian Rushton
p. cm.—(The master musicians)
Includes bibliographic references and index.
Contents: Salzburg and the grand tour : 1756–69—Works by an "almost supernatural talent"—Italy : 1769–
73—Opera seria : "fitting the clothes to the figure"—Salzburg : 1774–77—Sacred music : "I have thoroughly
acquainted myself with that style since my youth"—Mannheim and Paris : 1777–79—The "classical style" :
Mozart and the keyboard—Salzburg and Munich : 1779–81—Orchestral music : "the glorious effect of a
symphony with flutes, oboes, and clarinets"—Vienna : 1781–85—Singspiel : "music must never offend the
ear"—Piano concertos and chamber music in "the land of the clavier"—Vienna and Prague : 1786–88—
Chamber music : "the greatest composer known to me"—Opera buffa : "most important is that it must be
really comic"—The last years : 1788–91—The last works : "a rich possession, but even fairer hopes"—"—de
morte transire ad vitam".
ISBN-13: 978-019-518264-4
ISBN-10: 0-19-518264-2
1. Mozart, Wolfgang Amadeus, 1756–1791—Chronology.   2. Composers— Austria—Biography.   I. Title
II. The master musicians series.

ML410.M9R87 2006
780'.92—dc22
[B]   2005021058

Illustrations of insert courtesy of the Internationale Stiftung Mozarteum (ISM).

1 3 5 7 9 8 6 4 2

Printed in the United States of America
on acid-free paper

Contents

Preface

Mozart was prolific; he died when not quite thirty-six, but his essentially adult compositions span two-thirds of that short life. His works fall readily into categories—chamber, orchestral, church, or dramatic music—and the shorter units that make them up can usually be classified as variations, fantasias, sonata forms, rondos, arias, ensembles, finales. He had habits; no one could have written so much in so short a time without them. He adopted conventions more than he adapted them, and was certainly no reformer. But as he developed, in his middle years (from his late teens), each of his works becomes increasingly individualised rather than merely representative of a type. This must stand as an assertion; a book of this length cannot include the style analysis of his contemporaries necessary to support it. Nor, considering his life, can I report more than briefly on what we know of his lifestyle, beliefs, income and, most controversial of all, the cause of his death. I can only state what I believe on present evidence to be the case. There is no space for opera plots, and many favourite works receive no more than a passing mention. The works that are discussed are not immune from specific criticisms, for Mozart no longer needs an advocate before an uncomprehending world. For musical examples, I have tried to select passages to illustrate specific points, rather than for the pleasure of seeing them in print yet again. There are longer biographical and musical studies, and handbooks on individual works, but even these may be silent or reticent on aspects of, say, *Don Giovanni* or *Die Zauberflöte* that some feel to be of paramount importance, and others of transcendent beauty. The works themselves—not only the operas—appear inexhaustible, inspiring new insights that change their meaning with the passing of time.

My objective has been to supply an introduction and guide to Mozart's output, usable for reference, with the appendices (calendar, worklist, and personalia) usual in the Master Musicians series. The structure of the book itself attempts to simplify without being simplistic. I review genres of composition at gathering-points in between the chapters dealing with Mozart's life. The latter have dates in their titles, and can be read consecutively if the reader prefers. Some works are discussed a little ahead of their place in the biographical framework, but later works are given consideration on their own, in the 'life' chapters or in the final chapter on 'late works'. I have preferred this method to something more rational, but perhaps also more predictable and over-systematic. I would not go so far as the late Anthony Burgess if indeed he was speaking for himself when, in his bicentennial tribute *Mozart and the Wolf Gang,* he has Lorenzo da Ponte assert that 'Mozart's life is not worth presenting, since he neglected life for art'.[1] But nobody would take the slightest interest in Mozart's or his wife's illnesses, his debts, his relationship with his father—still less would anyone have invented love-affairs for him, and theories of his being poisoned—if his music did not compel attention to the man behind it. Conscious of my dependence on the scholarly work of many others, I hope to direct readers to some of the fascinating wealth of Mozartian literature—first, his music, but also what has been and is being written about it.

My debt to Mozart is not measurable, but is hereby acknowledged. I owe my love of his music to my parents, whose bookshelves housed a far-from-new Grove, and writings by Tovey, whose account of the piano and wind quintet (a work we could almost play en famille) fascinated me at about the age Mozart composed *Mitridate.* Several authors of literature on Mozart I am glad to count among valued friends and colleagues; other than Cliff Eisen and Dorothea Link, to whom a special thank you, I will not enumerate them, as they know who they are, but I am grateful to them all, as to others with whom I am less acquainted and some who, alas, are dead. I dedicate this work to the memory of four British Mozartians I feel honoured to have known: Bernard Williams, Alec Hyatt King, Alan Tyson, and the former editor of this series, who died just before I had the chance to submit any of my script for his scrutiny, Stanley Sadie.

Golcar, 2005   *Julian Rushton*

---

[1] Anthony Burgess, *Mozart and the 'Wolf Gang* (London: 1991), 79.

Abbreviations

Letters and contemporary documents

Letters are referred to by date and can variously be found in the comprehensive original-language publication, Bauer, Deutsch, and Eibl, *Mozart: Briefe und Aufzeichnungen*; and translated into English, the large selection, including many of Leopold Mozart's, in Emily Anderson, *The Letters of Mozart and His Family*, and a smaller selection, not quite complete even for Mozart himself, in Robert Spaethling, *Mozart's Letters, Mozart's Life*.

Documents of Mozart's life are referred to in the notes as *D-Doc* (Deutsch, O. E., *Mozart: A Documentary Biography*) and *E-Doc* (Eisen, C., *New Mozart Documents. A Supplement to O. E. Deutsch's Documentary Biography*).

Catalogues

Verzeichnüss	Mozart, *Verzeichnüss aller meine Werke*, manuscript list kept by Mozart from February 1784.
Köchel's catalogue	K1: Ludwig von Köchel, *Chronologisch-thematisches Verzeichnis sämtlicher Tonwerke* Wolfgang Amade Mozarts (Leipzig, 1862).
	K3: 3rd edition, ed. Alfred Einstein (Leipzig, 1937).
	K6: 6th edition, ed. F. Giegling, A. Weinmann, and G. Sievers (Leipzig, 1964)

Editions

NMA (Neue Mozart Ausgabe)	W. A. Mozart, *Neue Ausgabe sämtlicher Werke* (Kassel: Bärenreiter, 1955–91): the edition of Mozart's works was completed in 1991, but volumes of the critical commentary, and ancillary volumes, are still appearing.

Most notes give the name of the author and a full title, but for convenience some are abbreviated:

Halliwell, *Family*	Halliwell, R., *The Mozart Family*
Landon, *Golden Years*	Landon, H. C. R., *Mozart. The Golden Years, 1781–1791*
Landon, *1791*	Landon, H. C. R., *1791, Mozart's Last Year*
Link, *Court Theatre*	Link, D., *The National Court Theatre in Mozart's Vienna*
Link, *Words about Mozart*	Link, D., ed., with J. Nagley, *Words About Mozart: Essays in Honour of Stanley Sadie*
Sadie, *Wolfgang Amadè Mozart*	Sadie, S., ed., *Wolfgang Amadè Mozart. Essays on his Life and Music*
TNG2: (The New Grove 2)	Sadie, S., ed., *The New Grove Dictionary of Music and Musicians*, 2nd ed. (London, 2001), in 29 vols. Also available on line, edited by Laura Macy
Tyson, *Autograph Scores*	Tyson, A., *Mozart: Studies of the Autograph Scores*
Tyson, 'New Dates'	Tyson, A., 'Proposed New Dates for Many Works and Fragments Written by Mozart from March 1781 to December 1791', in Eisen, C., ed., *Mozart Studies*
Zaslaw, *Symphonies*	Zaslaw, N., *Mozart's Symphonies: Context, Performance Practice, Reception*

Zaslaw, *Piano Concertos*   Zaslaw, N., ed., *Mozart's Piano Concertos. Text, Context, Interpretation*

Full bibliographical details are in Select Bibliography.

Pitch notation: c'–b' represents the octave from middle C. Thus c–b forms the octave below; C–B the octave from the cello's lowest string; the octave from c''' begins above the treble-clef staff; the highest note for the Queen of Night is f'''.

CHAPTER I

Salzburg and the Grand Tour

1756–1769

THE COMPOSER'S FATHER, JOHANN GEORG LEOPOLD MOZART, was born in Augsburg, Bavaria, in November 1719; his mother, Anna Maria Walburga Pertl, was baptised on Christmas day 1720 at St Gilgen, an outlying settlement dependent on Salzburg. Leopold moved to Salzburg as a student, then as an employee: valet de chambre, then violinist and composer in the Kapelle of the ruling prince-archbishop of Salzburg and primate of Germany. After a long courtship, the 'handsomest couple in Salzburg' were married on 21 November 1747. Over the next ten years, they had seven children. The fourth, and the first to survive infancy, was Maria Anna Walburga Ignatia, known as Nannerl, born at the end of July 1751. She was a gifted musician, and if her importance in inspiring her younger brother by example cannot be measured, it was surely immense. When the family first went abroad, Nannerl was the keyboard prodigy. In adulthood she played and taught, but only locally, and domestically. What might have been her lot had Wolfgang died in infancy is speculative, for an international career was not impossible for a female pianist. Her compositions are unfortunately lost. In a letter from Rome (7 July 1770), Wolfgang praised one of her songs and urged her to write more. Leopold probably did little to develop her skills in that direction, but there is no sign that she resented this; her horizons, like her father's, were bounded by the expectations of the day, which made natural Leopold's concentration on the exceptionally gifted boy.

The seventh child and second to survive was the composer, born on 27 January 1756 and baptised the next day as Joannes Chrysostomus Wolfgangus Theophilus. As with his father, the first two names were normally not used. Instead of Theophilus, Mozart used the German equivalent, Gottlieb, but more often Italian versions: at first Amadeo, later Amadè (or, with characteristic indifference to diacriticals, Amadé), rarely the Latin Amadeus. In early publications he is J. G., J. G. W., A. or A. W. Mozart.[1] He was born into a household neither wealthy nor indigent. Leopold could rent a decent home in which his wife supervised domestic arrangements, assisted by a few servants. Leopold's duties allowed him enough freedom to cultivate a wide circle of friends among the minor nobility and Salzburg's merchant class, one of whom was his landlord. He also had time to educate his children; neither attended any school. Their home was a loving and stable environment that survived many absences and, in Mozart's teenage years, severance of the family into the travelling men and stay-at-home women.

The Mozarts' sense of nationality does not correspond to modern political boundaries. The ethnically diverse domains inherited, won, and married into by the ruling Habsburgs embraced modern Hungary and Bohemia (both nominally kingdoms), Slovakia, parts of Italy, and the Catholic Low Countries but did not include Salzburg or Bavaria. The Habsburg territories shared frangible borders with the Russian and Turkish Empires, and with Prussia; they were joined to the Catholic parts of Germany (this time including Salzburg and Bavaria) in a loose association, the Holy Roman Empire. Its head, for some centuries, was invariably a Habsburg.[2] Mozart, by modern criteria Austrian, counted himself a German composer.

The prince-archbishop of Salzburg was elected from the cathedral canons who, in turn, were drawn from noble families, not confined to the region; in their travels within the Empire, including Vienna, the Mozarts were to meet close relatives of people they knew in Salzburg. In childhood, through his father, Mozart formed a network of associations

---

[1] See Gertraut Haberkamp, *Die Erstdrück der Werke von Wolfgang Amadeus Mozart* (Tutzing, 1986).

[2] Strictly, the first emperor Mozart met, Francis, was from the house of Lorraine (Lothringen), but his elevation depended on his marriage to Maria Theresia, heiress of the Habsburgs.

with minor nobility that generally served him well, in addition to serving as a topic of gossip in the family letters. In 1753, Leopold's employer Archbishop Dietrichstein was succeeded by Siegmund, Count Schrattenbach, a man of kindly disposition who permitted Leopold Mozart to travel abroad with his gifted children. This generosity he could afford (he also paid some of the costs) because his musical establishment included another half-dozen composers competent to provide new music for the liturgy, for public entertainment, and for domestic consumption.

During the reign of Schrattenbach's successor, Hieronymus Colloredo, Wolfgang Mozart railed against the provinciality of Salzburg. But even then a less partisan observer might have rated the musical establishment highly among smaller German cities. A list of personnel, possibly supplied by Leopold Mozart and published by Marpurg in 1757, shows that musical activity was vigorous and varied.[3] The university, run by the church, allowed leeway for secular activities, and its annual summer celebrations were occasions for the performance of instrumental serenades, generally designated 'Finalmusik'. There was no opera company, but dramatic works were presented at court and in the university, which staged an annual graduation drama (Finalkomödie) until its theatre was closed in 1778. Operas could be presented on special occasions, such as the inauguration of a new archbishop or to impress visiting dignitaries. A public theatre was opened in 1775, and the city was included in the itinerary of travelling troupes performing German plays and operas (Singspiel). Beside what was introduced by visiting artists, music originating elsewhere found its way to Salzburg in published form or, more usually, in manuscript copies. Communications were generally good, and the city is close to Munich and, at least as the crow flies, Italy.

In a city ruled by a dignitary of the church, richly textured church music was part of the tradition, although nothing in the Mozarts' time matched the complexity of the Missa Salisburgensis in fifty-three parts (1682) attributed to Heinrich Biber. Marpurg lists only eight specialist violinists, but a larger string ensemble was available because several wind and brass players also played violin or cello; Leopold Mozart, if indeed he was Marpurg's informant, said that several of these instrumentalists

3 F. W. Marpurg, *Historisch-kritische Beyträge zur Aufnahme der Musik* (Berlin, 1757); an English translation of the information on Salzburg is in Zaslaw, *Symphonies*, 550–57.

played very well. There were no orchestral clarinets even in 1780, Mozart's last year in Salzburg, but other woodwind and horns were available as well as trombones, mainly used for church music; there were no fewer than ten trumpeters, with two timpanists. The singers comprised fifteen or so treble choristers, supported by adult male sopranos (castrati), and 'gentlemen of the choir'—three altos, eight tenors, and eight basses. Female singers, excluded from church, were available for dramatic and vocal chamber music, including two sisters called Lipp, one of whom married Johann Michael Haydn, and the other, the violinist Antonio Brunetti. Ernst Eberlin became Kapellmeister in 1749, succeeded in 1762 by Giuseppe Lolli. Eberlin's son-in-law, Leopold's friend Anton Cajetan Adlgasser (1729–77), was already the cathedral organist. Although prone to refer to themselves as 'Kapellmeister', neither Leopold nor Wolfgang Mozart could strictly be said to bear that title. In 1763, Leopold became deputy Kapellmeister, but this was to be his last promotion; Colloredo wanted his forces led by Italians (such as Lolli) who, to Leopold's justifiable annoyance, were paid more than Germans of equivalent or greater talent. In any case, he displeased Colloredo partly through overzealous promotion of his son.

Leopold Mozart is one of many composers who suffer from our retrospective division of the eighteenth century into 'high' baroque (Handel, Bach, Rameau) and mature 'classical'. Musicians in mid-century did not consider themselves to be working in a silver age; on the contrary, their world was filled with compositional innovation, mainly in opera and orchestral music, and in the development of new instruments and playing techniques. To Leopold's generation belong C. P. E. Bach, Gluck, and Jommelli, all born in 1714, as well as the short-lived Pergolesi. Several of the most famous opera composers of the century, including Piccinni and Traetta, were born in the late 1720s. From the next decade came Johann Christian Bach, Johann Schobert, and the Haydn brothers who lived long enough (notably Franz Joseph) to become identified with a 'high classical' style.[4] Long overshadowed by his elder brother, Johann Michael Haydn settled in Salzburg in 1763. Reference to Haydn in the Mozart family correspondence is usually to Michael, whose marriage and vagaries provided a source of gossip. Like Leopold, he was never a full Kapellmeister, but he

4 See for instance Charles Rosen, *The Classical Style. Haydn, Mozart, Beethoven.*

is now recognised as a considerable composer of symphonic and church music that certainly had an effect on his younger colleague.

The modern musical idiom, the 'style galant', was permitted in church, even encouraged by the presence of an orchestra and accomplished solo singers. The generation of Leopold Mozart and Adlgasser was well versed in galant idioms, while respecting the convention by which the learned style of counterpoint could be integrated into liturgical settings. The young Mozart was ready to conform to these church music traditions, and in his years in Salzburg he contributed Mass settings, litanies, vespers, and instrumental sonatas. Leopold Mozart composed more than thirty multi-movement instrumental collections of Finalmusik, combining characteristic pieces (marches, minuets) with symphonic and concerto movements; Wolfgang in turn contributed several more. According to the 1757 account, two of Leopold's colleagues, Caspar Cristelli and Ferdinand Seidl, composed only 'chamber music', a term including symphonies and concertos (performed in grand houses rather than concert halls) as well as smaller ensembles such as string quartets.

Despite extensive demands on their compositional and performing energies, Leopold and his colleagues also met privately to make music, surely a powerful factor in the rapid development of his children. He was keenly aware of intellectual developments, taking an interest in contemporary philosophers, some of them freethinkers, while himself retaining a strong allegiance to Catholicism. Recent research has partly removed Leopold's compositions from his son's shadow, but his most celebrated work, which shows his intelligence and industry and also his opportunism, was the violin tutor (*Versuch einer gründlichen Violinschule*) published in the year of Wolfgang's birth. Taking as models recent works by Quantz for flute and C. P. E. Bach for keyboard, Leopold filled an obvious gap. His compositions had mainly a local use and reputation, but the *Violinschule* aroused international interest, being translated into Dutch and French, and gained him a reputation that extended beyond the musical profession, helping to open doors when the family ventured abroad. Leopold's own development as a composer was eventually subsumed by his determination to devote himself to nourishing the 'gift from God', as he piously referred to his son.

Not long after Wolfgang Mozart's death, his public image became clouded in legend, often false but still part of the semipopular culture of 'classical' music. At least his brilliance as a young child is no legend: Mozart the prodigy, the *Wunderkind*, was a reality. His early success carried its penalty. In Paris, at the age of twenty-two, he complained that he was still considered a child; even after his death, his sister, whom he had hardly seen for ten years, disloyally claimed that, other than musically, he had never grown up. Whole books, mingling fact and fiction, have been written about his earliest years, glossing over the time when he wrote his greatest music. Maynard Solomon argues that Leopold's upbringing of Mozart, designedly or otherwise, enforced a childish dependence from which Leopold was reluctant to see his son escape.[5]

What distinguished Mozart's childhood from that of other *Wunderkinder* was less his musical accomplishment than the fact that he and Nannerl were displayed to the courts and the public at home and abroad. Mozart's exact contemporary Thomas Linley, who played a violin concerto in public at the age of seven, first went abroad at fourteen, meeting Mozart, already a seasoned traveller, in Italy. Leopold's activities were conditioned by the thought that having lost five children in early infancy, he might lose one or both of the survivors at any time. He may have risked their health and jeopardized their normal development by showing them off abroad, but in the context of the time his behaviour seems less exploitative than it would appear today. There seems no reason to doubt his sincerity in believing that it was his sacred duty to develop and make known his children's gifts.

Since Nannerl was taking lessons, her small brother naturally wanted to join in. Evidence of his precocity is contained in the notebook of simple keyboard pieces by various composers, intended for Nannerl, in which Leopold occasionally wrote that 'Wolfgangerl' had learned a piece in his fourth year.[6] In an age when performers, including Leopold, were also composers, it was just as natural that he soon started to scribble on music paper. Anecdotes of his childhood come from Johann Andreas Schachtner, one of the court trumpeters, who according to the 1857 report played the violin 'especially well'.[7] Perhaps we need not believe that Mozart wrote an intelligible piano concerto at the age of four, but stories of smudged MS paper and his love of arithmetic ring true.

---

[5] Maynard Solomon, *Mozart, a Life*, 5–18 and especially 11–13.

[6] *Notenbuch für Anna Maria Mozart*, dated 1759, and transcribed in NMA Series IX/27 (1).

[7] Schachtner's account was written in 1792 as a letter to Nannerl, and at her request. English translation D-Doc, 451–54. See also Nannerl's notes towards a biography, ibid., 454–63.

Direct evidence of his urge towards composition comes in the form of early keyboard pieces, which Leopold helped him write down. Unfortunately, the brief catalogue of his works prepared by Leopold in 1768 is perfunctory, without incipits, and starts only with his first publication, composed when he was already seven.[8] As a performer Mozart was to be best known as a master of the keyboard, but he was also a violinist, and during the family's stay in London he took singing lessons. He sang in public, with a small voice but with perfect taste, until his voice broke during the first visit to Italy when he was fourteen.[9] He learned to understand wind instruments thoroughly, and his writing for them is among the most rewarding in the repertoire. His habit of consulting instrumentalists and singers about their capabilities was probably founded early, during the family's Grand Tour of Western Europe.

Travels of a Wunderkind

In planning their travels, Leopold played a long game. Since neither child was old enough to be employed, he may have considered seeking an appointment for himself, in a city with greater resources; he clearly hoped for profit, notwithstanding the expense of travel and living abroad (it is not clear how much he did make).[10] His other objectives included his own reentry into the world of letters, by following the *Violinschule* with a book on the education of a musical genius; hence he kept travel notes and sent long letters back to Salzburg while they were abroad.[11] But his prime aim was to show the children to the world. He

---

[8] Sonatas for piano with violin accompaniment by 'Wolfgang Mozart, agé de Sept ans' (Paris, 1764). Leopold's catalogue (*Verzeichniss alles desjenigen was dieser 12jähriger Knabe seit seinem 7ten Jahre componiert*) claims to list 'what the 12-year-old boy has written since his seventh year' (actually his eighth). It was prepared to impress Emperor Joseph II, and is now in the Bibliothèque Nationale, Paris.

[9] On Mozart as a singer see Christoph-Helmut Mahling, ' . . . new and altogether special and astonishingly difficult: Some Comments on Junia's aria in *Lucio Silla*', in Sadie, *Wolfgang Amadè Mozart*, especially 377–79.

[10] Solomon argues that he salted away a good deal of money (*Mozart. A Life*; see chap. 4, 'The Family Treasure'); Halliwell argues more convincingly to the contrary (*Family*, 265 and elsewhere).

[11] On Leopold's ambitions, see David Schroeder, *Mozart in Revolt. Strategies of Resistance, Mischief and Deception*. Nannerl's diary, as much of it as survives, is mainly a record of events, useful but providing less insight into the feelings of the family than the letters. See Halliwell, *Family*, from 215; a few entries were written by Wolfgang.

did not treat them as performing monkeys but continued their education; he made sure that they too met interesting and important musicians, and encountered the best musical productions available. Nevertheless, their schedules were exhausting, and the children were sometimes unwell, starting with Wolfgang's bout of fever in Paris. Leopold and Anna Maria cherished the children and, by loving care more than the help of doctors, enabled them to win through some terrifying periods of illness.

They started modestly with a short journey to the nearest secular prince and potential patron, Maximilian III, elector of Bavaria, whose capital, Munich, was to play an important role in Mozart's life. The visit of less than a month, in January 1762, covered Wolfgang's sixth birthday. His mother stayed at home, and if Leopold wrote to her, the letters are not extant. It must have gone well enough, because at the end of the year the whole family decamped to Vienna, and Leopold began the series of bulletins addressed to his landlord, friend, and banker, Lorenz Hagenauer. This was the visit when Wolfgang, too young to understand class distinctions, was dandled on the Imperial knee by Maria Theresia, and proposed marriage to Archduchess Maria Antonia, later queen of France.

Schrattenbach then allowed Leopold to embark on his most ambitious project, although he did not expect an absence of over three years (June 1763 to November 1766). The Mozarts went first to Munich, then on to Leopold's native Augsburg, where 'I gained little or nothing' (11 Jul 1763); it did not help that he was on poor terms with his own relations. Their next target was Duke Carl Eugen of Württemburg, whose opera at Stuttgart and summer residence at Ludwigsberg had as musical director the great Jommelli. Leopold often complained of the aristocratic tendency to keep them waiting; in addition, he decided that Jommelli was determined to thwart the interests of German musicians. They were better received at Schwetzingen, the summer palace of the most lavish of musical patrons, Carl Theodor, elector of Mannheim.[12] The children were admired, and they met and befriended members of Europe's most famous orchestra.

[12] See Daniel Heartz, *Music in European Capitals*, for biographies of Carl Eugen and Carl Theodor.

They moved on in mid-July, intending to winter in Paris. On the way, they gave concerts in Frankfurt and Mainz, one with the fourteen-year-old Goethe in the audience. They were earning useful sums, as well as receiving a variety of presents, some curiously chosen: no doubt Nannerl could wear a nice English hat, but what would children do with snuffboxes and swords? No doubt Leopold was expected to go to the trouble of selling them—'we shall soon be able to rig out a stall' (17 Oct 1763)—but in fact these baubles were brought to Salzburg to be shown off and disposed of later.[13] They travelled through Rhineland cities, then to Aachen (where the resident Habsburg paid the children in kisses) and the Austrian Netherlands, reaching Brussels on 4 October. The ruling prince, brother of the emperor, followed family tradition by keeping them waiting, but they did give a successful concert.

They reached Paris on 18 November 1763. Leopold's last letter of the year, from Versailles, mentions Mme de Pompadour, more snuffboxes, and the triumph of his children; in February he describes their kind reception by the queen, and refers to the composers Schobert (jealous, envious) and Eckard (an honest man), both of whose enterprising keyboard music Nannerl could tackle, and Wolfgang assimilate. Wolfgang was composing sonatas for keyboard and violin, soon published as his 'Oeuvre 1'. Leopold, and Wolfgang after him, took a strong dislike to French music, but they had to remain until the spring before undertaking the dangerous crossing to England.

They reached London on 23 April 1764 and remained for fifteen months. In the wealthiest capital in Europe, not only the aristocracy but also mercantile and intellectual people had time and money for culture. The predominant musical style was Italian, although one of its chief representatives was a German, J. C. Bach, who had followed Handel's route from Germany to England via Italy. The drawbacks were the weather and religion; had London been Catholic, Leopold might never have gone home. Unlike most German rulers, the still-young George III and his queen received the musical prodigies soon after their arrival and paid promptly (although only twenty-four guineas).

It was now clear that Wolfgang's exceptional gifts, in sight-reading, improvisation, and composition, were outstripping Nannerl's; Leopold's

[13] *D-Doc*, 70.

letters are filled with 'our all-powerful Wolfgang' (8 June 1764). The boy extemporised, accompanied, played an organ concerto, and, passing for seven years old (he was eight and a half), attracted attention in a city where the media were freer and more in need of sensation than elsewhere, even Paris. They intended to return to the Continent later in the year, but in July Leopold fell seriously ill. The need to remain quietly at home—they were living in rural Chelsea—and, with a ban on playing the clavier, allowed Wolfgang freedom to compose his first symphony.[14] When he recovered Leopold decided to take advantage of the winter season to make money; his revived energies were devoted to arranging concerts and publicity, cultivating musicians and patrons, and publishing a second set of Wolfgang's sonatas.[15] If the winter concerts did not fulfil Leopold's most optimistic predictions, the educational advantage to Wolfgang was enormous. The castrato Giovanni Manzuoli gave him singing lessons, and the boy wrote his first aria. Besides studying the music of J. C. Bach, Mozart may have composed viol music for his colleague Karl Friedrich Abel.[16] Mozart's gift for assimilation may have extended to Handel, whose music was still popular (especially with the king), and a response to Baroque style informs much of his work, even before his encounter with the music of J. S. Bach.

The family moved to Frith Street, Soho (now opposite Ronnie Scott's jazz club). The public was invited for a fee to hear the young musicians and test them. One visitor was Daines Barrington, whose report for the Royal Society of London was eventually published in 1771, confirming that Mozart could perform such tricks as playing with the keyboard concealed, but more interestingly that he could ape the emotional content of serious operatic music, no doubt studied with Manzuoli.[17] The fruits of the London visit ripened over the years in instrumental music—for keyboard, chamber ensembles, and orchestra—and in serious opera; only Mozart's later originality in comedy had no foundations as yet.

---

[14] Information from Nannerl; *D-Doc*, 494. From this time probably also date the sketches in the 'London notebook'.

[15] Six sonatas for keyboard with violin (K. 10–15) published with a dedication to the queen, who gave thirty guineas.

[16] Leopold's catalogue mentions solos 'für die Viola da Gamba'. Abel seems the most likely reason for writing such pieces, now lost. I am indebted to Peter Holman for this suggestion.

[17] Barrington's report is in *D-Doc*, 95–100.

They finally left London in July 1765, after presenting the manuscript of a short four-part choral piece ('God is our refuge', K. 20) to the British Museum. There was a final money-spinning event in which the children were treated more like a circus act, playing duets in a tavern with the keyboard covered. They were persuaded to visit Holland, causing Leopold to abandon his plan to go to Italy before returning home. Wolfgang played at the court in The Hague in September, and his first symphonies were performed there, gaining the family supportive friends who saw them through their most serious crisis. First, Leopold was ill again, then both children; Nannerl nearly died and Wolfgang, who fell ill just as she was getting better, was reduced to skin and bone (Leopold's account to Hagenauer, in his letters of 5 November and 12 December 1765, is harrowing to read). Eventually they moved on, reaching Paris early in May 1766 and remaining two months, consolidating gains and demonstrating how greatly Wolfgang had developed in the meantime. Then they set off for Lyon and Geneva, spending a few weeks in each, and passed through Switzerland to Munich. In November, Wolfgang again had a bad fever: 'he couldn't stand up nor move his toes and knees . . . for four nights he couldn't sleep' (15 Nov 1766). Once he was better, the elector kept them waiting for an audience. Leopold affects to find this delay tiresome, but meeting patrons was the reason for the journey and was intended to sow seeds for future harvesting.

Back in Salzburg, the transformation of the child into a ten-year-old professional musician amazed their friends, and his development as a composer accelerated rapidly. Some difficulties remain over the dating and, indeed, authorship of early symphonies, including those of 1767. The archiepiscopal court needed placating with something sacred, so Wolfgang composed the first part of a German oratorio, *Die Schuldigkeit des ersten Gebotes* (of which the other parts were by Adlgasser and Michael Haydn), and the remarkable *Grabmusik*. In May, the University theatre staged his first musical drama, the Latin opera *Apollo et Hyacinthus*, designed for student performers—some only a little older than the composer himself.

In September, the family again set off for Vienna, passing through Melk where Wolfgang impressed by playing the organ in the great abbey. In Vienna they frequented the opera, which may indicate the train of Leopold's thoughts, directed towards the new emperor. Maria

Theresia's husband, Francis of Lorraine, had died in 1765, and their eldest son Joseph, now Holy Roman Emperor, ruled Austria jointly with
his mother. He was to be by far Mozart's most important Imperial patron—but not yet. Leopold hoped for something to arise from the
forthcoming marriage of an archduchess to the king of Naples, but the
bride contracted smallpox and died; the city went into mourning, cultural life was in suspense, and the Mozarts retreated, not to Salzburg but
northwards into Moravia. At Olmütz (Olomouc), both children contracted smallpox but survived (while Nannerl recovered Wolfgang may
have written a symphony, K. 43). They stayed with Count Podstatzky,
whose kindness, Leopold remarked, would do him 'no little honour in
the biography of our little one which I shall have printed later on. For
from a certain aspect there begins here a new period of his life' (10 Nov
1767). He was perhaps thinking ahead to a glorious début as an opera
composer in Vienna.

They spent the Christmas period in Brno, where the archbishop's
brother Count Schrattenbach received them kindly, and returned to Vienna on 10 January 1768. Leopold was concerned to inform Hagenauer
of the expense of staying there and of his difficulties with musicians and
patrons. The empress had partly withdrawn from public life, but she received them graciously; Leopold could count other members of the ruling classes as friends and patrons, but musicians and administrators were
another matter. Leopold claimed that Joseph II, who took the keenest
interest in the affairs of the 'theatre in the palace' (Burgtheater), had invited Wolfgang to write an opera. More probably he had made some
polite remark and thought no more about it. Composing the opera buffa
La finta semplice inevitably prolonged their stay, for which permission was
received from the archbishop, but once written, the opera was rejected
by the theatre administrator Giuseppe d'Affligio. Writing to Hagenauer
on 30 July, Leopold wildly pinned the blame on Gluck, who certainly
had no reason to hinder the child and in any case did not write opera
buffa. Wolfgang refuted malicious rumours that his father had composed
the opera by writing arias under the very eyes of the Kapellmeister
Bonno, the poet Metastasio, the senior composer Hasse, and others.
But—a refrain in all Leopold's complaints—at the court theatre, the Italians are in charge: 'a whole hell of musicians has arisen to prevent the
display of a child's ability' (14 Sep). Meanwhile his own position in

Salzburg was in jeopardy because, although the archbishop had condoned his extended absence, his pay was withheld.

In the midst of this diplomatic whirlwind, Leopold may have affronted the Habsburgs by his complaints, but Wolfgang serenely enough composed a second opera, *Bastien und Bastienne*. Thanks to its performance, possibly in the garden theatre belonging to Dr Mesmer, the period in Vienna ended more positively. Finally, his first full-scale mass setting (a *Missa solemnis*) was given before members of the royal family on 7 December in the orphanage chapel (hence it is called the 'Waisenhausmesse', K. 49=47a). It was around this time that Hasse reported that he found Mozart (already a 'maestro di musica') to be 'well-educated [. . .], good-looking, vivacious, gracious and very well mannered'.[18]

The family went home by way of the monastery at Melk, where again Wolfgang demonstrated his prowess on the organ. They had been away fifteen months, and Leopold had to petition the archbishop for back pay, claiming somewhat disingenuously that he had stayed away against his will: 'I could not leave Vienna before without loss of my own honour and that of my child'. Before the date of the petition, Wolfgang had helped the cause by his second Missa brevis (K. 65=61a); another large-scale mass soon followed.

The year 1769 established a pattern for the time Mozart spent in Salzburg over the next decade. He performed and composed incessantly to fulfil the requirements of court and city. Only in Salzburg does sacred music bulk so large in his output. To this year are ascribed a few symphonies, but none of certain authorship, and his first August serenades (Finalmusik), one in honour of the professor of logic, Fr Rufinus Widl (K. 100=62a), and another possibly for the medical faculty (K. 63). Before this, assuaging the wound sustained in Vienna, *La finta semplice* was performed at the court on 1 May. He had now produced music in nearly every important genre and was more than ready for a new adventure.

---

[18] Hasse was writing a testimonial to Giovanni Maria Ortes in Venice, in case he could be of use to the Mozarts. Translation from Landon, *Mozart. The Golden Years*, 14; the letter in full, with another translation, *D-Doc*, 92.

Works by an 'almost supernatural talent' [1]

MOZART'S PRECOCITY WAS FIRST EVIDENT IN KEYBOARD PLAYING and sight-reading, then in improvisation and composition. Composition, indeed, began with improvisation, followed by repetition to fix pieces sufficiently for his father to take them down. The earliest pieces imitate the music Leopold wrote in Nannerl's notebook. [2] Their two-part texture makes them playable by tiny hands, and for a budding composer, writing in such a spare texture while implying fuller harmony was excellent training. So was the imitation of good models, and this, following harmony and counterpoint on a cantus firmus, was to inform Mozart's own later teaching. He was quick to assimilate, and over the years honed his techniques to enable him to compose with remarkable speed and accuracy where musical grammar was concerned. Music written before the first Italian journey shows his natural ability in compelling notes to do his will, accompanied by a surprising degree of imaginative empathy with texts in vocal music. If works like *Grabmusik* and the operas of 1768 are based on mimicry—he can hardly have experienced the range of feelings implied—his skill in catching the right ac-

---

[1] Charles Burney, *The Present State of Music in France and Italy*, met 'the little German, whose premature and almost supernatural talents astonished us in London . . . ' on 10 August 1770 in Bologna. *The Present State of Music in France and Italy* (1771), in Percy A. Scholes, *Dr Burney's Musical Tours in Europe*, i, 162.

[2] Most of these pieces are not ascribed to a composer, and some may be by Leopold. Among attributed composers are Wagenseil, and C. P. E. Bach.

cents, for love and rage, for mourning and religious exaltation, are all the more remarkable.

Galant instrumental music

Mozart began composing in the shorter dance forms of the galant style. There is no question of originality, which is not to be expected in a child, least of all in a period when the music to be heard and played was nearly all contemporary. We can never know to what extent Leopold, in notating the earliest pieces, adjusted what his son played to conform to a standard. If he changed nothing, the little binary Allegro K. 3, composed at the age of six years and two months, is an epitome of devices Mozart was to use throughout his life (ex. 2.1). The first part makes a six-bar unit by repeating the third and fourth bars. In the balancing six-bar phrase, the fourth bar is an interrupted cadence; this makes the subsequent repetition necessary rather than gratuitous or merely playful, and the cadence is decorated melodically. The middle employs a simple sequence (supertonic minor to tonic major) and is typically shorter than the main sections; the recapitulation cadences rhyme with those of the first part. As well as satisfying a sense of form, the devices used in this modest piece eventually came to bear considerable structural and expressive weight.

Similar clean competence is on display in the numerous minuets, but the results are not always so satisfactory. A minuet composed in Paris and copied by Leopold into Nannerl's notebook (ex. 2.2) was subsequently published with a violin part within op. 1 (K. 7). The opening four bars present the simplest elaboration of tonic harmony. The chromatic touch in bars 5–6 enhances the modulation to the dominant; bars 7–8 are virtually identical, so that a balanced eight-bar unit could be obtained by omitting bars 5–6; the internal repetition, a delicate imbalance, gives life to the music. In the second half, however, the keyboard occupies too low a register, and the idea in bars 15–16, simpler than bars 5–6 but coming three times, restores phrasing in multiples of four, making twelve bars where ten would be ample. The violin part provides contrast of timbre and register by filling in the rests of the piano's right hand, but the movement remains disappointing.

Mozart composed innumerable well-chiselled minuets and movements in sonata form. Even in his late works, the minuet and its matching trio each normally maintains a single 'affect' or topic, with enough

Ex. 2.1   Allegro K. 3 (1762)

contrast in melodic shape and harmonic colour to impress, charm, or in rare cases disturb. Mature sonata forms, even if their binary origins resemble dance forms, are considerably longer, and one of their objectives seems to be the elaboration of contrasting ideas—whether melodies, rhythms, or textures—within a single tempo. The prototype of this kind of movement, however, may not have been available to Mozart in his earliest years, if indeed it existed. One tries to forgive the continual 'Alberti'

Ex. 2.2   Minuet K. 7 (1763)

figuration in the first movement of the op. 1 sonata in C (K. 6), which also exists as a keyboard piece in Nannerl's notebook: out of 224 crotchet beats, only ten do not use an identical left-hand pattern, precluding any significant textural variety. Unfortunately, the second movement is based on exactly the same figuration. The D-major sonata (K. 7) projects the flow of semiquavers in different hands with more enterprise and adopts a dotted figure as a cadential gesture; but the repeated-note triplets, a kind of drumming that runs almost throughout the second movement, miti-gate against lyricism or elegant delivery of the ornamentation.

Mozart's first symphony (K. 16) suggests that writing for orchestra helped him to present ideas of opposite character in a meaningful rela-tionship. No doubt he was remembering symphonies heard in Mannheim and other centres but also learning from the example of J. C. Bach, 'the first composer who observed the law of *contrast*, as a *principle*', as Burney observed.[3] The first idea contrasts a fanfarelike gesture with

3 Charles Burney (ed. Frank Mercer), *A General History of Music* (New York, 1935) ii, 866.

Ex. 2.3 Symphony K. 16 (1764), first movement

an exercise in strict counterpoint (ex. 2.3), a faint foreshadowing of later and grander openings to works in E♭. This asymmetrical period (three plus eight bars) is repeated, forming a larger symmetry. The *fp* markings, meaningless on a harpsichord, animate a true orchestral texture in the short bridge-passage, and the otherwise platitudinous closing material presented in the dominant. The second part of the movement defines a binary, rather than a full sonata, form (both parts are repeated): the opening idea is heard in the dominant, with a modulation to C minor, followed by the closing material in the tonic. The slow movement of the first symphony, in the C minor that he favoured for works in E♭, has a

EX. 2.4 Symphony K. 19 (1765), first movement, from bar 25

Allegro

mildly hypnotic quality, resulting from constant triplet motion and the repetition of the bass figure in almost every bar. The most enjoyable movement is the jiglike $\frac{3}{8}$ finale typical of Italian symphonies, in which Mozart contrasts lively diatonic matter with chromaticism.

The opening of the second symphony (K. 19) is livelier in its figuration, but perhaps as an experiment, the movement is not a full binary form and seems too short and amorphous. The return of the theme first heard in the dominant is decidedly less interesting (ex. 2.4), a bold plunge into the minor being simply forgotten. The design without repeats recurs in the symphony composed in The Hague (K. 22 in B♭), but

Ex. 2.4 (*continued*)

here the essence of the binary form remains, and Mozart colours his main idea with minor harmony in the second part; an extended repetition, with variation in harmonic colour, gives the music added breadth. Its slow movement is an early example of Mozart using the key of G minor, one seen as peculiarly significant for him.[4] There is brief foreshadowing of greater things—notably the slow movement of the last G-minor symphony—in a bridge passage that leads to a repetition of the opening idea in the major (ex. 2.5). Mozart also prepared to cultivate the piano concerto in 1767, by means of arrangements of solo piano movements by Raupach, Eckard, and others, presumably gathered abroad

[4] See Steven B. Jan, *Mozart's Music in G minor* (New York, 1995).

Ex. 2.5 Symphony K. 22 (1765), second movement

(K. 37, 39, 40, 41). Some of these composers show scarcely more textural inventiveness than the young boy, but the experience of working over the material and adding orchestral parts must have been excellent training.

Sacred and dramatic music

Although the Kyrie written in Paris is mainly homophonic, the first two masses show a determination to mimic his elders. In fugal imitation Mozart's technique was already reasonably secure, though not infallible (there are occasional forbidden consecutives and some crude unprepared dissonances). From this evidence it would appear that his later studies in Italy with Padre Martini were required only to polish his understanding of the 'learned' style expected in liturgical music and thus applied by Mozart to the end of his life, in the Requiem. It is also clear that he understood the topical traits and stylistic gestures appropriate to particular sections of the Mass text. This does not apply only to opera; both early masses, for instance, relish the contrast implicit in 'et exspecto resurrectionem mortuorum', halting the progress of diatonic counterpoint by a three-bar adagio; in the 'Waisenhausmesse' the bass moves by a diminished third, and the diminished seventh chord is resolved to a dominant seventh in third inversion (ex. 2.6). This Mass, Mozart's most ambitious composition to reach performance up to this time, never quite lives up to its first few bars, in which the plea for mercy ('Kyrie eleison') elaborates a move from C minor to E♭, using all the three possible diminished seventh chords (ex. 2.7); note also how Mozart, or the Mozarts together, exercised care in disposition of dynamic markings.

Ex. 2.6 'Waisenhausmesse', K. 139 (1768), Credo, bars 255–59

These liturgical works, and the dramatic works written for Salzburg in 1767, *Die Schuldigkeit des ersten Gebotes* and *Apollo et Hyacinthus*, are performable only as acts of Mozartian piety, particularly as he composed only one third of the oratorio. Considered as Lenten penance, the theatre being closed, *Die Schuldigkeit* is equivalent to abandoning red meat for caviar: a musical feast, if you like elongated arias not overly governed by the sense of the words. The *Grabmusik* is more interesting. We may smile at the naïve mimesis in the middle section of the long first aria, but operas of the same period by adult composers are no more sophisticated in their invocations of thunder, lightning, and fire, and seldom dare such violent modulations. To the self-lacerating virtuosity of the baritone

Ex. 2.7 'Waisenhausmesse', K. 139 (1768), Kyrie

Ex. 2.8 *Grabmusik*, K. 42 (1767), duet, from bar 67

* *sic*

'soul', the angel's gentle G-minor aria is a balm. The subsequent duet confirms the curiously pietistic message, the dialogue form recalling to us, though not to Mozart, certain duets in J. S. Bach's cantatas. This is epitomised in the modulation from E♭ to G minor, over a circle of fifths and with a wealth of chromatic detail, coming to rest as the angel floats down from the top register (ex. 2.8); the clash between bass singer and instrumental bass on the second group of semiquavers is, however, surely a mistake. Mozart was only a little over eleven when he composed this short cantata, apparently at the archbishop's behest; the attractive final chorus was added in 1773. Generally the scores of this period show how much less Leopold felt the need to intervene; to get someone else to look over a score for consistency, for instance in phrasing and dynamics, is a sensible precaution even for adult composers. One hopes Schratten-bach realised that, musically speaking, this boy was no longer a child and was surely ready for the dramatic composition soon to be undertaken in Vienna.

CHAPTER 3

Italy and Salzburg

1769–1773

O N 12 DECEMBER 1769, THE MALE MOZARTS SET OFF FOR ITALY,
aided by 120 ducats from the court treasury. Letters were now addressed to Maria Anna, with occasional postscripts from Wolfgang to
Nannerl. As they travelled, the prodigy was again on show as a keyboard
player and composer, but the prime objective was an opera commission,
following the examples of Hasse, J. C. Bach, Josef Mysliveček, and Florian
Gassmann, who had brought the young Antonio Salieri to Vienna in
1766. Italy was the cradle of opera, and its children had colonised every
European centre, even Paris; the Italian style of church music was also
widely disseminated. Handel would not have prevailed in London, nor
Hasse in Dresden, without a thorough grounding in the Italian musical
lingua franca.

The Mozarts gave their first concert in Verona at the end of 1769,
then travelled on to Milan. The Austrian governor, Count Firmian, a
relation of a former archbishop of Salzburg, was particularly supportive,
and he commissioned Mozart to write the main *opera seria* for the next
Carnival (between Christmas and Lent). There was no chance of starting work on it for several months, so the Mozarts headed south, sight-
seeing, performing, and learning. In Bologna they met and befriended
Mysliveček, but the main object of their visit was Padre Giovanni Battista Martini, historian and theorist of music, and former teacher of J. C.
Bach. Although Mozart already knew something of the learned style,
this more thorough grounding in counterpoint permanently affected

him, and not only in sacred music. Mozart worked hard at his exercises, and on a return visit in late summer he set the seal on his academic credentials by passing the entrance examination (possibly with some help from Martini) of the prestigious Bologna Accademia Filarmonica; he was later also elected to the equivalent institution in Verona (Leopold's letter of 12 Jan 1771).

The Mozarts moved on to Florence, where Archduke Leopold ruled as governor of Tuscany, and where Mozart formed his brief but close friendship with Thomas Linley; it included playing music together. The next objective was Rome, where they arrived on 11 April 1770, and Mozart notated from memory the music of Allegri's 'Miserere', a closely guarded secret of the Sistine chapel. They went on to Naples, where it was unconscionably hot. This city, despite the rival claims of Venice, had produced the dominant school of opera composers; it possessed a great conservatoire and, in the San Carlo, the largest opera house. In a couple of postscripts, Mozart offered his sister a developing view of *Armida*, one of the last works of the great Jommelli, who had recently returned from Stuttgart. Rather than the opera growing on him, Mozart implies that his liking diminished on a second hearing, concluding that it was too serious for the theatre, and 'old-fashioned'.

Back in Rome, Mozart was honoured by the pope who created him *cavaliere Speron d'Oro*, a Knight of the Golden Spur. The intense heat was relieved by a stay in the country near Bologna, thanks to the hospitable Count Pallavicini, but Mozart could still not start serious work on his opera. With the libretto of *Mitridate, re di Ponto* to hand, he could plan, study the characters, and perhaps compose recitatives and an overture. But the main job of a composer of opera seria was to write arias, and although he knew some of the singers from the first Milan visit, composing for them was best done in collaboration. Then, if they rejected an idea, Mozart could spare himself the labour of completing and orchestrating the piece. A number of instrumental works may have been composed, but without dated manuscripts it is uncertain what he wrote and when; perhaps the experience of Italy—Rome, Naples, Pompeii—and thinking about the opera was enough to keep him occupied, even when Leopold was laid up with a bad leg.

By October 20 they were back in Milan, and Mozart's fingers were aching from writing recitatives. Some of the singers were already there, but as late as 24 November, a month before the premiere, Leopold reported that the leading castrato has not yet appeared and 'Wolfgang refuses to do the work twice over and prefers to wait for his arrival so as to fit the costume to his figure'.[1] Leopold clearly had no qualms about his son's ability to compose rapidly to a deadline. The castrato Pietro Benedetti eventually arrived on 1 December, but the member of the cast who gave most trouble was the tenor, Guglielmo d'Ettore; he eventually performed one aria in a setting by Quirino Gasparini, whose *Mitridate* he had sung in Turin three years earlier. The prima donna Antonia Bernasconi honourably resisted blandishments to make a similar substitution. The performance night (on the first day of Carnival, 26 December) was a genuine success; swollen by a ballet, it lasted about six hours.

Before going home, the Mozarts explored other possibilities in northern Italy, visiting Turin and, in mid-February, Venice where they gave a concert on 5 March 1771. They reached Salzburg on 28 March, with high hopes for further success in Italy, for they had quitted Milan with an invitation to write another Carnival opera in two years' time; the contract, dated 4 March 1771, preceded the arrival of Archduke Ferdinand as governor of Lombardy and is qualified with 'the usual reservations in case of theatrical misfortunes and Princely intervention (which God forbid)'.[2] First, Mozart received two more commissions: an oratorio for Padua, *Betulia liberata*, which he composed and delivered (but it was not performed),[3] and from Milan, no doubt on the advice of Firmian, a short opera or *serenata* (*Ascanio in Alba*) for the marriage of Archduke Ferdinand to Maria Beatrice d'Este.

In the meantime, Wolfgang was raised to the rank of Konzertmeister in Salzburg, at first unpaid. During the summer he fulfilled this role by composing sacred music, including the first *Litaniae Lauretanae BVM*, and instrumental music including four symphonies. The vigour of Salzburg's musical life around this period is testified by Christoph Friedrich Daniel

---

[1] A few years later, Mozart echoed this remark when writing arias for Anton Raaff and Dorothea Wendling in Mannheim; letter of 28 February 1778.

[2] D-Doc, 133.

[3] A performance of *Betulia liberata* in 1775 in Munich may not have been of Mozart's work; the text was by Metastasio, whose texts were repeatedly set by all composers of Italian opera and oratorio.

Schubart, who particularly praised Mozart's keyboard playing.[4] The second and third Italian visits were confined to the north, and almost entirely concerned with the Milan operas. Mozart and his father left Salzburg on 13 August 1771 and proceeded to Venice, where Leopold negotiated another opera commission which would have required Mozart's presence early in 1773. Perhaps Leopold was hedging his bets; a failure with the Milan serenata might have led to cancellation of the opera seria for 1772. In the event, the Venice commission was abandoned. The Mozarts reached Milan before the end of August, and *Ascanio in Alba* was performed on 17 October, the day after the premiere of Hasse's last opera, *Ruggiero*. The old master was generous to Mozart, but when *Ascanio* was more warmly received than *Ruggiero*, Leopold's delight may have been a little too obvious; as he wrote home on 19 October: 'It really upsets me a lot, but Wolfgang's serenata has killed Hasse's opera'.[5] They lingered in Milan to wait on the archduke, Wolfgang filling in the time by writing at least one symphony (K. 112). Eventually, on 30 November, they were received by Ferdinand, who proposed to his mother that he employ Mozart. Memories of 1768, however, and news of Hasse's failure, may have piqued the empress, who told her son not to 'burden himself with useless people [. . .] who go about like beggars'; 'besides, he has a large family', added the mother of sixteen.[6]

A more immediate crisis was the death of Archbishop Schrattenbach on 16 December, the day after their return to Salzburg. A splendid Requiem Mass was composed by Michael Haydn, which surely made an impression on Mozart. There was a short interregnum during which Leopold successfully petitioned for back-payment of his salary, with the understanding that this was not a precedent. Hieronymus Colloredo, who took office in March 1772, was not a popular choice, but his relations with the Mozarts started well enough. The serenata *Il sogno di Scipione*, composed for the half-century of Schrattenbach's ordination, was performed instead for Colloredo's enthronement in May. In that month

---

[4] Zaslaw, *Symphonies*, 203.

[5] *Notizie del mondo* (Florence) reported 'The serenata, however, has met with great applause'. E-*Doc*, 21.

[6] D-*Doc*, 138. Three of Maria Theresia's children had died in infancy and three more when young, but in 1771 ten were still living.

Mozart wrote three more symphonies (K. 128, 129, 130), possibly with concerts in Italy in mind; the last and grandest in sonority adds a second pair of horns to the standard orchestra of two oboes, two horns, and strings. For the church, he produced some 'Epistle sonatas', single movements for strings and organ, sometimes augmented by trumpets, and the first *Litaniae de venerabili altaris sacramento*.

Colloredo ruled an independent principality, but one that could only survive by maintaining good relations with the Habsburgs. Even if he wanted to, he could hardly prevent the Mozarts from fulfilling the opera seria commission for Milan. Despite the labour of composing *Lucio Silla*, Mozart found time on the journey to begin a set of six string quartets (K. 155–160). Although none of the singers had taken part in *Mitridate*, the disputes of two years earlier were not repeated. The performance was again of inordinate length, with three ballets, and began two hours late because the archduke was sluggish with his correspondence. Nevertheless it was liked, and ran for twenty-six performances. The leading castrato, Vincenzo Rauzzini, was late in arriving and his demanding role was written in five weeks, but Mozart wrote for him the brilliant solo cantata *Exsultate, jubilate* (K. 165=158a). Mozart valued *Lucio Silla* highly enough to teach an aria to Aloysia Weber, and one of Giunia's arias was sung in Vienna ten years later.[7]

Mozart returned to Salzburg in March 1773 a recognised *maestro*, skilled on keyboard and violin, and an experienced composer with the necessary equipment to be a Kapellmeister. But he was barely seventeen, and so unemployable in a capacity where he would have the direction of older, possibly recalcitrant or self-opinionated, musicians. He surely hoped for more opera commissions from Italy. Presumably he could not know that, thanks to Maria Theresia's intervention, he could expect nothing more from Milan, and she perhaps said something similar to her son Leopold, grand duke of Tuscany, whom Leopold Mozart had approached. Did the Mozarts expect the success of *Lucio Silla* to resound throughout the Italian opera circuit? Italian opera was played in every major European city except Paris, and even that was about to change. Jommelli's day was over (he died in 1774), and Gluck was otherwise occupied, but the generation born in the 1720s and 1730s—Piccinni,

7 See Mahling, in Sadie, *Wolfgang Amadè Mozart*, 377–94.

Traetta, Sacchini, Mysliveček—had come into its own. Success by a teenager in Milan would hardly distract the attention of impresarios from mature composers with reputations established throughout Italy and beyond. In one of history's little ironies, the libretto of *Lucio Silla* found its way to Germany, and a new musical setting was commissioned for Carl Theodor's theatre in Mannheim with music by Mozart's mentor and model J. C. Bach in 1775.

CHAPTER 4

Opera Seria

'fitting the clothes to the figure'

OZART'S FIRST OPERA, THE LATIN DRAMA *APOLLO ET HY-
acinthus*, marked no great advance in the two months following
Die Schuldigkeit des ersten Gebotes, but it confirmed his ability to simulate
human emotions from tenderness to rage. Eighteen months later, writing comedies, he could vary the forms more than was normally allowed
in the procession of arias, laden with coloratura, that constitutes the
bulk of an opera seria; but it is into this latter genre, epitomised by
the librettos of Metastasio and the music of Hasse, that his other early
operas fall. There are few traces of the reformist tendencies which
had emerged mainly in Italian operas written for German centres (see
chap. 9).

Metastasio's libretti are masterpieces of rationalisation. Scenes in
recitative deliver the plot, and arias, carefully distributed according to
the prestige of the performers, are allotted to whichever character may
plausibly be the next to leave the stage. The topics of arias suit the pas-
sions that liberate the singer from the actual words, and the last line of
poetry is normally designed with a vowel-sound to suit high notes and
brilliant passagework. Barrington tells us that the boy Mozart could im-
provise scenes of love and rage to nonsense words in a manner 'above
mediocrity', and with 'extraordinary readiness of invention'. He soon
began composing scenes and arias, mostly to Metastasio's texts, for concert performance or insertion into operas by other composers, earning

his first Milan commission by writing for the singers who were there early in 1770.[1]

Some early arias are in the traditional full *da capo* form, in which the music of the first poetic stanza ends in the tonic and is repeated, entirely or in large part, after the second stanza. Mozart soon came to prefer the modified version in which the first stanza modulates; its repetition has to be recomposed like a sonata recapitulation, so that the aria ends in the tonic.[2] The middle section, or second stanza, is sometimes in a contrasting metre and tempo and may be more expressively intense, though also shorter, than the main section, a discrepancy noted in the dedicatory preface to Gluck's *Alceste*.[3] At the emotional high points of a drama, a principal singer is allocated a recitative with orchestral accompaniment (*recitativo stromentato*, or *obbligato*). Like an instrumental fantasia, these recitatives had no rules beyond what expression demands; as Rousseau defined it, 'the actor, agitated, carried away by a passion which prevents everything being said, breaks off and stops, leaving silences during which the orchestra speaks for him; and these [. . .] affect the audience far more than if the actor uttered everything that, through the music, it understands'.[4] The sequence of obbligato recitative and aria constitutes a 'scena'.

Mozart was happy to use texts previously set numberless times and enjoyed the challenge of making his own version; as he wrote to Leopold from Mannheim, he set

as a kind of exercise, the aria 'non sò d'onde viene' [. . .] I know the aria by [J. C.] Bach so well because I like it very much and can always hear it in my head. So I wanted to see if I would be able, in spite of all this, to write an aria that was completely different (28 Feb 1778).

---

[1] Anthony Pryer argues for a minor change in the dating of certain arias to accommodate this hypothesis. 'Mozart's Operatic Audition. The Milan Concert, 12 March 1770: a Reappraisal and Revision', *Eighteenth-Century Music* I/2 (2004), 265–88.

[2] This form is sometimes called 'modified *da capo*', because it can be used for texts designed for the strict *da capo* form, and sometimes a 'sonata form' aria despite the essentially instrumental nature of sonata form. With routinely positioned orchestral ritornelli, the aria is more akin to a concerto movement.

[3] Published in 1769, the dedication to the grand duke of Tuscany was probably written by the librettist Raniero da Calzabigi, but is signed by Gluck.

[4] Jean-Jacques Rousseau, 'Récitatif obligé', in *Dictionnaire de musique* (Paris, 1768).

This scena (K. 294) provided him with a further challenge, for he later set the words again, but for a bass singer instead of a soprano (K. 512).

In Milan, he strove to impress Firmian and the singer by the long scena 'Misero me . . . Misero pargoletto' (K. 77=73e), from Metastasio's *Demofoonte* (performed on 12 March 1770). The hero Timante is in despair because he believes he has married his own sister. Over 130 bars, the sympathetic orchestral gestures in the recitative pay diminishing returns. The aria, addressed to the child ('Misero pargoletto') of an apparently incestuous marriage, is an abbreviated *da capo*, the music returning to bar 38 rather than the very beginning after a too-short middle section (adagio). Anguish is inevitably subsumed by orderliness, and a few minor-mode inflections cannot save the aria from blandness. At least Mozart eschewed the empty-headed virtuosity of 'Fra cento affanni' (K. 88=73c), written about the same time. This is not to say that these arias are immature; similar criticism could be made of innumerable pieces by adults tilling the same artistic soil. Metastasian drama was a Baroque-period form to which the galant style could add little, and other composers—even Gluck and Jommelli—had problems animating it without recourse to alterations of the kind later effected for Mozart in *La clemenza di Tito*.

Mitridate rises above the level of the 1770 arias, not only because of Mozart's rapid maturation and intervening experience of opera in Italian theatres but because it is a complete opera; rather than being isolated specimens, the arias take on dramatic life because the characters' situations are known. Few eighteenth-century operas are tragedies, but a true opera seria will threaten to become one. *Mitridate* benefits from its basis in Racine's drama, filled with conflicts between the king and his sons, all in love with the same woman, and within the heroine's mind as she vacillates between her love for Sifare and her duty to the king. The drama unfolds under threat of a Roman attack; this is repulsed, but the king is fatally injured and becomes almost the only Mozartian hero to perish before the drama is over.

Betulia liberata, Mozart's only dramatic oratorio, is best considered a kind of opera seria, with the advantage of including real choruses. The main event, the murder of Holofernes by Giuditta (Judith), takes place offstage, and she tells her story in a lengthy obbligato recitative. Otherwise the main musical interest is in part 1, which shows Mozart experimenting with thematic integration. The three-movement overture in D minor, with four horns, is an early example of Sturm und Drang (storm and stress).[5] A contrapuntal middle section is succeeded by a presto that uses the same principal motive as the first movement. Within part 1, when the Israelites are in distress, Mozart frequently inflects the music to the parallel minor, and one aria and chorus are in minor keys. Giuditta's entry is marked by the first use of obbligato recitative, but the most intriguing feature is that part of the flowing melody of her first aria (contrasted in the ritornello, and later in the voice, with brilliant passagework) unmistakably recurs in her second aria (ex. 4.1); the two are separated by recitative, a repeat of a noble chorus, and an aria for the sceptical Achior. Mozart seems not to have repeated this unusual device, even within the motivic networks employed in *Idomeneo*.

The next two operas, *Il sogno di Scipione* and *Ascanio in Alba*, are of the courtly genre, in which the succession of recitatives and arias is relieved by chorus and ballet. Their situations are taken from Roman myth and history, but as *Il sogno* is a sententious allegory, and the text of *Ascanio* is necessarily sycophantic, neither takes off dramatically. *Ascanio* was performed first, but it was written immediately after *Il sogno*. However, the markedly greater interest of *Ascanio* may owe less to rapid compositional development than to Mozart's estimate of the capabilities of his singers and the taste of his audience. The lengthy arias of *Il sogno* are in *da capo* form, whereas those of *Ascanio* are more concise, and use the more modern tonal design. *Il sogno* does imply that the Salzburg singers had remarkable techniques, but it is old-fashioned beside *Ascanio*, where the orchestral writing is richer, and the shorter, more varied arias are relieved by pastoral dances and choruses, including one repeated, ritornello-like, in the manner of the earliest operas.

Mozart's Italian journeys reached a climax with *Lucio Silla*, his last full-length, orthodox opera seria. Unfortunately, the drama collapses when the tyrant decides to abandon revenge and retire into private life, a decision that appears unmotivated (although this is the only part of the libretto with a secure historical basis). The arias are more sharply

---

[5] Sturm und Drang as a topic of musical discourse has been first applied since the mid-twentieth century. See Leonard G. Ratner, *Classic Music: Expression, Form, and Style* (New York, 1980); *TNG2*, vol. 24, 631–33.

EX. 4.1 *Betulia liberata*, K. 118, ritornelli from Giuditta's arias

a. no. 5, bars 1–15

b. no. 8, bars 12–23

characterised and varied in form than in *Mitridate*, including experimental pieces, like Giunia's 'Dalla sponda tenebrosa', which twice
changes from adagio to allegro. This kind of thing Mozart must have
recalled from Gluck's *Alceste*, and the aria precedes the final scene of act
1, virtually a piece of 'reform opera'. It takes place in a graveyard, and
Mozart creates a sinister atmosphere by textures and harmony from the
complex of musical topics now identified as *ombra* (shadow), whose
greatest dramatic manifestation is the statue music of *Don Giovanni*.
The violent modulation from A minor to C minor begins a long recitative for Cecilio, but it does not lead to an aria; instead a procession enters, with a chorus, during which Giunia invokes her father, Marius, in
an expressive solo. She then mistakes Cecilio, who has been exiled and

whom she believes dead, for a ghost. Their rapturous duet seems to forget their extreme peril, and the rest of the opera never reaches the level of this remarkable scene. The fact that the tenor was a late substitute, with little stage experience, makes Silla's music, composed at the last moment, simpler than the rest; a weakness in casting becomes a dramatic weakness.

Metastasio's *Il re pastore* was slimmed down into two acts for Salzburg in 1775 and was presented as a serenata rather than a full-blown opera seria; as befits a work originally written to be sung by noble amateurs at Schönbrunn (1751), tragedy is hardly threatened. Mozart's music is more highly characterised than in the earlier serious operas, but he was now in his first maturity and had just completed the comedy *La finta giardiniera* for Munich. In both these operas characters of high estate mingle with humbler folk—in this case shepherds, one of them the rightful king. The aria 'L'amerò, sarò costante' for Aminta, the title role, is a lustrous rondo with obbligato violin and an orchestra with two cors anglais; perfectly positioned within the drama, its beauty led Mozart to introduce it into his Vienna concerts. Mozart's skill in characterisation shows up in two agonised arias for characters apparently about to be deprived of their lovers by the well-meaning meddling of Alessandro (Alexander the Great). Elisa's Andante ('Barbaro! oh Dio'), like Giunia's first aria, twice breaks from Andante to Allegro; Agenore's 'Sol può dir' maintains its C-minor Allegro throughout in an unrelenting Sturm und Drang—tremolo, syncopation, dynamic contrast, the melody strident and sighing by turns, without coloratura. The young Mozart is hardly to blame for his straightforwardly conventional settings of libretti supplied for an occasion, whether a courtly opera seria, a Lenten oratorio, or a marriage. In view of Mozart's vigorous intervention in the construction of *Idomeneo*, it is tempting to speculate that he may have played a part in paring the libretto of *Il re pastore* down to essentials. It is a surprising, polished, and charming minor masterpiece, showing that he was ready for a greater challenge. It must be counted one of the major frustrations of his career that the opportunity did not come for five more years.

Mozart wrote only two more wholly serious operas, *Idomeneo* and *La clemenza di Tito*. But he maintained contact with the style by continually producing arias on seria texts, and most of these are more interesting than the arias produced in Milan. His strong personal interest in Aloysia Lange accounts for the massive structure and vocal difficulties of the scena 'Popoli di Tessaglia . . . Io non chiedo' (K. 316=300b), the text drawn from *Alceste*; with Aloysia's arias, it is worth recalling that pitch in Mozart's day was generally at least a semitone lower than is normal today. The complexities of Josepha Dušek's 'Bella mia fiamma . . . Resta, o cara' (K. 528) may partly have been intended to tease the singer. Neither represents Mozart at his most ingratiating, but both, along with a number of other more seductive pieces written for Raaff, Wendling, and Adamberger, are among the lesser-known treasures of his maturity. The popularity of Mozart's comedies overshadows that of his serious operas, but without the experience of writing them, he would hardly have accomplished comedies of such human depth and complexity.

CHAPTER 5

Salzburg

1773–1777

E VEN IF ARCHBISHOP COLLOREDO'S REFORMING IDEAS WERE IN
harmony with those of Joseph II, he was no liberal. Like the emperor, he instituted a purge of inessential and ornamental elements in religious practice: simpler services in the cathedral, with shorter musical
settings of the Mass.[1] But he still required music for other purposes;
Mozart's wind divertimentos, composed on a regular cycle in January
and August from 1775 to 1777, were no doubt Colloredo's table-music.
Mozart composed two or more Masses each year from 1774 to 1777,
mainly of the short kind (*Missa brevis*), that conformed to the archbishop's requirements. In quantity, his output was reduced after his return from Paris early in 1779, but he can hardly be accused of laziness. In
1782, when Colloredo appointed Michael Haydn to fulfil some of
Mozart's duties, he added 'the additional stipulation that he show more
diligence'. This could be a dig at Mozart or at Haydn, whose occasional
drinking problem can hardly have been concealed (Leopold's letter, 29
Jun 1778). But Colloredo's musical requirements were insufficient to
keep his prolific Konzertmeister fully occupied, and despite his successes
in Italy, Mozart was asked for only one new dramatic work, *Il re pastore*,
in 1775.

The family began to enjoy an improved economic situation when

[1] Cliff Eisen, 'The Salzburg Symphonies. A Biographical Interpretation', in Stanley Sadie
(ed.), *Wolfgang Amadè Mozart*, 191.

Wolfgang's honorary title of Konzertmeister was confirmed by Colloredo in 1772, with a salary of 150 gulden. In the autumn of 1773 the Mozarts removed to the Tanzmeisterhaus, an apartment large enough for music-making and playing games, including shooting at targets—occupations for the whole family, whereas the mother was generally not involved in music. Colloredo was generally unwilling to allow his employees freedom to travel other than within his own entourage, but during his absence in the summer of 1773, Wolfgang and Leopold revisited Vienna, where they were received politely but gained nothing from the Habsburgs. This trip bore creative fruit in the form of a second set of six string quartets (K. 168–173). They are usually said to have been influenced by Joseph Haydn's remarkable op. 20, which had recently been published, but they were also a response to the popularity of the medium in Vienna, represented by Gassmann, Vanhal, and Ordonez. Certainly Mozart was not yet within shouting distance of Haydn's mastery in this medium. Back in Salzburg, he completed in December the quintet with two violas (K. 174), a texture he later made peculiarly his own, although the model here was probably Michael Haydn. Perhaps the idea that Vienna was the 'land of the clavier' became rooted in his mind, for his first original piano concerto (K. 175), finished in December, was well calculated to show off his growing mastery of the instrument.

Meanwhile, in October, Mozart had completed a brace of symphonies in the related keys of B♭ and G minor, the latter (K. 183) being the earliest to command a regular place in the modern repertoire. His intensive cultivation of particular instrumental forms (in these years, the symphony and violin concerto) was less a planned exploration of their potential than the fulfilment of the requirements of local concert life. In the long gap between opera commissions, he wrote few arias, but theatre music was never far from his mind. Probably in 1774 he composed the first parts of his only extended piece of incidental music, to Tobias Philip von Gebler's drama *Thamos, König in Egypten* (published in 1773); he supplied more music for later revivals. This and other music by Mozart found its way through Germany with Karl Wahr's and Johann Böhm's troupes of travelling actors. *Thamos* remains isolated within Mozart's oeuvre, but it provided valuable experience in secular choral writing to German words, as well as dramatic orchestral music.

Exceptionally, 1774 was spent almost entirely at home. In the winter, especially during Carnival, there were concerts, in which Mozart's new symphonies and the piano concerto could feature, alongside music by his elders (already, he cannot have regarded them as his betters). With the beginning of Lent, he would have to prepare the church music required after Easter and particularly in May, the month associated with the Blessed Virgin. In 1774, in her honour, he composed his second *Litaniae Lauretanae* (K. 195), a more mature score than the first. Concert life continued in the summer. Two new symphonies, in A and D (K. 201–202) were composed, and in May the Concertone (a concerto for two violins with obbligato parts for oboe and cello); the jolly bassoon concerto followed early in June. Mozart produced more short Masses, and music for Vespers (K. 193), though not yet a complete set of Vesper psalms. The August Finalmusik (K. 203=189b) is a substantial work in eight movements. The framing key is D, used for the associated March (K. 237=189c) and a concealed symphony with two minuets, formed of movement 1 (allegro with slow introduction), 5 and 7 (minuets in D), 6 (andante in G) and 8 (prestissimo finale). Enclosed within this, movements 2–4 form a three-movement violin concerto: andante in B♭, minuet in F, allegro in B♭. This pattern recurs with modifications in all the Salzburg Finalmusik.

During the first eight months of the year Mozart developed an individuality of style, which in due course acquired a reputation for being difficult. The high spirits of the A major symphony and the turbulence of the G minor mark him as a composer who was not going to allow routine production to quell a nature by turns impish and passionate— particularly when deprived of its natural outlet, opera. Posterity might agree with the archbishop in one respect: Mozart reserved his best musical ideas for other purposes than his employer's. The Epistle sonatas, instrumental works for use within the liturgy, lacked the scope for development and originality that emerges in the best symphonies and concertos of the period, and, comparatively, are hackwork.

At the end of the year Mozart was preoccupied with a welcome commission, an opera buffa for Munich, *La finta giardiniera*.[2] Mozart and Leopold arrived in Munich early in December, and were joined by

---

[2] *La finta giardiniera*, a title impossible to translate neatly, refers to a principal female (here the Countess Violante), disguised as a gardener (under the name Sandrina).

Nannerl in time for the premiere on 13 January 1775. The libretto (of uncertain authorship) is a characteristic production of the time, parallel-ing some of Haydn's operas of the period (*L'infedeltà delusa, La vera costanza*). This type of *dramma giocoso*, mixing serious and comic charac-ters of different social standing, had developed in Venice twenty-five years earlier in collaboration between the playwright Goldoni and the composer Galuppi. Like opera seria, these comedies consist mainly of arias. Ensembles, other than a few duets, are confined to the extended finales. At the end of the second act the situation is gravely entangled; in this opera, the leading soprano and tenor have lost their wits, believing themselves to be reincarnations of characters from Greek mythology. The short third act brings about the happy ending, uniting three pairs of lovers; only the comic Podestà (Mayor) is resigned to bachelordom. Mozart's fine instrumentation, sharply etched characterisation, and re-markably intense music in the arias of despair and the finales, make this his first mature *opera buffa*; but it is hardly characteristic of his maturity in this genre.

Mozart left Munich on 8 March with regret: as he wrote to his mother, he was happier in a city where he could breathe. Colloredo was also there, and heard without pleasure praises being showered on his young servant. Not for the last time, Mozart hoped in vain for an invi-tation to remain in Munich. At least, however, the new year in Salzburg brought some theatrical activity. The archbishop required a *serenata* for the visit of Maria Theresia's youngest son, Archduke Maximilian: the premiere of *Il re pastore* was on 23 April. The libretto by Metastasio was chosen as suitable for performance without elaborate theatrical machin-ery, as a 'serenata', like *Scipione*. The castrato Tommaso Consoli, who probably sang Ramiro in the Munich opera, came to Salzburg for the title role, together with the flautist Johann Baptist Becke, a friend of the Mozarts, for whom Mozart composed a limpid obbligato in one of Alexander the Great's arias. The remaining forces were local, and their music again demonstrates their capability in expressive and brilliant singing.

Later in the year, and once in 1776, Mozart seems to have supplied substitute arias for operas performed in Salzburg, but then the operatic well dried up again. The rest of 1775 may have seemed depressingly like 1773 and 1774, so it is not surprising that, apart from routine production of short masses, Epistle sonatas, and Finalmusik, Mozart's thoughts turned to escape. But what options were open to a former child prodigy, still too young to be a Kapellmeister? The travelling keyboard or violin virtuoso was an established member of the profession, but Mozart could not yet undertake such a career on his own. The solo recital was not cultivated until the nineteenth century; public keyboard performances consisted of concertos and improvisations, and concertos require an orchestra, adding to promotional expenses. In Munich, Mozart wrote his first surviving piano sonatas (K. 279–284), aimed at domestic consumption (including Nannerl's), teaching (Mozart liked to teach his own pieces), and publication.[3] In October, Leopold offered these and other works to the Leipzig publisher Breitkopf, without success; only one (K. 284) was published in Mozart's lifetime, and that only in 1784.

Mozart could not have contemplated life as a travelling violin virtuoso, for although he played well, he would not practice (as Leopold pointed out). He had written his first violin concerto in 1773, and in 1775 he added four more (but no new symphonies). While he may have been cultivating his own violin playing at this time, the concertos were probably written for the court violinist Antonio Brunetti. Later, in domestic chamber music, Mozart played the viola, although with arms in proportion to his stature (as an adult he was just over five feet tall), he must have used a relatively small instrument.

During the winter concert season (1775–76), the violin was again in evidence, and the brilliant fifth ('Turkish') concerto may have been supplied with a new Adagio, K. 261. The late winter and spring are notable for launching the great series of piano concertos. One of these (No. 7, K. 242) is for three pianists, Countess Lodron and her daughters (one part is distinctly less demanding than the others). A flurry of lighter compositions includes the popular *Serenata notturna* (K. 239), wittily composed for solo quartet (violins, viola, and double bass) with timpani and small string orchestra. Rather than Finalmusik for the university, he composed in July a substantial Serenade (K. 250) for a wedding in the noble Haffner family. And he did not neglect the church, adding three masses and the very fine *Litaniae de venerabili altaris sacramento*.

---

[3] Four sonatas probably from 1766 (K.Anh. 199–202=33d–g) are known from an entry in Breitkopf's catalogue.

1777 began more auspiciously, as Salzburg's music was enlivened by visiting musicians, including two women whose effect on Mozart was considerable. In January, he finished a fresh piano concerto, in E♭, for the French keyboard virtuoso Victoire Jenamy (K. 271).[4] Her influence on the work cannot be assessed, but Mozart produced something special, and knew it, for he later played it himself and tried to have it published in Paris. Posterity has endorsed his high opinion. Its abundant thematic invention, the melancholy passion of the C-minor slow movement, and the ebullience of the finale mark the first masterpiece among the piano concertos. Another visitor was the soprano Josepha Dušek. She and her husband became good friends of the Mozarts, and of his music; his first offering to Josepha was a large-scale scena (recitative and aria), 'Ah, lo previdi . . . Ah, t'invola agl'occhi miei' (K. 272), in effect two recitatives and two arias, the first stormy, the second a limpid lament. Drawn from an opera, *Andromeda*, previously set by Paisiello, its scale and beauty are tokens of Mozart's frustration at having no opera commission of his own to work on.

On 1 August 1777, the Mozarts summoned the courage to ask leave to travel. Their petition is nominally from Wolfgang, although Leopold wrote it. It refers to an earlier request, which the archbishop had ignored, in which he drew attention to his difficult economic situation, but this was surely disingenuous. The difficulty was that the world needed to be reminded of Mozart's genius, and—most important—offer him a better job so that the whole family could leave Salzburg. The letter reminds the archbishop that the Gospel requires us to use our talents well, and that a few years ago (during their visit to Vienna) he had 'graciously declared that I had nothing to hope for in Salzburg'. It was an own goal. After letting the Mozarts stew for a while, the archbishop on 28 August was graciously pleased to instruct his manager of human resources to tell father and son, 'in the name of the Gospel', that they were both fired.

---

[4] The name Jenamy, variously spelled in the correspondence, was assumed to be a misspelling of 'Jeunehomme', the name under which the concerto is often programmed (confusingly, since it means 'young man' and might therefore be assumed to refer to the composer). Information from Michael Lorenz.

CHAPTER 6

Sacred Music

'I have thoroughly acquainted myself with that style since my youth'[1]

M OST OF MOZART'S SACRED MUSIC WAS COMPOSED FOR THE
Salzburg liturgy. Although the finest pieces date from the later
years, the essential patterns were laid down earlier. As a boy in Paris he
composed an independent setting of the first section of the Ordinary of
the Mass, a Kyrie eleison, and in Vienna (1768) he contributed both
small and large types of complete setting (*Missa brevis* and *Missa solemnis*).
Colloredo's decree concerning the length of the liturgy may explain the
predominance of the Missa brevis in Mozart's output, but certain days in
the church year required more elaborate music, including the four C-
major masses composed between 1775 and 1780, the four Litanies and,
in his last two years in Salzburg, two sets of Vespers.

Colloredo's edict did not exclude decorative instrumental music;
Mozart's production of two or three church sonatas continued annually
into 1780. These are one-movement works in binary form, mostly in a
lively tempo, seemingly unfitted for their ostensible purpose of being
performed *during* the reading of the Epistle. The earliest are scored for
two violins, bass, and organ continuo, but a few have notated organ
parts, perhaps for when Mozart himself was not playing. The same
music could easily have appeared in a divertimento with harpsichord
continuo, but in the very last sonata Mozart treats the organ as a soloist.

[1] Mozart's petition of May 1790 to Archduke Franz (son of Leopold II and Emperor from
1792).

Two sonatas are in the style of opera overtures, with a full orchestra (oboes, horns, trumpets, and drums) but still no viola part; their exultant style, and composition in March/April (both in 1777 and in 1779), suggest the celebration of Easter.

The sonatas accord well with the music of the Mass, which Stravinsky called 'rococo-operatic sweets-of-sin'.[2] Mozart, like all his contemporaries, bathed the liturgical text in streams of galant violinistic brilliance fit for divertimenti and symphonies, but he also paid homage to the Church tradition of learned music—counterpoint and fugue—cultivated by Italian composers and teachers (such as Martini), a tradition only tenuously connected to the baroque counterpoint of northern Germany (Mozart's encounter with J. S. Bach came later). Another feature of Mozart's church music is the regular employment of trombones, which impart a dignified colouring, and which were seldom used outside the church, though they made an occasional appearance in supernatural scenes in opera. They almost always double the lower three choral parts and do nothing else, except for a dignified rising arpeggio played on their own, in double octaves, at bars 42 and 46 of the Agnus Dei in the 'Credo' mass (K. 257).

These stylistic and orchestrational routines leave little space for the individual composer's characteristics. Mozart studied the works of Eberlin, the former Salzburg Kapellmeister, and his own immediate seniors such as Leopold Mozart, Adlgasser, and Michael Haydn. The last two are praised as 'fine contrapuntists' in a letter to Padre Martini ostensibly from Mozart, but probably drafted by Leopold (4 Sep 1776); this letter also mentions that by the archbishop's orders, the entire Mass, including the Ordinary, the Offertory, and the Epistle sonata, should not last more than forty-five minutes. In contributing to the church repertoire, Mozart had no need to trouble himself with originality, but he still paid attention to the meaning of the words. His numerous settings of the Greek 'Kyrie eleison' (Lord, have mercy on us) mostly begin in a dignified style before the animated violins begin to energise the vocal lines and maintain momentum between clauses of the text. An unfinished Kyrie in E♭, composed probably in the late 1770s, begins with ceremonial brass and the briefest of imitation in the lower instruments beneath

[2] Igor Stravinsky and Robert Craft, *Expositions and Developments* (London, 1962), 77.

Ex. 6.1   Kyrie, K. 322, from bar 5 (wind from bar 9 by Maximilian Stadler)

galant violins; the choral suspensions lend an appropriate note of pleading (ex. 6.1).[3] Usually a faster tempo takes over, with some solo interventions at 'Christe eleison'.

In the Kyrie, repetition of the six-word text was essential to allow time
for the music to establish some kind of form of its own. With the Gloria
and Credo, composers had to impose a musical shape on the longer texts,
without much word repetition. The Gloria of the 'Credo' mass (K. 257)
maintains its bright *Allegro assai* throughout, returning to the opening at
'Quoniam tu solus (bar 81), but as there are more syllables, the original
syncopation is necessarily lost (ex. 6.2 A, B). In between, Mozart con-
trives a complete change of mood at 'Qui tollis peccata mundi' (bar 57,

[3] This Kyrie (K. 322=Anh.12 [296b]) was completed by Maximilian Stadler. If written for
Salzburg, trombones would probably have been included.

Ex. 6.1 *(continued)*

ex. 6.3): the burden of the world's sins is suggested by the dotted rhythm in the bass, emerging at half the speed of the dotted rhythm on 'Gloria'; off-beat violin parts convey a distinct anxiety, and the music soon modulates into related minor keys (G, D, A minor by bar 75).

The 'Credo' mass is so called because of its unusual handling of the opening four-note motive ('Credo, credo'). Although there is no call for it in the liturgy, this motive recurs throughout, in echo form or in counterpoint with other text (as from bar 47), anticipating Beethoven's treatment of the word in his *Missa solemnis*. At 'Et incarnatus est' the tempo changes to andante, and the key to A minor, the music for soloists having the character of a siciliano. At 'Crucifixus', Mozart brings back the chorus (and trombones), completely changing the character of the music without changing tempo; the pain of crucifixion is underlined by a throbbing bass, *fp* dynamics, and chromaticism (ex. 6.4). The main tempo returns at 'Et resurrexit'.

These masses last some twenty-five to thirty minutes, with ample time for the customary tender elaboration of the Benedictus, and a

Ex. 6.1 (*continued*)

Ex. 6.2 'Credo' mass, K. 257, Gloria

a. Opening

b. Quoniam

Ex. 6.3 'Credo' mass, K. 257, Qui tollis (Allegro assai) from bar 57

strongly designed Agnus Dei. If the 'Credo' mass is more experimental than later works, Mozart still invented new ways of setting the words, and of drawing masses to a close. Following a slow, pleading 'Agnus Dei', he normally changes to a genial allegro for the 'Dona nobis pacem', ending with a clangour of trumpets. But the 'Credo' mass ends whimsically, *piano*, an idea repeated in K. 337. In K. 317, the so-called Coronation Mass, the 'Dona nobis' is a reprise of part of the Kyrie, linking the end of the mass to its beginning.[4] A curiosity of the last two

[4] Bar 7 of the Kyrie, marked *più andante*, following *andante maestoso*. It should be remembered that andante is not a slow tempo, but implies motion (walking, not jogging); in Mozart, therefore, 'more *andante*' means faster, while *andantino* (literally 'a little *andante*') is slower than *andante*.

Ex. 6.4 'Credo' mass, K. 257, Crucifixus, from bar 103

masses is that the Agnus Dei movements, both for solo soprano (castrato), anticipate the Countess's arias in *Figaro*: in K. 317, the melodic shape of 'Dove sono', and in K. 337 of 'Porgi amor', which is after all a kind of prayer. Such intertextual connections in Mozart use the simplest building-blocks of his style and do not necessarily offer any interpretative insight.

Mozart's last completed mass, K. 337 in C, is unfairly overshadowed by its more famous predecessor. The scoring is unusual, with two bassoon parts but no horns. The Kyrie is a beautiful andante with a canonic opening (imitation at the unison). In the Gloria, Mozart drives through the 'Qui tollis' without changing speed, reflecting the text by other means such as marking the name of Jesus by a French augmented sixth

(D–F♯–A♭–C, bars 62–63), a chord he seldom used. He spins out the final 'Amen' by contrasting solo and chorus rather like a Baroque concerto grosso.[5] The Cr–edo has a slower 'Et incarnatus', and when the Allegro resumes it is mainly based on earlier material, making a satisfying musical design without excluding expression of the text. With no loss of momentum, 'Et expecto resurrectionem mortuorum' inspires an enriched harmonic palette and suspensions—a less mannered response to the text than in the 'Waisenhausmesse' (ex. 2.6). For the Benedictus, instead of the usual cantabile, Mozart wrote a sturdy fugue in A minor, followed by a Hosanna with a perhaps humorous silent pause, and for the Agnus, he plunges into the remote key of E♭, working his way back to C for 'Dona nobis'.

Perhaps the boldness of this last mass shows a certain impatience with his role as a Salzburg organist. In assessing these formal experiments, we should not overlook the fact that the works formed part of the liturgy and, as such, were not performed without interruption (as were concert pieces); the same is true of the multimovement Litanies and Vespers. The Litanies begin with yet more settings of 'Kyrie eleison', but the text is extended by additional Latin words. The remaining litanies each end with 'Miserere', providing a challenge of repeated setting of the same words to which Mozart rose with considerable resourcefulness. The later Litanies show his preoccupation with satisfying musical designs, falling into a kind of choral sonata form in which material first heard in the dominant is recapitulated in the tonic.

The expansive sets of Vespers, consisting of five psalms and the Magnificat, belong to the last Salzburg years. *Vesperae solennes de Confessore* (1780) overshadows its older sibling, partly because of the ravishing soprano solo, 'Laudate Dominum'; the equivalent movement in *Vesperae solennes de Domenica* (1779) is an ear-tickling piece of virtuosity, somewhat ridiculous in context. The first vesper psalm is 'Dixit Dominus', which Mozart had set earlier (K. 193=186g); the later settings confirm his ability to reconcile the expressive claims of the text with those of a developing musical design, its clear tonal architecture defined by

[5] The final cadence, bar 98, is characterised by, for Mozart, exceptionally crude parallel fifths, the treble moving g"-e" while the bass moves c'–a.

thematic development and recall. The 1780 Magnificat, in C major, begins with a ceremonial *adagio*. The second clause 'Et exultavit') begins
allegro, sustained until the end.[6] The main theme stands out as a soprano
solo; the tutti response brings a modulation to the dominant, G. In the
equivalent to a development section, adroit contrasts are made between
various images in the text; the quality of mercy ('Et misericordia') hints
at minor keys, while for divine strength ('Fecit potentiam'), a powerful
tutti makes a connection to the earlier 'qui potens est', with the same

Ex. 6.5 *Vesperae solennes de confessore*, K. 339, Magnificat, from bar 43

[6] The similarity to the second theme in the overture (1791) to *La clemenza di Tito* is another nonsignifying, but nevertheless intriguing, coincidence.

Ex. 6.5. *(continued)*

orchestral figure (compare bars 18, violins, and 33, basses). Humility ('humiles') is stretched over an ambiguous progression; the contrasted treatment of the poor (to be filled with good things) and rich (to be sent empty away) brings a strikingly literal musical response (ex. 6.5), the texture emptying for 'inanes' (the basses do not even complete the text). All this may have amused Mozart, and it still adds to the appeal of the music. At 'Suscepit Israel', the 'recapitulation' begins and the 'exposition' material is resolved and extended through the doxology ('Gloria Patri').

In the psalms, the recapitulation of the opening coincides with the doxology rather than, in the half-humorous Baroque practice, 'Sicut erat in principio' ('As it was in the beginning'). Since he had to set the same words repeatedly, Mozart's method relieved him of the obligation to find completely new music each time. Throughout the psalms, as in longer mass movements and litanies, vigorous choral writing is surrounded with the galant energy of the violins. For 'Laudate pueri', Mozart adopted an old-fashioned contrapuntal style. In the 1779 Vespers, the text is treated with new ideas for each successive clause, but in 1780 Mozart adheres to the same minor-mode fugue subject, with diminished seventh, adding new counterpoints and enjoying the learned devices of inversion and stretto. Padre Martini would have been proud of him.

The Kyrie in D minor (K. 341=368a) is one of Mozart's finest church compositions, but in default of an autograph, its date remains a matter for controversy. It seems most likely to have been written just after *Idomeneo* in order to impress Carl Theodor and win an offer of employment in Munich. The alternative date proposed is late in the 1780s, when Mozart was angling for a church appointment in Vienna, but it was not entered in his catalogue. If indeed it was composed early in 1781, Mozart had reached the end of a road where sacred music was concerned, although he cannot have known it. He never again had to compose the same texts, or the same sorts of text, time and again; and he never completed another full-length sacred work.

CHAPTER 7

Mannheim and Paris

1777–1779

NO DOUBT MOZART COULD HAVE EARNED A TOLERABLE LIVING in Salzburg had his ambition, stoked by Leopold's, been set a little lower. He most missed the chance to write operas, but it was as a keyboard player and instrumental composer that he had to make his way following his first resignation from the archbishop's service. Colloredo relented and retained Leopold so long as he stayed in Salzburg; Mozart set off, on 23 September 1777, with his mother who had mostly avoided the hardships of travel since 1770. Maria Anna was not a forceful character, and since women were not accorded the same social entrée as men, she could not emulate Leopold's watchful authority. He attempted to exert control by letters in which encouragement and advice mutates to exhortation and eventually exasperation. He was not helped by the fact that letters took several days to reach their destination and usually crossed with the reply to a previous letter.[1] Leopold could not take fully into account the fact that Wolfgang would be too excited by his new freedom to obey orders from afar; nor was it in his character to respond methodically to letters or to keep a diary. He wrote with a self-assurance not always justified by events. His mother either would not enforce orders or could not; and Wolfgang ran the trip as best he could. Driven by

---

[1] David Schröder suggests that Leopold intended the letters to continue his biographical project, and that Wolfgang's manoeuvrings made for letters impossible to publish. *Mozart in Revolt*, passim.

a correct estimation of his own outstanding talent, he did not realise that his superiority was not obvious to all of his contemporaries, nor that some who did understand it might feel threatened rather than friendly; and he was not free of an inherited lack of tact.

Leopold wanted Wolfgang to find a better patron in Germany, within the relatively secure economic and musical world that he himself understood best. At some point, however, Mozart decided to attempt one of the great capitals. Vienna had proved resistant; the Mozarts had visited neither Berlin nor St Petersburg, where they had no contacts; that left Paris and London. At first, Mozart made a real effort to gain employment in Germany, beginning as usual in Munich. There he again encountered Mysliveček, seriously ill as a result of syphilis; their conversation further whetted Mozart's appetite to compose operas. While trying to cover expenses by giving a concert and lessons, Mozart cultivated the court to no avail, and throughout this unhappy odyssey he may have offended as many people as he impressed. In Augsburg they visited Leopold's brother Franz Alois, and Mozart befriended his daughter Maria Thekla Mozart, known as 'Bäsle' (little cousin). We cannot know how intimate they became, but Mozart's subsequent letters to her contain puerile examples of the scatological humour that occasionally surfaces in the correspondence of the rest of the family. Augsburg had little to offer, and after giving a concert Mozart moved on to Mannheim.

And there he stayed, rather then directing himself through the Rhineland as Leopold intended (on 20 November he wrote supposing they were already en route for Mainz). Mannheim was Mozart's first rebellion, and for a while he must have thought himself in the right. No court had more fine musicians; several were very friendly. He was able to perform, compose, and teach Rosa, daughter of Kapellmeister Christian Cannabich. But Mannheim could not permanently support a musician not in the Electoral service, and Carl Theodor's surface politeness, as often with the powerful at that time, may have concealed a lofty contempt for Mozart's excessive eagerness to demonstrate his talents. Mozart was gratuitously rude, at least in letters, about the older Kapellmeister, Georg Joseph Vogler; it is unlikely that his attitude was hidden from those in Mannheim, and Vogler had the elector's ear.

Mozart's interest in German opera was revived by *Günther von Schwarzburg*, a recent opera by the senior composer Ignaz Holzbauer;

and Anton Schweitzer's *Rosamunde* was performed that winter. The famous orchestra, Burney's 'army of generals', included a group of woodwind players as remarkable for ensemble as for individual virtuosity. Mozart happily renewed his friendship with the Wendling family, among them the court's principal female singers. Dorothea Wendling's daughter Elisabeth Augusta, soprano, pianist, and mistress of the elector, was the dedicatee of Mozart's first songs of any significance, the only ones in French. Their company was made more congenial by the kind of verbal ragging he had enjoyed in Augsburg, but the major factor prolonging Mozart's stay was that he fell in love with the seventeen-year-old Aloysia, second of the four daughters of Fridolin Weber, a minor theatre singer who also had menial roles as prompter and copyist.[2] Mozart was so smitten that he professed to believe that Aloysia would conquer Italy with him as her guide and thus make the fortune of both families. When Leopold heard of this harebrained scheme, he was understandably horrified and commanded his son to concentrate on becoming famous in his own right—if necessary in Paris.

For the present, winter weather kept them in Mannheim where, despite the social round, Mozart found time to do what he most enjoyed: composing. But not all such work was to his taste, and he would surely have preferred to work on a larger scale. He was commissioned to write three simple concertos and some quartets for flute, not for Wendling but for his student, a much-travelled Netherlands doctor, Ferdinand Dejean. To Leopold's annoyance, Mozart could only bring himself to write two quartets and one new concerto, making a second by arranging his oboe concerto; nevertheless he was annoyed at receiving only ninety-six gulden rather than the agreed two hundred. His distaste may have been less for the flute than for having to write for an amateur while living among some of the finest professional musicians in Europe. It was more congenial to write keyboard sonatas, mostly with violin. The solo sonatas were used in teaching; Rosa Cannabich had to learn the sonata in C (K. 309=284b), and Mozart reported that the slow movement was a 'portrait' of her. Music of this kind might be sold for publication in Paris, where he had published his childish 'Oeuvre premier'; it was time

---

[2] Fridolin's Weber's brother Franz Anton was the father of the composer Carl Maria von Weber, who was thus a cousin of Mozart's children.

to reclaim that number for mature music. Six violin sonatas (K. 301–306), begun in Mannheim and finished in Paris, were indeed published as the replacement Opus 1, and optimistically dedicated to the electress in Mannheim. He also completed another piano sonata, in D (K. 311=284c); in Paris he composed a third in A minor (K. 310=300d), and a couple of sets of variations on popular tunes ('Je suis Lindor' and 'Lison dormait'). These works elevated Mozart to the ranks of the greatest living composers of instrumental music, the Bach sons and Haydn; but few people had the opportunity to notice it at the time.

The Mozarts reached Paris on 23 March 1778. The intellectual capital of Europe, with a little luck and at another time, might have provided Mozart with a living. But a war of words had begun in 1774 between the supporters of Gluck's reformed opera and those who favoured an authentically Italian style. *Idomeneo* would eventually show that Mozart could assimilate French as well as Italian elements and adapt the innovations of Gluck to his own more richly musical ends. But in Paris, nobody asked him to try. The collapse of the old French repertory opened the door to supporters of Italian opera who disliked Gluck as a German intruder, and a more famous German than Mozart, J. C. Bach, failed to bridge the divide. He visited Paris while Mozart was there to prepare his own French opera commission, but *Amadis*, presented in 1779, was a flop. Mozart's contemporary J. C. Vogel, who arrived in Paris in 1776, had to wait ten years before his avowedly 'Gluckist' opera *La Toison d'or* was staged. Piccinni's *Roland* was in repertoire during Mozart's visit, and Piccinni aroused Leopold's usual suspicion of the Italians: he is 'bound to become jealous of you (6–11 May 1778)'. But Leopold said the same of Grétry whom he presumably regarded as indigenous.[3] In fact Piccinni was a generous man, and Mozart might have done well to cultivate him. As it was, his only theatre commission was a short ballet, *Les petits riens*, choreographed by Noverre, an old acquaintance.

Pamphlets in the 'Querelle des Gluckistes et des Piccinnistes' use the word 'music' in their title but discuss only opera.[4] Parisian musical life was by no means exclusively focused on the theatre, but that was the best

[3] It is uncertain what Leopold knew of Grétry (who came from Liège, in modern Belgium), or any recent French music.

[4] See François Lesure (ed.), *Querelle des Gluckistes et des Piccinnistes* (Geneva, 1984).

arena in which to win fame and money. Meanwhile Mozart had to take whatever chances he could. Even Leopold had admitted in the 1760s that instrumental music, where German origins were no handicap, was making progress in Paris. Thanks to his Mannheim friends, the tenor Raaff, and the wind players, Mozart had hopes of the Concert spirituel, whose programmes of symphonic and vocal music were given when the theatres were closed. The Lenten season was nearing its end, but Mozart obligingly adapted and composed substitute movements for Holzbauer's *Miserere* (5 Apr 1778).[5] The director of the Concert spirituel (also principal tenor of the Paris opera), Joseph Legros, accepted a Sinfonia concertante for the Mannheim wind players (Wendling, Ramm, Punto, and Ritter).[6] But on 12 April, they played a Symphonie concertante by Giuseppe Maria Cambini (1746–1825), an Italian who had lived in Paris for several years. Mozart believed Cambini was responsible for Legros 'forgetting' his own work; and this is possible, for Mozart had crassly offended the Italian by another display of his own musical brilliance, playing his own music back to him with improvements (1 May 1778). At the Concert spirituel Mozart must have heard with mixed feelings music by Cannabich and solo concertos written and played by his Mannheim friends. Eventually Legros commissioned a symphony for the June concerts (the 'Paris', No. 31, K. 297=300a). By this time, Mozart had completed his piano and violin sonatas, and a double concerto (K. 299= 297c) for the Comte de Guines to play with his daughter. He also had some pupils, but as he pointed out, it took more time than it was worth to get about such a large and expensive city to teach them in their homes, and some, including Guines, behaved as if they were doing Mozart a favour, and were slow to pay.

Mozart's mother gently complained in May that she hardly ever left their rather chilly lodging, although she had recovered from various minor ailments. The following month, as Mozart was preparing the symphony for performance, she became more seriously ill. Among the

[5] Mozart's music is lost. It is likely to have been performed on 16 or 17 April, but programme details do not survive. A Mozart aria was sung on 21 April by 'Savoy'. See Constant Pierre, *Histoire du Concert spirituel* (Paris, 1975), 308–9.

[6] Mozart's work has not survived. The Sinfonia concertante for oboe, clarinet, horn, and bassoon (K.Anh. 9=297B) may be an arrangement. See Robert D. Levin, *Who wrote the Mozart Four-Wind Concertante?* (Stuyvesant, NY, 1988).

viler Mozart legends is one that says he let her die unattended. In fact, she saw a priest and received extreme unction before falling into delirium, dying unconscious in the presence of her son, a nurse, and a friend, the musician Franz Joseph Heina. Medical treatment had been delayed by her own insistence on having a German doctor; Heina eventually found one, but she deteriorated meanwhile. In any case her fever (Mozart said 'internal inflammation', unwittingly anticipating the vague diagnosis of his own final illness) was something doctors could do nothing about beyond their ineffectual panacea of repeated bleeding, which probably hastened her end.

By then the 'Paris' symphony had been performed, and Mozart wrote home in the early hours of 3 July, considerately preparing his father for the worst by telling him his mother was merely very ill, then going on to relate the good news of his first and only success in Paris. He wrote by the same post to Abbé Bullinger, who had helped finance the journey, asking him to break the news gently and save Leopold a period of agonised waiting. Among the uncertainties of this painful period is the exact date of composition of the A-minor piano sonata. It has been associated with the pain and turbulence of the period of his mother's illness and death but may have been written earlier, affected by a turmoil of feelings connected with Aloysia or his severance from the guiding hand of Leopold. Or he may have written it because he felt like writing that kind of piece. Not every joy and pain perceived in Mozart's music can possibly originate from events; he was an artist, not an autobiographer, and his custom, as with other composers of the time, was to salt a collection of pieces mainly in major keys by including one in the minor. With the new op. 1, this role is fulfilled by the haunting violin sonata in E minor (K. 304); Mozart probably hoped to publish the piano sonatas as well.

Baron Grimm has been criticised for not helping Mozart more, but while a busy literary man, diplomat, and socialite, he had little influence in musical circles, and Mozart's attitude towards all things French may not have ingratiated him with a Francophile German intellectual. After the death of Anna Maria, Grimm offered Mozart hospitality; it was accepted somewhat gracelessly because Mozart liked Grimm's mistress, Mme d'Épinay. Through overconfidence, or poor preparation for his assault on Paris, Mozart had failed in his fight for recognition. He rationalised this by informing Leopold of active hostility towards himself, or at best indifference; he complained that 'they take me for a beginner—except for the real musicians'. This was written on 31 July 1778, when he still hoped for the return of Raaff to gain him a foothold with the establishment. Through the kindness of Jean-Joseph Rodolphe, he may have been offered an organist's post at Versailles, but given the distance from Paris, it must have seemed a dead end, and despite Leopold's advice he rejected it.

The organ proved his saviour, nevertheless. Leopold, who understandably wished to reunite his remaining family, succeeded in gaining Wolfgang the post in Salzburg left vacant by the death of Adlgasser. By now he had received from Grimm a firm but fair account of Wolfgang's prospects, not helped by his too amiable and easy-going ways; echoes of this comment find their way into letters years later, written when Mozart was settling in Vienna. Mozart hoped to avoid going back to Salzburg, and having delayed until 26 September, he moved as slowly as he dared. His letters are filled with disgust at the provinciality of his native town and the slovenliness of its musicians (for instance, that of 15 Oct 1778 from Strasbourg). He returned via Nancy and Strasbourg, where he gave a concert, and then Mannheim, only to have confirmed what he must have known: Carl Theodor, raised to the electorate of Bavaria, had removed to Munich. Mozart renewed various acquaintanceships, staying with Mme Cannabich; as an excuse to linger, he gave some lessons, protesting on 12 November that there were real employment prospects, as the elector would surely not endure Bavarian manners for ever. Leopold would have none of it, and on 19 November he resorted to moral blackmail: 'your whole intent is to ruin me [. . .] I hope that, after your mother had to die in Paris, you will not burden your conscience with the death of your father'. On 23 November he struck a subtler or more conciliatory note, pointing out that Aloysia was now employed in Munich, which was not far from Salzburg; Italy was also nearer, where Wolfgang might hope to build a career in opera. On 9 December Mozart headed for Munich to try his luck with Carl Theodor once more—and with Aloysia. He was almost without means but stayed with the Webers and offered Aloysia the ambitious recitative and aria 'Popoli di Tessaglia . . . Io non chiedo'. But his double mission failed. There was nothing to be had from Carl Theodor, and Aloysia received him coldly. The flautist Becke took on the role of comforter at this, perhaps the lowest point of Mozart's life. He wrote to Leopold on 29 December as his son's advocate. Given the fury or anxiety expressed in Leopold's letters, Mozart was understandably worried at the reception he might receive at home; but surely it was the loss of Aloysia that made him weep bitterly for an hour.[7]

---

[7] Halliwell, *Family*, 327–29; Robert Gutman, *Mozart, a Cultural Biography*, 473–72.

CHAPTER 8

The 'Classical Style'

Mozart and the Keyboard

COMPOSITION APART, MOZART'S PROFESSIONAL ASPIRATIONS WERE
nearly all centred on the keyboard ('clavier'). He developed his
manual technique on the harpsichord, but by the time he wrote home
from Augsburg after visiting Johann Andreas Stein's organ and piano
workshop, his preferred instrument was the piano: the 'Cembalo col piano
e forte', nowadays called 'fortepiano' (14 and 16 Oct 1777).[1] He sometimes composed at the keyboard, developing his technique as well as his
compositional ideas by improvisation. When he wrote down fantasias, cadenzas, and variation sets, fugues, and perhaps also sonatas, he fixed a version of music originally improvised, so others could use it—Nannerl,
students, performers lacking his inventive facility—but also for sale (posterity was not in his thoughts). Variations on 'Non più andrai' from *Figaro*
were performed in Prague but unfortunately never committed to paper;
there were surely more 'lost' works of this kind. What were ostensibly improvisations may have been partly worked out in advance, but we cannot
say how closely notated works correspond to what his amazed audiences
may have thought he plucked out of the air.

The practice of improvisation may explain occasional lapses in patterns of modulation that with Mozart are usually smooth, ingenious, or

---

[1] 'Fortepiano' is used today to distinguish the revived eighteenth-century instrument from
the modern one. Mozart played only on contemporary instruments, here simply termed
'piano'.

if startling, expressively so. The first movement of the D–major sonata K. 311 (284c) may suffer from his experimental tendencies. There are fascinating aspects to this movement, such as his use of a new and ano-dyne closing motif (bar 38) as the basis of the development, and the re-turn of themes in the recapitulation in a different order from the exposition. But part of the retransition from the development rudely brushes aside an elegant B–minor cadence to continue in G (ex. 8.1). In view of Mozart's practice elsewhere, it seems we are dealing here with

Ex. 8.1 Sonata in D, K. 311, first movement, from bar 52

Allegro con spirito

arbitrary behaviour more suited to a fantasia than a sonata. Not that brusqueness is always arbitrary; in the much later Adagio in B minor (K. 540), similarly harsh gestures (three modulating chords) recur as a form of punctuation, becoming part of the work's character.

Mozart's music is routinely said to be easy for unformed players and difficult for mature artists, since every note, jewel-like, must be perfectly placed. This view is affected by the virtuosity of subsequent generations, composing for progressively larger instruments; it makes sense only within today's museum culture. In his own day, Mozart's brilliance was remarked upon as much as his cultured taste and, at times, his fondness for harsh and difficult progressions. Late in 1781, his contest with Clementi, who had also trained on the harpsichord, showed him technical possibilities he himself could not match (see chap. 11), particularly in the right hand; Michael Kelly, who met him in 1785–86, reported that the heart of Mozart's virtuosity lay in 'his feeling, the rapidity of his fingers, the great execution and strength of his left hand particularly'.[2] We might infer as much from the sonatas, for example the striding left hand of the finale to K. 310 (ex. 8.2a), or the triplet run over two octaves in the finale of K. 576, accompanying the reiteration of a seemingly innocent melody (ex. 8.2b). A good left-hand technique is a requirement in concertos, including those written for others, as in the second variation in the finale to K. 453, written for Barbara Ployer. His daring is also displayed in rapid switches of register, as in K. 309 (ex. 8.2c). Absolute equality of hands is apparent throughout his mature work, for which the sonata K. 533 may stand as example (ex. 8.2d).

Mozart's earliest published works were keyboard solos with accompaniment for violin, and piano trios in which the violin and cello are more ornamental than independent. Such works had a domestic market, whereas the solo piano sonata, before the age of the recital, lacked the sociability of these small ensembles, to which should be added the piano duet (four hands on one keyboard). The journeys of 1777–79 produced a stream of sonatas, some with violin, the first flowering of his maturity in these genres. The C-major sonata (K. 309=284b), written for Rosa Cannabich, shows his confidence in handling this intimate yet demanding medium. The first movement is an excellent example of the maturity

[2] Michael Kelly, *Reminiscences* (as *Solo Recital*, London, 1972), 123.

Ex. 8.2

a. Sonata in A minor, K. 310, finale, from bar 211

b. Sonata in D, K. 576, finale, from bar 9

of techniques associated with what is now usually called 'the Classical Style'. The opening theme consists of disparate ideas (ex. 8.3a), a stern arpeggio similar to the opening of the next sonata (K. 284=205b), where it is followed by vigorous drumming with patches of lyricism among brilliant figuration. K. 309 presents a more marked contrast through its answering phrase, *piano* (bar 3), which nevertheless maintains the logical ascent of the arpeggio to g". The sequential falling phrase concludes in bar 8, but the end is elided with a return to the opening. This time the

Ex. 8.2 *(continued)*

c. Sonata in C, K. 309, first movement, from bar 54

d. Sonata in F, K. 533, first movement, from bar 176

answering phrase does not resolve, instead breaking off; the *forte* c''' completes the arpeggio, and its accompaniment maintains the quaver motion. At bar 21, the ascent reaches e''' and a gradual descent brings a strong half-close on D, the dominant of the dominant, a key-change carefully engineered by the part-writing (and thus the kind of progression that attracts the commendatory term 'organic', unlike ex. 8.1). The new theme in G brings a new rhythmic character. The closing phases of the exposition climax on a dissonant chord (diminished seventh, bar 50), using the

Ex. 8.2 (*continued*)

highest note available (f'''), before a short brilliant passage culminating in a trill, and the coda already quoted (ex. 8.2c).

Development is a musical process that may occur anywhere, but its concentration towards the middle of movements leads us to identify a 'development section' in sonata form. This part of K. 309 shows how a striking idea can be transformed while retaining its identity. The music modulates by rising fifths, led by assertions of the opening theme in G minor, D minor, and A minor, where, however (bar 73), the motive changes intervals and is directed upwards (ex. 8.3b). Subsequently the second bar of the motive is treated in isolation. The original contour is restored at bar 86, the retransition to the recapitulation.

Mozart was seldom content with recapitulations that merely adjust the exposition to maintain the tonic rather than modulate to the dominant. In K. 309, the recapitulation is actually four bars longer than the exposition. From its eighth bar (bar 101) Mozart initiates a short secondary development with the opening motif in C minor and takes us on a considerable journey before resolving at bar 110 into the music of bar 15. The original bars 27–28 are removed, but one more bar is needed to extend the transition and end on G instead of the exposition's D. With material originally in the dominant, the composer has to decide whether to transpose down a fifth, to a duller register, or up a fourth, where it could go beyond the instrument's range; Mozart usually deals with this problem creatively, by

Ex. 8.3 Sonata in C, K. 309, first movement

a. Opening, from bar 1

Allegro con spirito

transposing part of the material down, and part of it up. In K. 309 the theme (bar 129) reappears first in the left hand, *below* its accompaniment. For much of the closing period, downward transposition was the only option, and example 8.2c recurs without skipping between registers. Mozart compensates for this lessening of interest by a coda, repeating the opening theme and adding further emphatic cadences in the upper register.

Ex. 8.3 (*continued*)

b. From bar 73

The slow movements of the piano sonatas and duets are among Mozart's most intimately expressive. In K. 309 Mozart claimed to be portraying Rosa Cannabich, or at least her keyboard skills, including a delicate touch, the ability to vary dynamics without exaggeration (there are many *fp* markings), and the fantasy needed to make the ornamentation of the recurrent theme sound spontaneous. The tempo *Andante un poco Adagio* warns that the potentially lively rhythms of the opening are the easy form of the theme; at bar 17, grace notes are added, and at bar 25 the theme becomes a flurry of demisemiquavers. In the final stages a tiny chromatic figure has to be played in spread octaves (bars 72–74); the dynamic is, helpfully, *forte*, but the passage must not sound rough. The transitional episode from bar 40 requires firm playing of three-part counterpoint, in the manner of a trio with two violins playing a chain of suspensions over a steadily moving bass; on its recurrence (bar 60) the bass is transformed into flowing triplets (slower and less far-ranging than ex. 8.2b). Mozart was fond of this Baroque texture, of which another example forms an episode in the F major rondo (K. 494); when adding this to two new movements to make a sonata (K. 533), he enriched the coda with more counterpoint based on the rondo theme, a cadenza-like passage which forms a worthy climax to one of his finest sonatas.

The finale of K. 309 is headed Rondeau and is an example of 'Sonata rondo', a form Mozart is said to have invented, in a string quartet (K. 157 in C) from his last Milan visit.[3] But the early piece is a primitive affair, lacking in contrast between themes, and in transitional material, whereas by K. 309 the material is fully worked out. The distinguishing feature of this design is its wedding of an essential component of sonata form onto the episodic structure of a rondo; the first episode (B) is usually in the dominant, but is recapitulated in the tonic (the second episodic theme, if any, is not). In K. 309 B follows a transition at bar 40 and is recapitulated at bar 143. Its original glittering summit, the right-hand tremolo (d"–d"') of bar 58, is necessarily transposed down at bar 162, as the keyboard did not extend to g"'. Following the last return of the rondo theme (A) from bar 189, Mozart returns to this tremolo over more intense harmony; it rises to c"' as a springboard for climactic emphasis on e"', the highest available note of the tonic chord. Having made

---

3 *TNG2*, xxi, 653.

Ex. 8.4 a. Sonata, K. 310, first movement, with contrapuntal background

his point by this ingenious variation of a formal template of which he may, in practice, have been scarcely aware, Mozart wittily follows the forceful series of cadences with a lower-register restatement of A, ending *pianissimo*. Sonatas were not intended for public performance; the grandly expanded rondo K. 494/533 ends the same way as K. 309, with both hands low down, written in the bass clef, an example of a dry wit with which Mozart is not always credited.

Whatever the cause of the passionate character of the A-minor sonata (K. 310=300d), the driving rhythms of its outer movements remain ex-

Ex. 8.4 *(continued)*

b. Rondo in A minor, K. 511, from bar 116

ceptional, as does its dissonant opening, based on a bold projection of a contrapuntal sequence (ex. 8.4a). The sombre middle section of the slow movement (in C minor, from bar 37) can be matched in major-key sonatas, but only in later years, notably K. 333 (315c), where the second part (bar 32) brings some of Mozart's tartest dissonance, and K. 533, where the contrapuntal sequences from bar 60 are scarcely less harsh; the apparent serenity of the main theme is itself clouded by the diminished seventh in the second bar. Several slow movements in the form of a main theme and episodes are afflicted by a similar melancholy, usually in the form of a minor-mode episode (as in the last two piano sonatas, K. 570 and 576). The apogee of Mozartian melancholy is the A-minor rondo K. 511; the division between the private, passionate Mozart and the artful pomaded image is never clearer than in the formidably daring sequence near the end (ex. 8.4b). Such works were surely meant for the connoisseur without too much regard to the amateur.

Music for Violin and Piano

A growing equality between the instruments is perceptible in the violin sonatas written in Mannheim and Paris, but as twelve years had intervened since K. 31, this development is hardly surprising. The first of the sonatas published as Mozart's second op. 1 and op. 2 (in G, K. 301=293a) begins with the melody in the violin and repeated by the keyboard, a scoring neatly reversed at the recapitulation. The sonatas closely resemble those for solo keyboard in their formal structures, but except for the last, in D (K. 306=300l), they have only two movements, lacking the cantabile slow movement like that of the contemporary solo sonatas K. 309 and 310. The extended slow movement of the fifth sonata, in A (K. 305=293d) is a set of six variations, the fifth in A minor and the sixth back in the major, in triple metre and allegro, a version of the pattern common to most of Mozart's variation sets.

The apparent exception to the comparatively light-weight manner of the op. 1 sonatas is the fourth, in E minor (K. 304=300c): apparent because the texture remains pellucid and the atmosphere nostalgic, quite unlike the turmoil of the A-minor piano sonata. Only the allusion to the opening theme at the end of the exposition and recapitulation (bars 77 and 183) is sternly contrapuntal, and the coda returns to this theme in wistful reminiscence. The second movement is a minuet and trio. The minuet uses complex textures, mainly delicate and in higher registers, but with a few bars of striding bass at the end (bar 78), resembling the A-minor sonata (ex. 8.2a). The full harmony of the major-mode trio, at the centre of the keyboard, makes a contrast as emotionally telling as similar music by Schubert.

The last sonata of the group (K. 306) begins its slow movement with a piano solo, the violin providing a counterpoint before taking it over and expanding its range; the violin twice takes on the duty of varying register in the recapitulation (bars 75 and 81; compare 24 and 30). In the finale the opening theme is played in unison, at first with the violin an octave below the piano, then with it an octave above. The timbre in both inversions has a disarming charm matching the gentle swing of the melody. This movement veers between its opening $\frac{2}{4}$ allegretto and allegro in $\frac{6}{8}$, resolving or brushing aside problems of integration by a composed cadenza.

The sonatas written early in Mozart's Vienna years follow the gains made in Mannheim. The sonata in G (K. 379=373a) is one of his most original. It opens with a richly ornamented adagio in which the last bars are coloured by minor-mode inflections; the movement never properly ends, merging into a minor-mode allegro where the twelve-bar development is short even by Mozart's standards. This disturbing start is moderated by the second movement proper, a set of variations. Otherwise the Vienna sonatas all have three movements, though with great diversity of form; after sonata-form opening movements come variations as central and final movements, rondos, and a *Tempo di minuetto* finale to K. 377 (=473e). The set published as op. 2 concludes with the dashing rondo finale of the E♭ sonata K. 380 (374f), in the hunting style best exemplified by finales to horn concertos. The remaining sonatas for violin and piano came singly over the next few years. They confirm the maturity of a genre that by now has left the domestic ambience for performance in Viennese salons, becoming true chamber music. The solo piano sonatas and those for violin and piano fed into the work of Beethoven along with music by Clementi and others. Largely ignored when nineteenth-century pianists and violinists began to form a concert repertory, they have been underrated by twentieth-century critics even as they have been loved by musicians.

CHAPTER 9

Salzburg and Munich

1779–1781

CURSING THE PEOPLE OF SALZBURG EVEN IN HIS LAST LETTER FROM Munich (8 Jan 1779), Mozart set off for home. He was offered free travel in the coaches of various dignitaries, whose schedules he had to follow. In Salzburg, he found the petition for him to succeed Adlgasser, written by Leopold and awaiting his signature. His appointment was approved in February, with the condition that he compose more music than his predecessor. The gloom of the family, reunited but without Maria Anna, may have been alleviated by Bäsle, Wolfgang's cousin, who visited him in Munich and Salzburg; but whatever her feelings, Mozart was not interested in her as a possible mate, no doubt to Leopold's relief.

After his glimpse of freedom, Mozart must have felt that the waters were closing over his head. Composition, a possible means of escape, was also balm to his bruised feelings. He was later to complain, from Vienna, that he could not do serious work in Salzburg (6 May 1781). Nevertheless, during this period he produced his finest works to date in every field he cultivated, not least church music—although he may not have considered that his highest priority. By March 1779, he had completed the Mass in C (K. 317), still one of his best-known sacred works, followed a year later by the Missa solemnis in C (K. 337), his last complete setting of the Ordinary. In each of these years Mozart also supplied the cathedral with full Vesper settings, in duration equivalent to a Mass, and he continued to produce 'Epistle sonatas'. What more the archbishop expected is not clear, but presumably Mozart played a full role in performing music by his colleagues, and reviving his own, during his twenty-two-month tenure as organist.

This last period in Salzburg is most notable as that in which Mozart became a complete master of prevailing orchestral genres. He produced three excellent new symphonies. The first in G (No. 32, K. 318) is a short symphony in the form of an Italian overture, but the others (Nos. 33 in B♭, K. 319, and 34 in C, K. 338) are four-movement works. The 'Posthorn' serenade K. 320, with two attached Marches, served as university Finalmusik in 1779 and contains a symphony and two fine concertante movements. A new concerto for two pianos (No. 10, K. 365), supposedly for Nannerl and himself to play, was good enough to be revived publicly in Vienna. He abandoned a concerto for violin and piano, intended for a concert society in Mannheim, and a sinfonia concertante in A for violin, viola, and cello, instead composing the magnificent Sinfonia concertante (K. 364) for violin and viola, one of his finest orchestral works of any period, a more eloquent brother to the 'Jenamy' piano concerto (K. 271): both are in E♭, with C-minor slow movements of haunting melancholy. Dialogue is always a feature of Mozart's concertos, but usually between soloist and orchestra rather than between two individual 'characters', and the Sinfonia concertante may briefly have consoled him for the lack of an opportunity to write opera.

The Mozarts were keen theatregoers, enjoying the work of various troupes of travelling actors who passed through Salzburg. Mozart's acquaintance with the actor and impresario Emanuel Schikaneder, eventually to bear extraordinary fruit, may be dated from 1780, when Schikaneder's repertoire in Salzburg included *Hamlet*. It was probably in 1779 that Mozart added the remarkable orchestral entr'actes to the choruses for *Thamos* composed some years earlier. And inspired by his experience of German opera and melodrama in Mannheim and elsewhere, he began composing a German opera despite having no actual commission. He could have offered it to the touring companies, for in 1780 Johann Böhm's troupe gave *La finta giardiniera* as a Singspiel, with spoken dialogue; Mozart may have had a hand in adapting it, and it was perhaps performed in Salzburg before the known production at Augsburg.[1] But

---

[1] Other German productions are known, with various titles. Modern revivals were in Singspiel form until the lost Italian act 1 reappeared in the late twentieth century.

for the new opera, Mozart surely had Vienna in mind, for Joseph II had recently established a German opera company, the Nationalsingspiel, to vary the repertoire of plays at the Burgtheater. Mozart's MS has no title, but the work is known by the name of its heroine, *Zaide*. It is too substantial to be considered a fragment and is fully orchestrated as far as it goes. *Zaide* and *Thamos* were valuable training in extensive composition to German words, so that Mozart was well prepared for the Vienna commission that eventually came his way. More immediately, composing music of such dramatic intensity prepared him for his next operatic challenge, when seeds sown in Mannheim and Munich finally grew into an opera seria commission for the 1781 Carnival.

Idomeneo

It may have been Anton Raaff who persuaded Munich to offer Mozart the commission for a serious opera on the grandest scale. Although Carl Theodor never offered Mozart a job, he recognised something remarkable in him, and doubtless agreed to the commission; but Mozart was less sure of the goodwill of the theatre intendant, Count Seeau. On his return journey from Paris he had written from Mannheim that this 'cursed scoundrel [Seeau] said my opera buffa [*La finta giardiniera*] had been booed off the stage in Munich!' (12 Nov 1778). Mozart even had doubts about Raaff, whose Bernacchi-school bel canto style was not, he had declared while in Paris (12 June), to his taste. Nevertheless, they were firm friends; he had greatly pleased the tenor with the aria 'Se al labbro mio non credi' (K. 295), and Raaff, at sixty-six, had been engaged to take the title-role in the new opera. The friendship of the Wendlings, and Cannabich and his orchestra, stimulated Mozart to give of his best. The outcome is an opera sui generis, almost too rich in invention, its dramatic situations so elaborated that severe cuts were made before the first performance to allow time for an ample final ballet. Perhaps it is not surprising that it took some 150 years for Mozart's extraordinary achievement to be fully appreciated.

The commission indicates the eclectic nature of Carl Theodor's operatic interests, for rather than an existing Italian libretto, Munich chose a French text, *Idoménée* by Antoine Danchet.[2] Translation and adaptation

---

[2] It was composed by André Campra for Paris in 1712.

were entrusted to Gianbattista Varesco, the archbishop's chaplain in Salzburg; he had to turn a five-act *tragédie lyrique* at least half-way towards the moral drama of Metastasio, as well as into a three-act form. The result is a hybrid—thanks to the music, a magnificent hybrid—but not a new type of opera. The first important Italian operas based on translated French librettos were composed by Traetta in Parma in the 1750s, followed by his *Armida* for Vienna (1761). The next year Gluck composed *Orfeo ed Euridice* for Vienna, followed by *Alceste* in 1767; this the Mozarts had seen, and even before witnessing Jommelli's *Armida* in Naples they may have had some inkling of his 'reform' works composed for Stuttgart. Some of Jommelli's works had been performed in Mannheim, and it is he who comes closest, at his best, to the language of *Idomeneo*. Mozart had also experienced the reverse process, the Italianisation of French opera, at the hands of Piccinni. All these models, and *Zaide*, contributed to the unprecedented richness of the orchestrally accompanied recitatives in *Idomeneo*.

Mozart's assumption of control over the libretto can be followed in a fascinating exchange of letters that continued until Leopold, with Nannerl, came to Munich for the performances. Leopold usually took Varesco's part, urging Mozart to set all the words in scenes that, especially when slowed by orchestral participation, were expanded beyond what could be effective dramatically. Mozart made the point succinctly, referring to the unexpected intervention of the god Neptune who brings about a happy ending: 'If the ghost's speech in Hamlet were a bit shorter, it would be far more effective' (29 Nov 1780). As much could be said of other scenes, including the meeting of the king Idomeneo and his son Idamante by the seashore, and the climactic scene, where the sacrifice of Idamante is interrupted by the arrival of his beloved Ilia, intent on replacing him on the altar. Varesco seems to have considered that removing lines from his text was mutilating a monument; everything had to be printed for the edification of the audience. But Mozart was far more experienced in the theatre than Varesco or his own father. He used Raaff as the excuse for insisting on a revised aria text, but it was his own initiative to cut to the bone those scenes that would be ineffective because neither Raaff nor the 'molto amato castrato' Vincenzo dal Prato (Idamante) were good actors. For both, Mozart tailored the arias to avoid overtaxing them, which may explain the equivocal views some have expressed concerning Idamante's music.

Mozart was enthusiastic about Dorothea Wendling who sang Ilia. He had written a scena for her on a text from Metastasio's *Didone abbandonata* ('Basta vincesti . . . Ah, non lasciarmi', K. 295a). His careful tailoring of music to the strengths of singers is apparent when this aria is compared to the opening scene of *Idomeneo*; likewise a scena for Wendling. Raaff's final aria, 'Torna la pace intorno', can be compared to music by Hasse on whose work Raaff's reputation had been built.[3] And Mozart did not forget his friends who had been deprived of their Sinfonia concertante; Ilia's second aria, 'Se il padre perdei', has beautiful solos for flute, oboe, horn, and bassoon.

Altogether, this period of collaboration with friends who were expert musicians was among the happiest of Mozart's career.[4] But there were problems: Dal Prato's musicianship appealed to Mozart no more than his acting, although his singing must have been competent by most standards, and Munich retained his services thereafter. The role of Idomeneo's confidant Arbace was expanded at Mozart's request by a recitative ('Sventurata Sidon', in act 3), because Domenico Panzacchi could act and deserved the chance to shine; as the character is minor, Arbace's two arias are often omitted, but the recitative is too good to lose. Mozart was also firm with Raaff, insisting that the dramatic crux of act 3 must be a quartet—perhaps the single most beautiful number in the opera—rather than an aria, and refusing to contemplate an aria at the end of act 2; he must confront Neptune's rage in a *recitativo obbligato*, for which Varesco must supply the text. In the end, Raaff's last aria was omitted, along with last-act arias for all the singers except Dorothea Wendling.

The orchestral writing is a crowning glory of *Idomeneo* and, with the writing for chorus, is perhaps the feature that most obviously differentiates it from conventional opera seria. Mozart had seen the sea, although only the English Channel, and this perhaps helped him evoke its wrath in the first act. He also uses the orchestral development to make a metaphorical point, for the storm music emerges directly out of Elektra's furious aria 'Tutto nel cor vi sento', and thus from the wrath of Agamemnon's daughter, spurned by Idamante for the enslaved princess

---

[3] See Daniel Heartz, 'Raaff's Last Aria: a Mozartean Idyll in the Spirit of Hasse', *Musical Quarterly* 60 (1974): 517–43.

[4] This was confirmed by Constanze; see Medici and Hughes, *A Mozart Pilgrimage*, 94.

Ilia. The most original twist to this D-minor aria is the return of the opening in C minor. Elektra quickly recovers her original key, but the rent in the musical fabric is not so easily repaired, and a modulation at the end of the aria—Mozart left no time for applause—brings back C minor for the storm, in the same tempo. In the storm music, the dynamic flux, agitation in the strings, sustained blasts of woodwind and four horns, antiphonal scurries in the violins, plaintive woodwind scales, are tricks of the trade, superbly handled; their originality, here and in the still more extraordinary music near the end of act 2, lies in the concentrated application of such techniques over a harmonic pattern that verges, in the latter scene, on tonal incoherence—itself a metaphor for the terror of the Cretan populace, menaced by a monster from the sea.

Despite such wild imaginings, Mozart's concern with an overarching coherence is never more apparent than in *Idomeneo*. Like all his mature operas, it begins and ends in the same key, D major; exceptionally, each act also ends in this key. Mozart was delighted to compose the ballets himself, after acts 1 and 3, and he included in them thematic as well as tonal references to other parts of the drama.[5] Thematic connections have been detected between several numbers, forming something like a network of leading motives.[6] Not all these elements can have got there by accident, but Mozart's intentions remain unfathomable; nothing quite like this has been detected in any earlier opera, even those of Gluck.

Mozart again found time for new composition once the opera was completed. No doubt currying favour, he composed a fine scena ('Misera, dove son! . . . Ah! Non son io', K. 369) for Countess Paumgarten, the elector's current 'favorita', or mistress (13 Nov 1780).[7] For Ramm, who had played his oboe concerto, Mozart wrote an excellent oboe quartet (K. 370); and he may also have written the noble Kyrie in D minor (K. 341=368a). Uniquely among Mozart's church music it uses an

---

[5] The final ballet received a separate Köchel number (367). It is hard to be sure how much of it was performed, or in what order.

[6] For discussion of the thematic and tonal aspects coherence of *Idomeneo* see *inter alia* Heartz, *Mozart's Operas*; Julian Rushton, *W.A. Mozart: Idomeneo*; Idem., 'A Reconciliation Motive in *Idomeneo*?', in Dorothea Link, *Words about Mozart*.

[7] FAVORITA is spelled out as a crude acrostic. Mozart liked K. 369 well enough to have it performed by Adamberger in 1783.

orchestra with clarinets and four horns—the orchestra of *Idomeneo*—and it may have been part of a plan to demonstrate his all-round competence to the elector. In a letter of 13 November, well before the production of *Idomeneo*, Mozart says 'I should like to be known here in that [sacred] style of composition as well', and asks Leopold to bring scores of three of his masses, specifying one in B♭ (probably K. 275=272b); the others were perhaps the most recent, K. 317 and 337.

Despite Carl Theodor's approval, there were only three performances of *Idomeneo*. Composing for such connoisseurs and professionals may actually have created a problem for Mozart. Music of equally glorious vocal and instrumental elaboration recurs in *Die Entführung*, and gave him the reputation of favouring the orchestra at the expense of the voices, although few complain today. But for the present, no doubt glowing from the assurance that he had achieved something beyond the power of his contemporaries, Mozart bid farewell to Leopold and Nannerl, who returned to Salzburg. Having overstayed his own leave by several weeks, he obeyed the archbishop's summons to join him in Vienna.

Mozart's birthplace, now the Mozarts Geburtshaus museum.

Leopold Mozart. Portrait attributed to Pietro
Antonio Lorenzoni, c. 1775.

VUE DE LA VILLE CAPITALE DE SALZBOURG AVEC LA FORTERESSE.
Dédié à l'Illustre Chapitre de l'Eglise Metropolitaine de Salzbourg.

View of Salzburg in 1791. Engraving by Anton Amon after Franz von Naumann.

The Wunderkind in formal dress. Portrait
attributed to Pietro Antonio Lorenzoni,
c. 1763.

Nannerl in formal dress. Portrait attributed to
Lorenzoni, c. 1763.

Hieronymus Joseph Franz de Paula,
Count Colloredo, Prince-Archbishop
of Salzburg. Anonymous portrait.

Nannerl, Wolfgang, and Leopold Mozart, with the portrait of Maria Anna.
Attributed to Johann Nepomuk della Croce, c. 1780–81.

Piano by Anton Walter, c. 1780, owned by
Mozart.

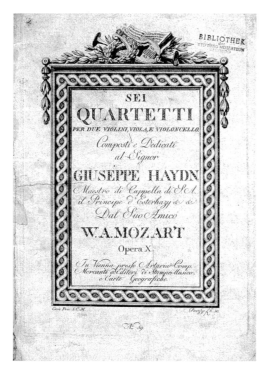

Title page of Mozart's quartets Op. 10, dedicated
to Joseph Haydn and published by Artaria,
Vienna, 1785.

Mozart at the keyboard. Unfinished portrait by Joseph Lange, c. 1789.

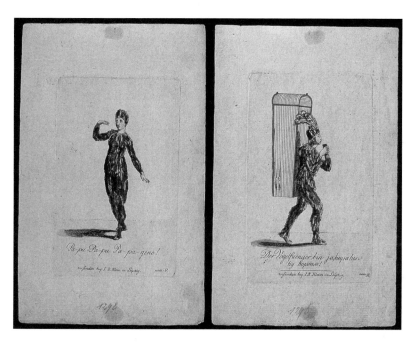

Costume designs for Papagena and Papageno in *Die Zauberflöte*. Engraving by Salomon Richter, Leipzig, 1793.

Theater bill announcing the premiere of *Die Zauberflöte*.

Constanze Mozart. Portrait by Hans Hansen,
1802.

Mozart's sons Carl Thomas and Franz Xaver
Wolfgang. Portrait by Hans Hansen, c. 1798.

CHAPTER 10

Orchestral Music

'the glorious effect of a symphony with flutes, oboes, and clarinets'

W HEN MOZART RETURNED TO SALZBURG IN 1766, HE HAD COM-
posed half-a-dozen symphonies and the seventeen-movement
Galimathias musicum (K. 32). Other than piano concertos, the majority of his
orchestral works date from periods of residence in Salzburg, with a few symphonies composed for concerts in Vienna and Milan. His Salzburg output
also includes violin concertos and orchestral divertimenti—serenades, cassa-
tions, and Finalmusik for summer festivities. The usual count of forty-one
Mozart symphonies, derived from the nineteenth-century Breitkopf and
Härtel edition, is an underestimate, and the situation is complicated by
doubtful authorship in a few cases, and because what constituted a symphony was not defined as an exclusive category. The sinfonia (overture) of
Italian opera was indistinguishable from a three-movement symphony (fast–
slow–fast), and could be taken from the theatre to the concert-room, and
movements extracted from Finalmusik were recycled as symphonies and
concertos.[1] Mozart added a conventional finale, a jiglike Presto in $\frac{3}{8}$(K. 120),
to make a symphony of the two-movement sinfonia of *Ascanio in Alba*. Beside the other Italian opera overtures, two of the eight symphonies written
in Salzburg in 1771–72 are in this three-movement form (K. 128–129), apparently without theatrical connections; the other six have minuets, with finales mostly in duple metres.

---

[1] The roster of Mozart symphonies in NMA and listed in Zaslaw, *Symphonies*, includes those
derived from opera overtures and Finalmusik.

It is too easy to define a divertimento as a piece with a couple of minuets on each side of a slow movement, but this is the form of the wind serenade K. 375, and may have been of *Eine kleine Nachtmusik*, for which Mozart listed a second minuet in his catalogue. The 'Haffner' symphony (K. 385) seems originally to have had two minuets and an attendant march and to have been commissioned, and treated in Salzburg, as a serenade (27 Jul 1782). But as already indicated (see chap. 5), Salzburg Finalmusik had more than five movements. The inclusion of concerto movements begins with the very first cassation (K. 63, from 1769). The grandest of all Finalmusik is the 'Posthorn serenade' K. 320 (1779), which includes material Mozart adapted for a three-movement symphony in D (the first, fifth, and seventh movements), and two charming concertante movements (the third and fourth, Andante and Rondo); associated with this, and other Finalmusik, are a couple of marches. The genre does not preclude seriousness. The first movement of K. 320 has more breadth than many pieces designated 'symphony', and its fifth movement is an elegiac Andantino in D minor, reminiscent of the slow movement of the piano concerto K. 271.

None of Mozart's earlier symphonies begins with a slow introduction. The first allegro, and the finale, of a divertimento or symphony is a binary sonata form, with or without repeats; rondos are rare in symphonies. Slow movements adopt binary forms, but some are sets of variations, as they are occasionally in concertos and divertimenti. Mozart's orchestration is founded on the string section; some symphonies include movements without wind. Some string divertimenti (e.g. K. 136–138) may be intended for soloists but are still effective when played by a standard string orchestra. The popular 'Serenata notturna' (K. 239) may point to a wider performing practice, as the bass of its solo quartet is a violone (according to the autograph), playing at contrabass rather than cello pitch. Divided violas, quite common in earlier Mozart, were possibly played one to a part, but are still given thematic material as well as in-filling. The standard orchestra included two oboes and two horns, but a bassoon would normally be there, doubling the cellos. Natural trumpets are used in C, D, and E♭, but were difficult to accommodate in other keys. This partly explains the unconscionable amount of D major in Mozart's overtures and divertimenti, but this was also the violinists' favourite key, or certainly Leopold's: 'I know you prefer that key',

Mozart comments, perhaps with a hint of malice, on sending the hastily composed 'Haffner' symphony (27 Jul 1782). Trumpets may imply the presence of timpani, but no parts are notated in the majority of the early scores, and the trumpetless timpani in 'Serenata notturna' are as exceptional as the posthorn in K. 320 (it plays only in the trio to the second minuet). There is usually no need for a continuo to fill out the texture. Nevertheless, orchestral groups were usually directed jointly by the first violinist and a keyboard player, who was unlikely to remain silent.

Mozart's expression of delight in the full sound of an orchestra with flutes, oboes, and clarinets in addition to bassoons, horns, trumpets, and drums, comes in a letter written from Mannheim, but he was probably thinking of Paris and belittling the resources of Salzburg (3 Dec 1778). Even in Vienna, he seldom mustered such forces outside the theatre. Nannerl reported that he asked her to remind him, while writing his first symphony, to keep the horns busy; the tale is borne out by the musical evidence. Mozart's writing for wind instruments quickly outstripped his contemporaries', reaching a climax in the Viennese symphonies and concertos. But he was always concerned to vary the scoring as much as was feasible in Salzburg, and when four horns were available, or there were enough woodwind players to use flutes and oboes, he took advantage of the circumstance.

Theatrical associations may explain the presence of flutes and oboes, along with notated bassoon parts and trumpets, in the E♭ symphony of March 1773 (No. 26, K. 184=166a). This unusually serious piece is in overture form, and its three movements run together without interruption, the first two movements having no final cadence. The work was used by Böhm's company as an overture to a drama—not, however, *Thamos*, although it would be reasonable to use it that way.[2] A symphony in D (No. 19, K. 181=162b), less fully scored, has the same form but no known theatrical associations. The same is true of the last of these compact symphonies, in G (No. 32, K. 318), which has been associated without evidence with *Zaide*. It anticipates the overture form used in *Die Entführung*, a sonata form interrupted by a slow movement; rather than a new tempo, the last section resumes and completes the first. It uses an orchestra of theatrical size, exceptionally, for a work in G,

[2] Zaslaw, *Symphonies*, 250–51.

Ex. 10.1 Symphony in G, K. 199, first movement
a. Opening

including trumpets (in C), but these were possibly added later, for performance in Vienna.[3]

The remaining eight symphonies of 1773–74 include four in three
movements and four in four movements. They are the last symphonies
Mozart produced in bulk, and include the first of real originality. No. 27
in G (K. 199=162a) is a charming piece, using flutes instead of oboes,
and is a good example of Mozart's early symphonic manner, and of his
burgeoning sense of musical humour. The first movement begins with a
call to attention and conventionally vigorous gestures over a drumming
bass (ex. 10.1a). The music drives to the strong dominant chord of bar
19, insouciantly established as the local tonic by an engagingly singing
period for strings (ex. 10.1b). This consequent phrase is *forte* and its continuation, reinforced by tremolo (from bar 36), is repeated *piano*. Rather
than developing this material, the centre of the movement forms a chain
of new ideas, with a more rapid changeover of instrumentation and key
(A minor, G major, E minor, C major, ex. 10.1c). The recapitulation is
exactly the same length as the exposition and identical up to the strong

3 Zaslaw, *Symphonies*, 345.

Ex. 10.1   (*continued*)

b. Second theme, from bar 20

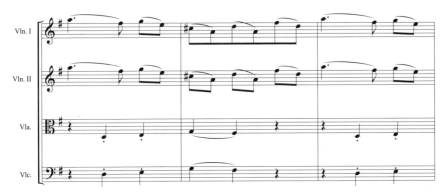

dominant chord, but the music proceeds in the tonic, and the only variation is within the second theme; the *piano* antecedent is transposed
down a fifth, the *forte* consequent up a fourth.

The deliciously light texture of the Andantino grazioso of K. 199 is
obtained by muted violins and pizzicato basses; the violas vary doubling

Ex. 10.1 (*continued*)

c. Development and retransition, from bar 59

the bass with occasional bowed in-filling (ex. 10.2a). The repetition with added flutes and horns leads to a cadence in A, twice interrupted by F; this resolves back by way of the dissonant augmented sixth, marked *fp*. The violins ponder the continuation (ex. 10.2b), but leave it open, their octave generating the melody of the middle section. Drawing their

Ex. 10.2 Symphony in G, K. 199, second movement

a. Opening

Andantino grazioso

b. From bar 21

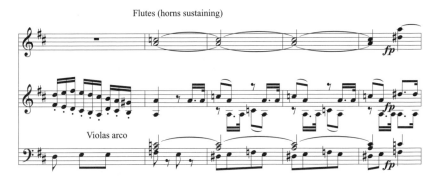

bows, the basses prepare the reprise with this octave, and the movement ends in the air, with bars 32–34 transposed to D. The second violin counterpoint at the start of the finale may answer this comical question.

After composition of the 1773 Finalmusik in Vienna, two sharply contrasted symphonies followed in October. No. 24 in B♭ (K. 182=173dA),

Ex. 10.2 (*continued*)

in three movements, is light, even frothy in character; No. 25 in G minor (K. 183=173dB) is Mozart's unwitting contribution to the movement retrospectively identified as 'Sturm und Drang', and most associated with minor-key symphonies composed about the same time by Joseph Haydn (his Nos. 44 and 45).[4] The elements denoting storm and stress—minor mode, driving, syncopated rhythms, dynamic contrasts—have no identifiable social or personal cause, and do not constitute a 'Romantic crisis'. Rather Sturm und Drang represents the symphonic cultivation of musical possibilities, derived in part from the dance of furies in Gluck's ballet *Don Juan* (1761), an influence here more potent than Haydn's. Mozart uses two pairs of horns in different keys, increasing the number of notes

---

[4] On this see Barry S. Brook, 'Sturm und Drang and the Romantic Period in Music', *Studies in Romanticism* 9 (1970), 269–84; Leonard G. Ratner, *Classic Music*; Zaslaw *Symphonies*, 261–63.

available, and these substitute for the blasts of trumpet and trombone in Gluck's score. The first movement, minuet, and finale have striding unison themes, so that the whole work is governed by a dourly purposeful forward drive, with the finale as uncompromisingly stressful as the first movement. The slow movement (not without tension) is enriched in sound by obbligato bassoons, and the G-major pastoral trio to the minuet, scored for wind instruments only, is an incident of repose, just as in the later G-minor symphony (K.550).

The early G-minor symphony is only one step in the breakthrough in Mozart's symphonic output to a personal style for which 'galant' appears a demeaning adjective—as does 'classical', except in the sense of 'canonical masterpiece'. The three symphonies of 1774 consolidate the gains in works of less turbulence. No. 28 in C (K. 200=189k), whose date is uncertain (it could be 1773), and No. 30 in D (K. 202=186b) are relatively neglected, whereas the third major-key piece from 1774, No. 29 in A (K. 201=186a), is frequently performed; and although the first two mentioned are never tedious, it is easy to see why. The symphony in A is as original as the G minor, not for its effect on our emotions but for its sophisticated entertainment value. Its fund of distinctive ideas is typical of what raises Mozart above the best of his contemporaries (always excluding Joseph Haydn). Although Mozart could do more than most with conventional motifs, his output from the mid-1770s is distinguished by the quality of individual ideas. The sinuous motif that opens the symphony, its octaves accompanied by augmented reflections of itself in a lightly chromatic texture (ex. 10.3), does not come to dominate the movement like the more athletic octave theme of the 'Haffner' symphony. At this stage, Mozart still prefers to seduce his listeners by a plethora of ideas of equally engaging charm. The slow movement continues in this vein, subtly mounting a counterpoint above the melody in the second violins (ex. 10.4); never one to waste a good idea, Mozart used an identical counterpoint above a different motif in the slow movement of the A-minor piano sonata (K. 310). The minuet's courtly dotted rhythm is rudely mocked as a wind fanfare, which arbitrarily ends each section. This bit of humour spills over into the sparkling finale, whose energy is repeatedly distracted by a rocketlike violin scale, followed by a pause for thought, until Mozart finally slams the door.

Until he had the opportunity to enjoy the sweets of the Parisian

Ex. 10.3   Symphony in A, K. 201, first movement

ensemble, with flutes, oboes, and clarinets, as well as bassoons, horns, trumpets, and drums, Mozart's attention turned from symphonies to concertos. He was amused by the expectations attached to the first bow-stroke ('premier coup d'archet'), for 'they all start together, as they do in other places'. Mozart decided to test his French audience, of which he expressed a low opinion ('oxen'), by starting his finale quietly, contrary to custom, and then bring in the tutti: 'as I expected, the audience said "hush" at the quiet beginning, but when it came to the *forte* they immediately began to clap' (12 Jun 1778). He agreed to replace the original slow movement, although he himself was happy with it (3 Oct 1778).[5]

[5] Mozart says in a letter written on the way home from Nancy that Legros has bought the sinfonia concertante and two 'overtures' (symphonies), but he will write them out again from memory. On the alternative slow movements, and the question of a second 'lost' Paris symphony, see Zaslaw, *Symphonies*, 323–34.

Ex. 10.3 (*continued*)

Ex. 10.4   Symphony in A, K. 201, second movement

Andante (violins con sordini)

The first movement draws broad contrasts between tutti and quieter sections mainly for strings, with relatively little solo woodwind work. Although there is no exposition repeat, Mozart shows his listeners the way with firm returns to the opening flourish: one in the dominant (bar 110) marks the central development, otherwise mainly a pretty tune in F major, and the next marks the recapitulation where the now familiar material is boldly developed. The brilliance and grandeur of this three-movement D major symphony brought something new to Mozart's armoury, and although the two later D-major symphonies ('Haffner' and 'Prague') are finer, the instrumental and rhetorical lessons of the 'Paris' inform much of his later work.

No such grandeur was required, or even possible, at home. Apart from the 'overture' K. 318 (see 87), the last two Salzburg symphonies return to a basic orchestration for the B♭ symphony (No. 33, K. 319), with added trumpets and timpani for the symphony in C (No. 34, K. 338). The lighter scoring of K. 319, a favourite of chamber orchestras, places the onus on musical invention, and by this date (July 1779) Mozart was unlikely to fail; it is a delight from its melodious beginning to its witty conclusion; further comment seems superfluous. K. 338, from August 1780, is closer in spirit to the 'Paris', building contrast into its opening period (fanfare, quiet response with trills, forte with minor-mode echo, crescendo to a sustained tutti). In such dramatically paced movements, Mozart was increasingly prepared to expand the lyrical period first heard in the dominant (bars 42–64), here followed by a longer crescendo: the lessons of Mannheim have been well learned and digested, and he now excels any model. The slow movement does without oboes and horns, as if to save them for the brilliantly jigging buffo finale.

Concertos

The progress of Mozart's concertos parallels that of the symphonies: the pleasant, even admirable, breaks through into music of individual and unforgettable charm and originality. The solid labour of works written to mid-1775, the first two violin concertos and the 'Concertone', gave way to inspiration in the last three violin concertos. The first ritornello theme of the G-major concerto (K. 216, ex. 10.5), subsequently given to the soloist, shows how Mozart, in a single thread, could combine an arresting gesture and an irregular response, even though a symmetrical consequent

Ex. 10.5   Violin concerto in G, K. 216, first solo, bars 38–68

would have been possible; the second phrase runs into its seventh bar, against the antecedent four, and introduces new rhythms and a new musical character. The soloist's second phrase inaugurates the modulation to the dominant, established by a more whimsical idea (bar 64).

In each of these concertos, a slow movement replete with melodic charm and elegant ornamentation is followed by a boisterous Rondo finale, the form making space for sections contrasted in mood, metre, and speed. In the G-major concerto, the headlong jig is interrupted by a nostalgic andante and a common-time allegretto; in the D-major (K. 218) the rondo theme itself mixes andante in $\frac{2}{4}$ and allegro in $\frac{6}{8}$, and its last big episode is an andante in $\frac{4}{4}$; and in the last concerto, in A (K. 219), a thoroughly mid-European Tempo di Minuetto is threatened by the allegro *alla turca*, whose brilliant figuration, leaping motifs, and chromatic slides are partly humorous but also a little sinister. Without any transition, the 'Turkish' music simply stops, and the minuet resumes as if nothing had happened . . . but the possibility of anarchy is not forgotten. These last three concertos, unlike the earlier ones, end self-deprecatingly, *piano* or *pianissimo*.

Mozart's wind concertos, despite respectable Baroque precedents, have become the foundation of their soloists' repertories in a way the violin concertos have not. Apart from a lost trumpet concerto, the first is Mozart's only concerto for bassoon, an engagingly tuneful piece, perhaps ahead of the violin concertos in solving the problem of combining virtuosity with charm. In 1777, Mozart wrote his C-major concerto (K. 314=271k) for the Salzburg oboist Giuseppe Ferlendis. He later adapted it for the flautist Dejean, a move not entirely cynical, for he had to transpose it up to D and rearrange the figuration to make less use of the lower register (relatively weak on the flute); a narrower range is compensated for by reworking triplet passages as semiquavers. Hardly more effort would have been needed to write a new concerto, but perhaps ideas came sluggishly after the completely original concerto, in G (K. 313=285c). Mozart had to swallow his passing distaste for the flute when asked in Paris to write a double concerto for the Comte de Guines on flute and his daughter on harp, his only extended music for the latter instrument. In all these concertos he treats his soloists with care, providing melodic opportunities and the chance to show off, but without reaching the imaginative level of the last violin concertos or the great Sinfonia concertante for violin and viola.

The draft of a triple concerto for violin, viola, and cello was abandoned, as was his wont with projects that seemed not to take wing, less than half-way through the first movement. To match the sound of the other instruments, the viola, which is normally too small for its pitch and so has relatively slack strings, was to be tuned up a tone, playing in G but sounding in A. Assuming the extra tension could be achieved without the strings breaking, it would be hard to keep in tune. Perhaps, too, three performers, none of whom had to breathe, was too many to keep active over a long period. In the Sinfonia concertante (K. 364), the viola, more practically, is tuned up a semitone, to sound in E♭ while playing in D, a key that takes advantage of open strings unavailable to the violinist. The work is marked as special by the first solo entry, in octaves, above the orchestra's completion of its ritornello; thus the two impose themselves with subtlety before intruding upon orchestral motifs— including engaging interventions from horns and oboes—with decorations that seem to become their musical raison d'être. Necessarily, because two instruments are involved, Mozart wrote out the cadenzas, and the two-part lament in the slow movement is particularly poignant. The ebullient finale is a rondo in a single tempo, all the jollier for having no complete episode in the minor mode. Apart from a Rondo for Brunetti composed in 1781, Mozart wrote no more string concertos.

CHAPTER 11

Vienna

1781–1785

MOZART AND HIS FATHER COULD NOT HAVE PREDICTED THAT after parting in Munich, they would spend so little time together. Colloredo summoned Mozart to Vienna as a Konzertmeister, composer, and keyboard player, to entertain his guests. Had Mozart returned to Salzburg, the tensions that led to his discharge would undoubtedly have broken out in a place where Mozart was less able to take advantage of the situation. Colloredo surely noticed Mozart's interest in exploiting Vienna for his own benefit: for Mozart it was 'the land of the Clavier' (2 Jun 1781). Probably Colloredo believed he could control a young man of twenty-five, with his father in Salzburg as hostage; more than once, Mozart expressed anxiety that Leopold might suffer in the cause of his own freedom. Colloredo's attitude was entirely feudal; he would not even tell his musical servants when they might return home, and although he required very little of them, he was not interested in whether they might feel they were wasting time.

With Mozart in Vienna were the castrato Francesco Ceccarelli, a friend, and the violinist Brunetti, whom Mozart did not trust; he rewrote his letter of 8 April 1781, which Brunetti was to carry to Salzburg, to disguise or render ambiguous anything that might be considered seditious. Brunetti left after a concert given for Colloredo's father on 8 April, in which Ceccarelli sang a new scena, 'A questo seno . . . Or che il cielo' (K. 374), and Brunetti played a new Rondo for violin and orchestra (K. 373) and a new sonata (K. 379), in which

Mozart played the piano part without yet having written it down. Mozart's indignation at his menial status is everywhere apparent, even though he knew his letters might be read by the archbishop's minions (he occasionally used a crude cipher). He was plotting his escape almost from the moment of arrival. He reviewed the chances of gaining a foothold at court, such as might have satisfied even Leopold, but there were no vacancies. The posts were mainly held by Italians, about whom Mozart occasionally shared his father's paranoia, although he became friendly with several. Leopold insisted that the sensible course was to return home, rather than finding little work amid the temptations of an expensive city. Mozart replied with plans for survival, while awaiting changes in the Imperial Kapelle, where the principal composer, Giuseppe Bonno, was already seventy (11 Apr 1781).[1] He would sell his compositions and teach, but teach only the wealthy; two paying well would match his Salzburg stipend (although this would be hopelessly inadequate in Vienna); he might find a pupil within the royal family (perhaps Princess Elisabeth of Württemberg, but someone else was appointed). His calculations conveniently overlooked the aristocratic custom of deserting Vienna for the country in the summer. But once freed from servitude, he could give concerts. With proper professional acumen, he set about cultivating acquaintances with money to spend, including those related to people in Salzburg and, like Countess Thun, with influence in Vienna and Prague. He associated with other musicians with a view to future collaboration and exchange of favours in benefit concerts, and he made many acquaintances among richer families, some recently ennobled, who welcomed him into their homes as a gifted performer and entertaining guest. Another ambition, never realised, was an annual opera commission. With that, he could support Leopold in Vienna, and he encouraged Nannerl to marry Franz Armand d'Yppold (a suitor who did not have Leopold's blessing) and bring him to Vienna, where his chances of employment were slight.

Leopold saw that success on all these fronts was improbable. He conferred with the elder Count Arco in Salzburg, in general a supporter of the Mozarts and father of Countess Lodron. The younger Count Arco, in Vienna as the archbishop's chamberlain, was thus reinforcing both

---

[1] More than usual in this letter is in cipher.

fathers' views when he urged Mozart to be sensible and return to Salzburg. Mozart's insubordinate attitude led the archbishop to fire him in May, but only orally, and his release took a month's negotiation. Arco withheld his formal petition for release; Mozart was furious, and the count, losing the moral argument, helped him out of the door with a kick. This, at least, is what Mozart told his father.

Unfortunately, Leopold's replies are lost, or destroyed. They certainly contained hurtful comments on Mozart's rashness and character weaknesses, no doubt the more painful for containing a grain of truth. Leopold's anxieties, simmering since the return from Paris, now boiled over, and he found it all too easy to believe malicious gossip about Mozart's idleness and dissolute ways. Mozart moved early in May from the archbishop's quarters to lodge with the widow Weber at the 'Eye of God' near St Peter's Church. The Weber family had removed to Vienna in 1779, when Aloysia obtained a contract to sing at the Burgtheater. Fridolin had died soon afterwards, but in 1780 Aloysia became the second wife of the painter and actor Joseph Lange, so Mozart was not under the same roof as his former idol. Admitting a residual attraction, he criticised her to Leopold as 'false' and 'coquettish', though quite soon they were on good enough terms for him to compose arias for her. Joseph later painted the portrait that, though unfinished, Mozart's widow considered the best likeness.

To quell rumours of his involvement with Constanze Weber, he removed again, eventually to inferior lodgings (round the corner in the Graben), and told Leopold that gossip coupled him with his talented pupil Josepha Auernhammer, in whose parents' house he had lived for a few days, and whose physical attributes he described in unflattering terms (22 Aug 1781). He denied rumours spread by Peter Winter, and counterattacked by informing Leopold that Winter had offered him immoral advice, saying that keeping a mistress was cheaper than marrying. Mozart insisted that he lived chastely and frugally, and maintained his religious observances (15 and 22 Dec 1781).[2]

In fact he worked extremely hard to realise his intention to support

---

[2] Winter may have been a worry to Mozart, as he had some success with operas performed in Munich; following *Idomeneo*, Mozart might have retained the hope of another commission there.

himself on a freelance basis. He finished the six violin sonatas published by Artaria in 1781 as op.2, dedicating them to Josepha Auernhammer. A less homogeneous selection followed, published by Torricella in 1784, containing two B♭ sonatas (K. 330=315c of 1783 for piano, and K. 454 for piano and violin) and the earlier piano sonata in D (K. 284=205b, of 1775). He composed variation sets for violin and piano and for piano alone. Since the emperor had formally established a fashion for 'Harmoniemusik' (a wind ensemble typically including two each of oboes, clarinets, horns, and bassoons), Mozart, ever sensitive to opportunity, composed three masterpieces for wind ensemble. The first was the serenade in E♭, written as a sextet but soon improved by adding oboes (K. 375); it was followed by the austere C-minor octet (K. 388=384a), and the astounding seven-movement work for twelve wind instruments and string bass (K. 361=370a).[3] No doubt he especially relished the chance to write for clarinets, missing from the Salzburg ensembles, as well as enjoying the company of the virtuoso Anton Stadler, and the music was liked: Mozart reported that he was serenaded on his name-day, 31 October, with the first version of K. 375 (7 Nov 1781).

The summer was also spent in pursuit of an opera libretto. Mozart hoped to mount *Idomeneo* in Vienna, in which case he would adapt the title-role for the bass Ludwig Fischer, and rearrange the castrato part (Idamante) for the tenor Valentin Adamberger. This prospect soon faded, to be overtaken by composition of a new Singspiel. Mozart already knew Johann Gottlieb Stephanie, who was currently running the German opera company at the Burgtheater. Despite some initial suspicion on Mozart's side, Stephanie gave him valuable assistance. He advised that *Zaide*, which Mozart had intended for the Nationalsingspiel, was too serious for Vienna (the alleged frivolity of Viennese audiences is a recurring motive in Mozart reception), and instead adapted (without permission) a similar libretto, *Belmont und Konstanze* by Christoph Bretzner, as *Die Entführung aus dem Serail*. Mozart was working on it by August and overoptimistically expected to finish it for September when Grand Duke Paul, heir to the Russian Empire, was coming to Vienna on behalf of his mother, Catherine the Great, to seal an alliance against

---

[3] The title 'Gran Partita' is written on the autograph score of K. 361, but not in Mozart's hand. There is no certainty about its date, which may be as late as 1783.

the Ottoman (Turkish) Empire. Joseph II declined his chancellor's suggestion that they import an Italian opera company for the occasion, on grounds of expense and his own distaste for *opera seria*.[4] *Die Entführung* was topical, with a Turkish setting and a plot-line that reinforces the perceived superiority of European over Muslim customs, including the freedom afforded to women (*Zaide* has no European characters).

In the event Gluck, who had produced no new opera since 1779, revived his Italian *Alceste* and his Paris masterpiece, translated into German by J. B. Alxinger as *Iphigenia auf Tauris*.[5] Mozart hoped Alxinger might translate *Idomeneo*. A performance of either of his new operas would have greatly enhanced Mozart's standing, but postponement of the Singspiel to 1782 gave him the chance to complete it to his satisfaction. Differences from Bretzner's text increase noticeably as the action develops, but even in act 1, Mozart added an aria for the harem overseer Osmin, making Stephanie write words to music already composed, as he wished to take full advantage of Fischer's wide range and resonant low notes; they can create casting problems to this day (they are also exploited in 'Così dunque tradisci . . . Aspri rimorsi atroci' (K. 432=421a)). Adamberger, the highest-paid singer in the company, was to be the heroic lover Belmonte, with Cavalieri as the aptly named heroine Konstanze. It may seem surprising that Aloysia Lange, the highest-paid female singer, did not take this role.[6] She had given birth to her first child in May 1781 and perhaps was not available when the opera was being composed. She did, however, adopt the role in 1784 when she presented *Die Entführung* at a benefit night in the Burgtheater and also in revivals at the Kärntnertortheater.

During 1782 Mozart was much occupied with the keyboard-based projects that maintained him over the next three years. He was encouraged to believe that he might support himself by piano playing when, during the winter 1781–82, Joseph II arranged a performing contest with the Italian virtuoso Muzio Clementi. Mozart prevailed, doubtless through the ingenious stylistic contrasts to which his music is prone, and

---

[4] Heartz, *Haydn, Mozart and the Viennese School*, 26–27.

[5] *Alceste* (Vienna, 1767) had no topical relevance, but *Iphigénie en Tauride* (Paris, 1779) characterises the barbarous Scythians by means of 'Turkish' percussion.

[6] Adamberger was paid 2,133 gulden, Aloysia 1,706, Fischer and Cavalieri 1,200, and the music director Umlauf only 800 gulden. Thomas Bauman, *W. A. Mozart: Die Entführung aus dem Serail*, 16

through the expressiveness and imagination of his playing. Clementi seems to have been a generous foe, whereas Mozart sneered in letters to Leopold (partly for Nannerl's benefit) at his rival's enviable facility, for instance in rapid scales in thirds: Clementi was merely a 'mechanicus', lacking in taste (17 Dec 1781; 12 and 16 Jan 1782).

Mozart was not the only virtuoso in Vienna, and his activities may have been looked on with a jaundiced eye by people such as Kozeluch. But for most of the 1780s, he was recognised as the finest keyboard player in Vienna. He could play for hours in the drawing rooms of wealthy patrons, but concerts for which he wanted to sell tickets had varied programmes, including vocal items and symphonies, and he needed a larger repertoire than even he could furnish on his own. Besides performances of works by composers such as Michael Haydn and Gyrowetz, he sent for his own earlier symphonies from Salzburg and revived arias from *Lucio Silla*, *Il re pastore*, and *Idomeneo*; the presence in his concerts of important singers like Adamberger and Lange was an added attraction. The first symphony (No. 35) to be composed in Vienna was written in frantic haste in the summer of 1782 for the ennoblement of Sigmund Haffner in Salzburg. Mozart soon performed it in Vienna, adding flutes and clarinets. Viennese listeners may have noticed an echo of Osmin's final aria in the presto finale, which Mozart said must be played as fast as possible (7 Aug 1782). The most remarkable feature of the 'Haffner' symphony is the first movement's concentration on a single motive; two-octave leaps for the violins, immediately developed to elaborate a descending fourth. Despite Mozart's care to provide contrast, this figure crops up at every significant juncture, inverted for the arrival in the dominant (bar 48, under a quaver motif remembered from the A-major symphony; see ex. 10.3), reshaped in the following tutti (bar 59), and used for remarkable contrapuntal exercises in the development (from bar 95). The brilliance, intellectual and instrumental, of this symphony seems like a lesson from Mozart to his father, who had exerted moral compulsion to write it when he was terribly busy (20 Jul 1782).

It was in December 1781 that Mozart finally admitted to Leopold that he was intent on marrying Constanze Weber. Despite posthumous rumours, there is no evidence that, once married, he turned his amorous attentions elsewhere; the few letters he wrote her in his last travels, or from Vienna when she was away, mingle news and anxiety about money with many expressions of affection. He told Leopold that her mother and guardian had plotted to compromise them and force the marriage, but after he signed an agreement, Constanze tore it up because she trusted him. He admitted that she was not pretty but insisted she was the sensible Weber daughter (slighting remarks about Josepha and Aloysia were made to underline the point). The marriage, which took place quietly on 4 August 1782, must be accounted a success. Constanze's competent handling of Mozart's estate, admittedly with help from his friends, even displayed a streak of ruthlessness; she was certainly not the featherbrain that some biographers have represented. There is no more reason to blame her for their financial difficulties than for her six pregnancies (hardly exceptional in nine years of marriage). As so often with Mozart, the least salacious interpretation of the available evidence is probably the least inaccurate.[7]

The first performance of *Die Entführung* took place just before the marriage, on 16 July. This was a period when Mozart was much preoccupied with wind instruments, so to avoid piracy and make a little money, he arranged favourite numbers for 'Harmonie'. The opera's success encouraged him to send copies to other theatres, and there were productions in Prague, Warsaw, and three German cities before the end of 1783. In late 1784, to Leopold's delight, it reached Salzburg, and even the archbishop was impressed, or so Leopold told Nannerl (9 Nov 1784). In all it appeared in over thirty theatres in Mozart's lifetime. He particularly hoped for an early production in Berlin, perhaps with a view to impressing his name upon the Prussian court, but this did not materialise until 1788. Had he received royalties in the modern fashion, his financial problems would have been greatly eased or his spending power correspondingly greater.

Another important factor in his development was exploration of older music and the cultivation of fugues. On Sundays at least from early 1782 he frequented the house of Baron Gottfried van Swieten, a court official who collected the music of Handel and of J. S., W. F., and C. P. E. Bach (10 Apr 1782).[8] Mozart had long been adept at fugal writ-

---

[7] On this and other Mozart legends see William Stafford, *Mozart's Death*.

[8] In this letter, Mozart also laments the death of J. C. Bach.

ing in an Italian-based textbook style. Now, mainly through studying instrumental fugues by J. S. Bach, he began experimenting with more daring subjects. He improvised fugues to please Joseph II and, it seems,
Constanze. While a skilled improviser can gloss over technical peccadil-
loes, Mozart's artistic pride required him to labour at polishing his ideas
when writing them down. Many fugues were never finished, perhaps
because he was short of time for work that was hardly saleable.[9] He
completed a grand fantasia in C, followed by an almost perversely complicated fugue (K. 394=383a) with a deliberately dissonant countersubject, and sent them off to Nannerl, telling her about his sessions with
Swieten and adding the injunction not to play the fugue too fast (20 Apr
1782). He arranged a number of keyboard fugues, mainly by J. S. Bach,
for strings, preceding some of them with new preludes (K. 404a, 405),
and began composing a neo-Baroque suite (K. 399=385i), unfinished
but one of his weirdest pieces (see chap. 19, p 237). In 1783 he composed another gritty fugue for two pianos (K. 426), later arranged for
strings with a splendid Adagio prelude (K. 546), which like the prelude
to the suite is replete with the majestic dotted rhythms of the French
overture. Perhaps no composer since the young Purcell had so fructified
his own style by earnest wrestling with the practices of a bygone era.

The effects of this study can be heard in the most magnificently
Baroque torso Mozart ever sculpted: the Mass in C minor intended as a
thanksgiving for his marriage. Composing it was a propitiatory sacrifice,
for neither Vienna nor Salzburg required such an immense liturgical
work; its dimensions, had it been finished, might have matched those of
Bach's Mass in B minor, and it displays every aspect of his style, from the
galant to the severest counterpoint. Yet even while working towards
these diverse and serious objectives, he found time to write the first of
his genial horn concertos for Joseph Leutgeb, a friend with Salzburg
connections, and in Vienna a useful acquaintance (he sold cheese).
Mozart may also have met Ferdinand Dejean, now living in Vienna; the
flute quartet in C (Anh. 171/285b) was written at this time.[10]

---

[9] Alfred Einstein attributed Mozart's failure to finish fugues to a lack of interest in doing
something mainly for Constanze. *Mozart, His Character, His Work*, 152.

[10] Tyson, 'New Dates', 216. The style of flute writing conforms to that of the earlier quartets.
Its second movement (of two) adapts the variations from K. 361.

Mozart's energy was phenomenal, but his concern to earn money may have come into conflict with his musical spirit, the best of which went into work like the C minor Mass, which promised no immediate reward. In 1782 he returned to the string quartet, doubtless under the impact of Haydn's newly published op.33, both composers having abstained from quartet-writing for about a decade. Impact need not imply influence: the new quartets were more resistant to Haydn's model than the earlier set (K. 168–173). Mozart eventually completed this project in 1785, and it was published as op.10 with a dedication asking Haydn to be godfather to these children, 'fruit of a long and laborious study'. It does indeed appear from the autographs that writing for quartet in a new style did cause difficulties to a composer accustomed to block out his textures through use of the piano.

For public consumption, and with remarkable success, he resumed composing and playing piano concertos. He performed the double concerto (K. 365) with Auernhammer in November 1781, along with a brilliantly fresh sonata for two pianos (K. 448=375a). In February 1782 he revived his first Salzburg concerto (K. 175) with a new finale (K. 382), which was much liked, and in the following winter season, 1782–83, he began the astonishing series of concertos so prominent within his output up to the production of *Figaro* in 1786.

For a few years his pattern of activity was governed by the additional opportunities afforded by closure of theatres during Lent, which added to the venues available for concerts; many of the benefit concerts in which Mozart played, on his own or on others' behalf, fall at this time of the year. The first new Vienna concerto, K. 414 in A, comes from late in 1782, as does the separate Rondo in A (K. 386), possibly a rejected finale.[11] K. 413 in F and K. 415 in C were composed early in 1783. Mozart wrote to Leopold that these concertos should please both 'connoisseurs and amateurs' (a distinction drawn already by C. P. E. Bach), for they are

a happy medium between what is too difficult and too easy—they are very brilliant—pleasing to the ear—natural without being vacuous—some passages only connoisseurs will fully understand—yet the ordinary listener will also find them satisfying, without knowing why (28 Dec 1782).

---

[11] K. 386 is reconstructed from partial autograph score and a piano arrangement by Cipriani Potter. See Tyson, *Autograph Scores*, 262–89.

He was selling them by subscription for six ducats, perhaps too ambitious a price, quickly reduced to four. No sales ensued.

In February 1783, when Mozart might have expected an invitation to follow *Die Entführung* with another German opera, Joseph II disbanded the Nationalsingspiel and assembled a troupe to perform opera buffa, while maintaining a company to act German plays.[12] This appeased Viennese musical appetites, but it was not entirely an Italian enterprise run by Italians: local talent was also recruited, including Lange and Adamberger. Nevertheless, Mozart hoped to find a place in the scheme of things, and he was encouraged by the theatre intendant, with whom he had been long acquainted, Count Rosenberg-Orsini. Mozart was reading librettos (he says about a hundred) in the hope of finding something to suit him; a disgruntled letter to Leopold, ever open to suggestions that Italians were not to be trusted, mentions the excellent buffo, Francesco Benucci, and the new court poet, Lorenzo da Ponte, who has promised a libretto; but 'if he is in league with Salieri, I'll never get a poem out of him' (7 May 1783). In the same letter Mozart enquires whether Varesco might be willing to write a comic libretto, with three contrasted female roles (a significant feature of the eventual Da Ponte-Mozart collaborations). When the buffo troupe presented Anfossi's *Il curioso indiscreto*, Mozart was asked for three new arias, to replace ones unsuited to Lange and Adamberger. Lange's (K. 418–419) were performed, but Adamberger's (K. 420) was not, apparently through an intrigue of Salieri (21 Jun and 2 Jul 1783).[13] Perhaps these pieces were out of scale within Anfossi's opera, although it was fashionable type of opera buffa with serious elements.[14] The excuse for inserting the arias may have been disingenuous; such show-pieces were surely meant to reflect glory on the singer and composer, who took pains to excuse himself from any such intention; he quotes the text of his disclaimer in a letter of 2 July, which also hints at a conflict of interest between Lange and a new English soprano, Nancy Storace.

[12] See Link, *Court Theatre*.

[13] Mozart states that Salieri affected to pass a message from Rosenberg, asking Adamberger to drop the aria; but Rosenberg knew nothing of the matter.

[14] *Il curioso indiscreto* (Rome, 1777) is loosely based on *Don Quixote*, and is a 'dramma giocoso', a subset of *opera buffa* rather than a different genre, first used for operas that mixed serious and comic characters; it is used by Da Ponte for *Don Giovanni* and *Così fan tutte*, both of which Mozart called 'opera buffa'.

Meanwhile, Mozart had many other preoccupations. In June he was at work on the second of the 'Haydn' string quartets (K. 421=417b), the only one in a minor key. Constanze was about to give birth, and she later said that the chromatic minuet was inspired by her labour pains (this leaves unexplained the airy trio in the major). Raimund Leopold Mozart was born on 17 June 1783. Six weeks later, the young couple left for Salzburg, a visit often mooted and often postponed, leaving Raimund with a wet nurse.

The visit to Salzburg and after

The visit lasted from July to October. Lacking family letters, we can only guess at the real feelings of Leopold and Nannerl on meeting Constanze. Mozart's letters over the previous months are touchingly filled with messages from her to Leopold and Nannerl, but the responses are not extant. Perhaps the atmosphere was strained at times; nevertheless, Nannerl's diary notes a great deal of social activity.[15] Constanze was introduced to friends and to the city where she eventually lived in her second widowhood. There was theatre and music-making, public and domestic. The forces available at home (four Mozarts and Leopold's resident pupils) were considerable, and friends came, including Michael Haydn, to play chamber music. Mozart himself worked hard, finishing the quartet in E♭ (K. 428=421b) and taking the Mass as far as it ever went. He composed two duets for violin and viola as a favour to Haydn, and probably worked on the three fine piano sonatas (K. 330–332=300h–k) published in 1784 as op.6.[16] Parts of the Mass were performed in St Peter's Church, with Constanze singing one of the difficult soprano solos; this must have been more a musical than a liturgical occasion. Mozart also wrote some social dances and discussed with Varesco the development of their opera project *L'oca del Cairo* (The Cairo Goose).

On the journey home, the Mozart couple reached Linz on 30 October, where he met several friends and was invited to the home of Count

---

[15] Nannerl's diary is summarised by Halliwell, *Family*, 408–23.

[16] These sonatas were previously allocated an earlier date (hence the K. numbers), through confusion with those written on the Mannheim-Paris journey. The date 1783 is suggested by paper studies; the autographs were not dated. Tyson. 'New Dates', 215–16.

Thun. A concert was fixed for 4 November: 'I didn't bring a single symphony with me, so I'll have to write a new one in a hurry' (31 Oct 1783). Haste notwithstanding, Symphony No. 36 in C (K. 425, 'Linz') includes a minuet and is the first Mozart symphony with a slow introduction. In calibre it belongs with Mozart's last and finest symphonies, with a haunting slow movement set off by one of his most ceremonial minuets.

Back in Vienna, they found that their healthy son had died, a common fate for babies separated from their parents. A new pregnancy soon followed. Varesco's libretto was not turning out well, and at some point in 1784 Mozart abandoned it and turned his attention to *Lo sposo deluso*, subtitled 'the rivalry of three women for a single lover'. With more immediate promise of reward, he concentrated on preparing the winter concert season. During 1784, an *annus mirabilis*, he composed no fewer than six piano concertos. Mozart told Leopold on 3 March that he had three concerts of his own in the Trattnerhof during the remainder of Lent, so 'you can well imagine that I must always offer something new'. To fill the programmes he called upon friends among Vienna's singers, writing a new scena for Adamberger ('Misero! O sogno . . . Aura, che intorno spiri', K. 431=425b), and performed symphonies, presumably including the 'Linz' and one by Michael Haydn, to which he added a slow introduction.[17] Programmes were also completed by filleting appropriate movements from his Salzburg serenades. Impressing upon Leopold his continuing importance in Viennese musical life, Mozart listed twenty-two concerts in which he was involved between 26 February and 3 April, mainly in the grander houses of Count Esterházy and Prince Galitzin, but also three 'private' concerts in the Trattnerhof, where he was living, and two public concerts he promoted himself in the Burgtheater.

The first concerto of 1784 (No. 14: K. 449), written for Babette Ployer, is the first work Mozart entered in his 'Verzeichnüss aller meiner Werke', his personal catalogue, in February 1784.[18] This systematic record

[17] This was long assumed to be Mozart's Symphony No. 37. On the date, see Tyson, 'New Dates', 219.

[18] The normal spelling is 'Verzeichnis', but Mozart often wrote vowels according to their sounds (for instance 'Leitgeb' and 'Siessmayr').

of his output may have reduced the threat of piracy, and it allows us to date the completion of works with reasonable confidence, even if a number of entries were made retrospectively and a few, usually short, works were left out. The catalogue also provides a terminal date for the composition of, for example, the serenade K. 361, too large to have been overlooked and thus surely completed before the inception of the catalogue; the only known performance was at a benefit concert for Anton Stadler, whose clarinet and basset-horn playing so inspired Mozart, on 23 March 1784, a day not accounted for in Mozart's list of concerts in that period.

Among the immediate successors of K. 449 were two more concertos and a chamber work Mozart designed for himself, the beautiful quintet for piano and wind (K. 452), which he called his best work to date (10 Apr 1784). How long he held to that opinion one cannot tell, but he presumably rated it above the second concerto for Ployer (No. 17: K. 453 in G, mentioned in the same letter). Other splendid works followed, including the violin sonata K. 454 and the piano concertos K. 456 and 459, so the favour accorded K. 452 may not have outlasted the year. K. 454 is remarkable for its expansive scale, unusual in the violin sonatas; it has an imposing slow introduction to the first movement, a richly ornate slow movement, and a full-blown sonata-rondo finale. It is possible that, as with the sonata performed by Brunetti, Mozart played it before writing out the piano part—and this time in the presence of the emperor.[19]

Alongside the piano concertos and other concertante music such as the quintet, music for smaller groupings continued to occupy Mozart with a view to publication and performance. He finished a large-scale set of keyboard variations on a theme of Gluck (K. 455), the C-minor piano sonata (K. 457), and the 'Hunt' quartet (K. 458), so called because of the first movement's arpeggio theme in six-eight, a motif and a metre strongly associated with hunting-horns and more commonly used for finales. The sonata was finished on 14 October. Its fierce temper stands out among its genial contemporaries, and from the other sonatas, and it does not form part of a group (it was published in 1785 with the fantasia K. 475). Nothing in his life is known to have determined the charac-

---

[19] The violinist was Regina Strinasacchi. This concert was on 29 April 1784 at the Kärntnertortheater, but the entry in *Verzeichnüss* is dated 21 April. However the MS itself suggests the story may be true and the catalogue entry, one of the earliest, may be retrospective.

ter of this work, but Mozart may have been going through a difficult period. On 23 August 1784 Nannerl became the third wife of a government official, Johann Baptist Franz von Berchtold zu Sonnenberg, and moved to St Gilgen, her mother's birthplace. Leopold kept in constant touch with his daughter, and on 14 September he wrote that her brother had been very ill in August, perhaps with a rheumatic fever. On 21 September Constanze gave birth to their second child, Carl Thomas, who was properly cared for and lived into adulthood; and in December, the month in which he also completed a splendid piano concerto with fugal finale (K. 459), Mozart was formally admitted to the Freemasons' Lodge 'Zur Wohlthätigkeit'.

Masonry is not a religion, although it was deist, and it was unfairly suspected of hostility to the Catholic establishment and of being subversive of the political order. Mozart took an interest in philosophical approaches to understanding his place on earth, but repudiated neither Catholicism nor the Habsburg Empire.[20] Something in Freemasonry—its beliefs and practices, the solemn meetings, and support for brother Masons—aroused a powerful response and led to a commitment a little behind that to his family, although well behind that to his art. The nature of the relationship between his Masonic leanings and his music remains cloudy. Symbolism represented by tonalities, instrumentation, and especially rhythm, has been detected in surprising places; but excepting works composed for the Masons, and perhaps *Die Zauberflöte*, there is usually little reason to believe that these references are not incidental and arbitrary.[21] Cryptology seems an unlikely preoccupation for a composer as prolific as Mozart, and one who wrote for present consumption, out of economic necessity, as well as from an inherited sense of obligation for his musical gifts. No annotations in his surviving sketches suggest that he engaged in intellectual games while composing, unless we count the non-symbolic *Musikalisches Würfelspiel* (K.Anh.294d=516f), a way of constructing elementary minuets by joining sections of music selected by throwing dice.

[20] In 1785 Leopold Mozart and Joseph Haydn were admitted to Viennese lodges. Although neither was able to attend meetings as assiduously as Mozart, their membership is testimony to the absence of any religiously subversive element.

[21] A concise summary of Masonic symbolism, with further references, is given by Philippe A. Autexier in Landon, *The Mozart Compendium*, 132–34.

The Masons included nobility, including members of the powerful Esterházy family; businessmen, including those like Michael Puchberg and Joseph Goldhahn who were helpful to Mozart; scientists like Ignaz von Born; priests, and artists. Mozart was invited to join 'Zur Wohlthätigkeit' in 1783, but he must have known about the 'craft' since first contributing to Gebler's *Thamos, König in Aegypten*. Some wind pieces have been associated with Masonic meetings because they feature basset-horns, but their dates of composition are uncertain and they may have been written for domestic use.[22] The cantata (*Die Maurerfreude*, K. 471), written in April 1785 in honour of Born, is rather bland; most of Mozart's explicitly Masonic pieces are on a smaller scale, and none is of outstanding quality except the remarkable *Mauerische Trauermusik* (Masonic funeral music, K. 477), icily ritualistic rather than moving but fascinating for its use of a plainchant and for its instrumentation, which in the final version includes three basset-horns and a double bassoon.[23]

Leopold Mozart arrived in Vienna, accompanied by his student Heinrich Marchand, on 11 February 1785. He had taken the Marchand children into his household, perhaps in part as surrogate for Wolfgang.[24] With Nannerl's marriage, the children had returned to their parents in Munich; Leopold collected Heinrich on his way to Vienna. His only visit to his son's household coincided with the height of Mozart's prosperity; Leopold reported to Nannerl on his activities, contacts, and position in the capital's musical life, on the flat he occupied (Schulerstrasse No. 846), on young Carl, and, with appreciation, on the food. No doubt Constanze exerted herself to make the best impression and partly succeeded (16 Feb 1785). This year, Mozart was giving concerts in the Mehlgrube hall, which he managed to hire cheaply; his piano was taken 'a dozen times at least to the theatre or some other place', usually with

[22] The works for clarinets and basset-horns include two Adagios, K.410 and the exceptionally beautiful K. 411=384d, and a number of more secular sonatas (including minuets and fast finales) for three basset-horns.

[23] The very first version may not even have been meant for a funeral, but for an induction, and included voices. See Zaslaw, *Mozart's Symphonies*, 443–44. The remaining instruments are horns, from which Mozart gets extra notes by having one in E♭ and one in C, two oboes, one clarinet (a low-lying, modest part, perhaps for an amateur performer?) and strings.

[24] The younger child was Gretl, a singer. Leopold was especially proud of Heinrich's performance in Salzburg of Mozart's difficult D-minor piano concerto (K. 466).

the 'large pedalboard [. . .] which sits under the instrument and is a couple of feet longer and very heavy' (it is not certain what Mozart used this pedal for) (12 Mar 1785).[25] Two of his most splendid concertos, K. 466 in D minor and K. 467 in C, were first performed during Leopold's visit.

In March, Mozart's only mature oratorio *Davidde penitente* (K. 469) was performed twice at the Burgtheater as part of the Lenten oratorio season. Leopold had heard most of the music in Salzburg in its original form, for it is none other than the C-minor Mass, parodied with Italian words. There were, however, two new arias for Cavalieri and Adamberger, the latter particularly attractive, with four obbligato woodwind instruments. Besides renewing acquaintance with several old friends, and finally meeting Baroness Waldstädten with whom he had earlier conducted a bantering correspondence, Leopold was introduced to the British musicians, Nancy and Stephen Storace, Michael Kelly, and Thomas Attwood, whose composition exercises with Mozart form the most substantial record we have of his teaching methods; they amount to a complete course of elementary composition: harmony, strict counterpoint, free composition in strict forms.[26] Another visitor was Joseph Haydn. Mozart had just finished the quartets dedicated to him, and the most recent (K. 458, 464, 465) were played through; according to Kelly, Haydn and Dittersdorf played the violins, Mozart the viola, and Johann Baptist Vanhal the cello. Haydn was more than pleased; he was hugely impressed, and Leopold reported him as saying: 'Before God and as an honest man I tell you that your son is the greatest composer known to me either in person or by name. He has taste and, what is more, the most profound knowledge of composition' (16 Feb 1785).

[25] On the pedal-board and its possible use in K. 466, see David Rowland, *A History of Piano Pedalling* (Cambridge, 1993), 87–90; David Grayson, *Mozart: Piano Concertos Nos. 20 and 21* (Cambridge, 1998), 108–11.

[26] Attwood's notebooks are preserved in the British Library; they and the exercises of Ployer and Freystädtler are included in the NMA.

Singspiel

'music must never offend the ear'

OZART WOULD NOT USUALLY BE INCLUDED AMONG MUSICAL
nationalists, and most of his vocal works are in Latin or Italian.
But he several times expressed the wish to write more in his own language,
and the main genre using German texts was Singspiel, a term now generally understood as meaning German opera with spoken dialogue. Unfortunately, however, his desire to develop this genre seldom coincided with
the demands of the theatres; and after *Bastien und Bastienne*, he completed
only two more German operas.

For much of the eighteenth century, German opera was dependent
on foreign genres, both Italian and French. *Bastien und Bastienne* was
translated from an opéra comique by Charles-Simon Favart, who had
been sending libretti to Vienna since the 1750s to be adapted or freshly
composed by Gluck.[1] A pastoral tale of a lovers' tiff, cleared up by artful
use of bogus magic, it demands the simplest of musical support, well
within the scope of a twelve-year-old. Besides the short arias, Mozart
included his first developing ensemble, a 200-bar duet in which the
lovers are reconciled.

Mozart's outburst of enthusiasm for 'melodrama', the technique of
delivering speech punctuated by music (more rarely, speech through
music), came as the result of experiences in Mannheim, on his journey

---

[1] Favart's *Les Amours de Bastien et Bastienne* (1753) was derived in turn from Jean-Jacques
Rousseau's *Le Devin du village* (1752).

home from Paris. He was astonished by the effectiveness of George Benda's *Medea* and wrote to Leopold that 'one should do most operatic recitatives in this way'(12 Nov 1778). If he began the melodrama he planned, *Semiramis*, the music is lost; but he used the technique in two scenes of his next German opera, *Zaide*, for which the spoken dialogue is otherwise missing. Mozart did not return to melodrama in later operas, even those in German. A few passages in *Die Entführung* require the music to be punctuated by speech; in Osmin's first aria this is because Belmonte is trying to attract his attention, and during Pedrillo's act 3 'Romanze' it reflects the stage function of the music—the signal for the elopement—in which the orchestra imitates a guitar.

Zaide is among the most fascinating of Mozart's unfinished works. Unlike the C-minor Mass and Requiem, written to liturgical texts, we cannot be sure about its eventual complete form. What survives amounts to two acts, with no overture. The last number is an extended quartet which makes an excellent act finale, as the action freezes with three sympathetic characters in defiant opposition to the fire-breathing sultan. But the final diminuendo is unusual for the end of an act; maybe after all it was to be a two-act opera with a perfunctory change of heart from the sultan (rather as in *Lucio Silla*). There are two melodramas. One for the sultan forms an operatic scena, culminating in an aria, but the first and far more expressive one is for the exhausted Gomatz, and ends with him falling asleep. Zaide's love for him is expressed in the serenely beautiful 'Ruhe sanft', a melody in minuet time with a tensile elegance reminiscence of J. S. Bach, of whose music Mozart then knew little or nothing. Had Mozart, like Handel and Gluck, habitually hoarded ideas from unperformed works, it would surely have been used again.

Die Entführung aus dem Serail has obvious similarities to *Zaide*, but pasha Selim, equivalent to the sultan in *Zaide*, is a speaking role, an arrangement Mozart seems to have accepted without demur. Yet it is surely odd, and a weakness, to have the character on whom everyone's fate depends unrepresented in the music. Instead Mozart expanded the harem overseer Osmin's role with a third aria in the final act, and characterises him throughout by 'Turkish' music, which is also more traditionally deployed in the overture and choruses. Osmin's exotic otherness is a political as well as a cultural statement, and since it is he who thwarts the lovers' escape, he is a serious menace, despite his obstinacy, ill temper, and naivety in allowing Pedrillo to get him drunk.

As with *Idomeneo*, Mozart's enthusiastic messages to Salzburg offer precious insights into his conception of dramatic music. His letter of 26 September 1781 is one of the most interesting he ever wrote. He changes the first scene so that Belmonte sings before he speaks (the music is a major-key version of the middle section of the overture). The account of Osmin's rage most catches our attention, as a basis for a consistent aesthetic of musical drama:

> Osmin's rage will be funny because I use Turkish music [. . .]. As his anger grows, the allegro assai, which starts just when one the aria seems to be over, will make a splendid effect, because it is in a different tempo and in a different key. Anyone who gets into such a violent temper transgresses every kind of order, moderation, and limit; he hardly knows who he is any more. In just this way, the music must no longer know itself. But because passions, however violent, must never be expressed until they become revolting, and music must never offend the ear, even in the most horrid situations, but must always please—in other words, must always remain music—I have not chosen a key foreign to F, the key of the aria, but one that is related to it; but not its nearest relative, D minor, but the more distant A minor.

Mozart goes on to explain that in Belmonte's A-major aria 'O wie ängstlich, o wie feurig' the violins in octaves represent the beating of his loving heart; the piece is written

> specially for Adamberger's voice; we can see him trembling—faltering—we can see his heaving breast—this is expressed by a crescendo—we can hear the whispering and the sighing, expressed by the muted first violins and one flute playing in unison.

Such direct associations between musical figuration and the specifics of the text may perhaps be applied elsewhere in Mozart's works, but it is worth noticing that that the features he picks out for illustration either concern motion (trembling, faltering, heaving—or with Osmin, the movements of rage) or actual sounds (whispering, sighing). More traditional associations between the minor mode and sorrow are also deployed, so that minor inflections within pieces in the major mode take on more than the aesthetic value of chiaroscuro. But to apply musical symbolism to abstract conceptions, such as love, which itself can bring joy or sorrow, might be going beyond what music can reasonably be held to convey. Any notion that Mozart's music speaks like words is not only wrong, but diminishes it; and Belmonte's aria may represent an extreme position within his oeuvre.

Mozart also expressed regret at having sacrificed Konstanze's first aria, 'Ach ich liebte, war so glücklich', 'to the flexible throat of Mademoiselle Cavalieri [. . .] I tried to be as expressive as an Italian bravura aria allows'. The piece is ingenious and original; he dared to precede the voice entry with a single note on the oboe, and the short slow introduction is recomposed to form the middle section of the sonata-type allegro Mozart had learned to use in opera seria. The change of speed is associated with Konstanze's change of fortune ('wie schnell schwand meine Freude' ['How quickly my joy disappeared']). The florid passages, as musical sense dictates, come in the cadential sections, but following 'und nun schwimmt mein Aug' in Thränen' ('now my eyes are filled with tears'), the sentiment 'Kummer ruht in meinem Schooss' ('Grief dwells in my breast') would not naturally inspire vocal fireworks, with several ascents to c''' and d''' (ex. 12.1). Nevertheless, if the aria is taken as a whole, the contrast between expressive melody with minor inflections and brilliant *passaggi* embodies its meaning, which is to contrast Konstanze's past happiness as a woman freely engaged to her lover, and her present misery as a captive; the more expressive phrases are laden with appoggiaturas, and the orchestral outbursts are enough to make one clutch one's heart (the student of orchestration will note how Mozart manages this with a three-part texture, as indicated in example 12.1, in which the upper parts are doubled and trebled in octaves; note also the small-scale but intense variation in the second outburst, from bar 30). This conflict is central to the whole opera, which despite Mozart's efforts with Osmin and the pert English maid Blonde, turns out almost wholly serious.[2] The form of the finale, a vaudeville, makes a nod towards comedy: the Europeans, nobles and servants alike, sing the same tune and refrain, whereas Osmin breaks out into a repetition of his rage aria, which this time does indeed seem ridiculous. But the happy ending cannot extinguish the acute sense of danger, fully articulated in the

---

[2] See Matthew Head, *Orientalism, Masquerade and Mozart's Turkish Music* (London, 2000).

Ex. 12.1 *Die Entführung*, act 1, aria, 'Ach, ich liebte' (Konstanze)
Allegro section, from bar 18 ('Trennung war mein banges Loos')

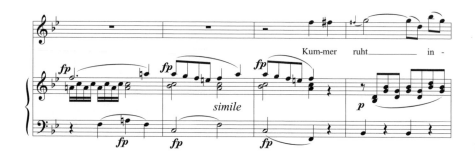

beautiful duet in which Konstanze and Belmonte, about to be executed, bid each other farewell.

'Too many notes, my dear Mozart', was the emperor's reaction (but it may be apocryphal). He could have been referring to the elaboration of the orchestral accompaniments or to the length of the score, especially the arias: three each for Konstanze, Belmonte, and Osmin, two each for

Ex. 12.1 (*continued*)

Blonde and Pedrillo (although the latter's second 'aria' is the weird serenade). In a structural curiosity anticipated in *Zaide*, Konstanze has two
long arias in act 2 separated only by dialogue. As a result, the opera is
closely focused on her. The G-minor 'Traurigkeit' still requires an 'agile
throat', but is sorrowful throughout and uses melisma entirely for expressive effect, like Ilia's first aria in *Idomeneo*, in the same key. Then the
pasha offers her a choice: love him, or endure 'torture of every kind':
'Martern von allen Arten'. She picks up these words for her 300-bar aria

Ex. 12.1 (*continued*)

in C, 'Martern aller Arten', notorious for its 60-bar introduction and
virtuosity, not only from Cavalieri but from the solo quartet of flute,
oboe, violin, and cello. Vocal brilliance here signifies defiance, as she re-
joices in the prospect of martyrdom. The ensembles include three duets
involving Osmin, who is also involved in the comic trio that ends the
first act. A multisectional quartet for the European characters ends act 2,
exploring feelings of joy, jealousy, indignation, forgiveness, and faith in

love. At one point Blonde sings in compound ($\frac{12}{8}$) time to the others' $\frac{4}{4}$, a device Mozart may have picked up from opéra comique by Philidor or Grétry.

Since Mozart himself alluded to Italian influence (although German by birth, both Cavalieri and Adamberger had studied under Italians), *Die Entführung* is sometimes accused not only of too many notes, but of excessive diversity of style. Although such reactions may turn on the qualities of a particular performance, this eclecticism may add to its appeal; it was certainly no obstacle to its early reception, which made Mozart famous all over Germany.

Incidental music

Thamos is Mozart's only extensive piece of incidental music, but the two stages in its composition suggest a serious interest in this now neglected genre. Instrumental music was required for entr'actes, and for the later revival there must have been not only a competent chorus but a solo singer (High Priest), for whom words were added to Gebler's drama. Perhaps, however, the choral items are less the anticipation of *Die Zauberflöte* they are sometimes made out to be than examples of a genre to which both works paid tribute. Its other most striking feature is the development of a gesturally expressive orchestral style. Annotations on the autograph in Leopold Mozart's hand suggest music intended to convey specific emotions, and that speech was to be superimposed, making this a melodrama (Sais emerges from the temple of young maidens of the sun; the coast is clear, but she has doubts (the change to minor, with *fp* markings); when she speaks, the music reflects her anxiety and an access of confidence at the last major chord (ex. 12.2). Mozart exploited the shock effect of augmented sixth chords, his favourite chromatic shapes, and dynamics which, although seldom other than *p*, *f*, and *fp*, are meticulously indicated and have a sharpness in delineating musical character more usually associated with Beethoven.

Mozart's only other music to a play was *Der Schauspieldirektor*, sometimes optimistically classified as an opera although there are more spoken than singing roles, and the target of Stephanie's mild satire is spoken as well as sung theatre. Within what passes for a plot, the two arias are audition pieces and do not express the characters' own feelings. These arias put paid to the idea that Mozart's occasionally extravagant virtuosity was

Allegro

Sais allein kommt aus dem Hause der Sonnenjungfrauen,
sieht sich um, ob sie allein ist

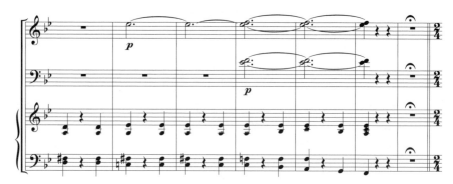

"Nichts hindert den Vorsatz..."

Allegretto (strings)

(geräth in Zweifel)

Ex. 12.2 (*continued*)

("O Menes, ist's wahr...")

("Ja! schon hörst du mich!")

designed to make fun of the singers he disliked (notably his sister-in-law Hofer, and Ferrarese). It is not credible that he would have endangered the success of his work by holding his performers up to mockery, and thus antagonising them. The success of *Der Schauspieldirektor*, a vocal equivalent to his later Musical Joke (K. 522), depended on open mockery of singers' pretensions, and the musical farce is entirely different from the vocal acrobatics of real characters like Fiordiligi or the Queen of Night—notably within the trio, when Lange shows her paces on the words 'Adagio' and 'Allegro'. But as with *Thamos*, the revival of the play which provoked Mozart's splendid music would be a high price to pay for hearing it in its original context.

'The Land of the Clavier'

Piano Concertos and Piano Chamber Music

MOZART'S MATURE PIANO CONCERTOS WERE CENTRAL TO HIS musical and economic being in the early Vienna years, combining his brilliance in execution with unprecedented orchestral sensitivity, formal inventiveness, and an inexhaustible variety of mood. The dramatic qualities of the concertos, metaphorical if not literal, are often remarked upon.[1]

Mozart's first piano concertos are arrangements of sonatas, one group mixing movements by different composers, another using whole sonatas by J. C. Bach, with orchestra of two violins and bass, and thus domestic rather than concert music.[2] Together with his first original concerto (No. 5, K. 175), these arrangements provided the first-movement formal template which Mozart employed with such resourcefulness. Bach's binary first movements are turned into concerto forms by omitting the repeats and adding orchestral ritornellos and space for a cadenza, conforming to a 'concerto form' that synthesises the baroque ritornello principle with the dynamic of sonata form.

Concerto form divides into: (1) a ritornello in the tonic and a first solo that establishes a complementary key, like a sonata exposition;

---

[1] James Webster observes: 'Mozart's concertos may be "dramatic", but only his operatic music is dramatic'. 'Are Mozart's Concertos "Dramatic"', in Zaslaw *Piano Concertos*, 107–38, cited 133.

[2] Sonatas 'for Piano-forte or Harpsichord', from op.5 (facsimile edition, preface by Christopher Hogwood, Oxford, 1973).

(2) a central ritornello and a second, developmental solo; (3) a third solo equivalent to a sonata recapitulation, and a closing ritornello prolonged by the soloist's improvised cadenza. The normal procedure in (1) is for the soloist to enter after the ritornello, playing the opening theme; new ideas introduced during or after the modulation underline the sonata-dynamic of the solo section. In (2) the ritornello is like a coda, empha-sising the new key, but may modulate ready for the fantasia-like explorations of the second solo. A point of interest in (3) is that the re-capitulation may refreshingly reorder the themes, a kind of variation more common in the later concertos.

The formal types employed in slow movements and finales are more diverse. For the slow movements, Mozart's cultivation of a singing style for the piano is well suited to the delicate, melodically dominated man-ner he sometimes called 'Romanza'. The finale is usually an entertain-ing rondo. But variation forms occurs in both these positions (the variation finales of Nos. 17 and 24, K. 453 and 491, and the variation slow movement of No. 18, K. 456). The finale sometimes incorporates changes of tempo, like the later violin concertos, or a complete change of mood, as when the agitated D-minor rondo of No. 20 (K. 466) yields to a glittering major-mode coda. These, however, are works of Mozart's later ascendancy in public performance, and it is possible that aspects of these works proved 'tough meat for the Viennese', as (ac-cording to legend) the emperor said of *Don Giovanni*. Certainly the last two concertos represent, in terms of formal and emotional range, something of a retrenchment.

Given the considerable literature on Mozart's piano concertos, no catalogue résumé will be attempted. The mixture of convention (even if his own convention) and novelty can be illustrated by selected examples. Several concertos begin ceremonially. Numbers 17, 18, and 19 (K. 453 in G, K. 456 in B♭, K. 459 in F) set out with the same potentially martial rhythm, yet each in a very different character: K. 453 lyrical, the bass en-tirely G until the tenth bar; K. 456 the most nearly military, with its no-nonsense tonic and dominant bass; and K. 459 accelerating in rhythm in its second phrase over a bass line that makes the texture contrapuntal (ex. 13.1 a). In K. 459, sixteen bars in this style precede a suave contrast (theme B), lightly coloured by the neighbour-note G♯ (ex. 13.1 b). A third idea (theme C) partly restores the martial rhythm through wood-

Ex. 13.1   a. Incipits from piano concertos, K. 453, K. 456, K. 459

K.453

K.456

K.459 theme "a"

wind interjections and is characterised by a more broken texture and dynamic contrasts (ex. 13.1 c). Ideas suited to cadences follow (theme D): an antiphonal idea (ex. 13.1 d) with a dramatic tutti (two diminished sevenths); string scales answered by tutti fanfares; and an opera buffa close from bar 62.[3]

---

[3] On the relationship of Mozart's concertos to opera buffa, see Wye Jamison Allanbrook 'Comic issues in Mozart's Piano Concertos', in Zaslaw, *Piano Concertos*, 75–106.

Ex. 13.1 (*continued*)

b. and c. K. 459, first movement, from bar 16 (themes b and c)

theme "c"

d. K.459 antiphonal idea "d", and first cadence theme

How can the solo impose itself on such a plethora of ideas? First, it plays the martial theme A, adapted to its own instrumental character, then it adds a triplet accompaniment to a woodwind restatement. Another type of dialogue has the suave B theme in the orchestra against a wide-ranging piano counterpoint (from bar 87).[4] The piano thus appears to control the

---

[4] See also Simon P. Keefe, *Mozart's Piano Concertos: Dramatic Dialogue in the Age of Enlightenment.*

Ex. 13.1   (*continued*)

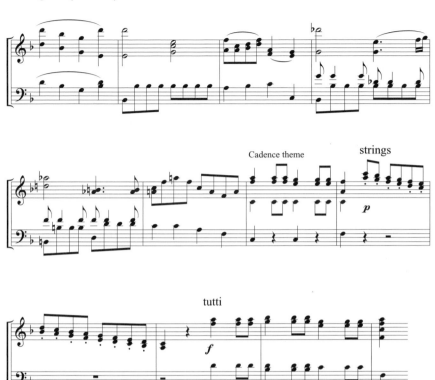

rapid modulation to the half-close at bar 95, whereat it introduces a new theme of its own (E). The woodwind, as if liberated by the soloist's intervention, make their own version of A, with copious imitation (from bar 106), and the piano develops this in liquid sequences before reaching a simple cadence (bar 130). For fullest confirmation of the complementary key (the dominant, C), the strings introduce another new theme (F), which the piano repeats with decorations. Only after some more work on A (from 149) do the final stages (D) of the ritornello again come into play (from 163); the solo continues to its closing trill in bar 188.

Replete with contrast, dialogue, harmony and just a little conflict, this immense expositional space is now concluded, but the tutti (second ritornello) breaks into the resolution of the cadence, anticipated by the basses which play the martial rhythm under the trill. The orchestra treats A to strict imitation, with a quieter response, then unexpectedly veers to the relative key, A minor (bar 211). Here the piano enters for its second solo ('development')—short, as usual with Mozart. The instability of the harmony is balanced by the continuous flow of piano triplets, over which the woodwind pipe tentative versions of A. The tonality is drawn back to D minor, relative minor of F, before a short but startling modulation brings the reprise (ex. 13.2; note the grip of the semitones, then the fifths, in the bass). In the third solo (recapitulation) Mozart's template allows themes to return in a different order, with renewed, but different, kinds of dialogue; some of the most fascinating music occurs just where a composer might be tempted to avoid modulating and recapitulate the themes in due order (as Mozart does in some concertos, starting with K. 175). In K. 459, after theme A divided between solo and orchestra and B much as in the first solo, the woodwind imitation on A follows at once, with the piano's liquid sequences. Bar 297 corresponds to the dominant cadence at bar 130, followed as before by F (in the tonic), the D themes, and the cadential trill. Themes C and E, having served their purpose in the exposition, are forgotten. The last ritornello begins like the second but in the tonic (bar 379 corresponding to 189). This time, the music lands on the dominant with the invariable grand six-four chord, destined to be resolved obliquely at the end of the cadenza. A final tutti brings back the closing scales, fanfares, and the opera buffa ending of the first ritornello, not heard for more than 300 bars.

Mozart's redistribution of themes operates on the level of detail accessible to the connoisseur and student, rather than to the casual listener, fulfilling the principles he expressed in his letter about the first Viennese concertos (see chap. 11, p 110). Changing the order of themes is of little importance if the connecting links are unbroken by arbitrary disconnections; Mozart could keep the line of continuity or thread ('filo') intact, while changing his handling of the smaller components of form. Like the operas, the concertos display Mozart's experimental temperament and avoidance of repeating himself. In No. 9 (K. 271, 'Jenamy') he impudently brings the piano in to share the opening theme with the orchestra, a call to attention he never repeated. Another variant is to bring the piano in after the ritornello with a new theme, as in Nos. 20, 22, and 24 (K. 466, 482, and 491).

Piano concerto No. 20 (K. 466 in D minor) enters a new emotional world, at least for the concertos; earlier works in minor keys, notably the

Ex. 13.2 K. 459, first movement, retransition, from bar 241

A-minor sonata (K. 310) and the D-minor quartet (K. 421), have something of its restlessness. The opening appears purely orchestral in character,
although during the first solo the piano finds ways to assimilate its mood
while complicating its texture (from bar 95). K. 466 contains a strange example of Mozartian intertextuality: at the peak of its magnificent first
paragraph (bar 28) the rhythm of K. 459 (ex. 13.1, A theme) reappears, and

the contrasting idea within the ritornello (bar 32) is a slower but less seductive version of example 13.1, theme B. In No. 21 (K. 467 in C), a sunny sequel to K. 466, the piano begins with brilliant *Eingang* (lead-in), and the orchestra enters with the main theme under the soloist's trill.

Mozart cultivated simplicity and directness in most of his concerto slow movements. Several are a type he called 'Romanza', in which a lyrical main theme is passed from piano to orchestra (or the other way), and returns after one episode to make a simple ternary form, or after two, to make a rondo. In K. 466, only in the second episode reflects the sombre hue of the outside movements; wind instruments sigh above the soloist's perpetual-motion triplets, with much crossing of hands. Romanza types recur in such widely contrasted concertos as K. 491 and No.26, the 'Coronation' (K. 537). The slow movement of K. 459 is unusual for being in concerto form, $\frac{6}{8}$, and allegretto rather than andante or adagio. A uniquely expressive slow movement is the other-worldly F-major Andante of K. 467. Mozart's counterpoint forms daring progressions which Leopold Mozart thought might be the result of copying errors; nowadays, the movement has become almost emblematic of Mozartian serenity (Leopold to Nannerl, 14 Jan 1786).[5]

The normal finale for concertos is a rondo in the $\frac{6}{8}$ hunting rhythm, as in the B-flat concertos Nos. 18 and 27 (K. 456 and 595). But Mozart often adopted other styles, using common time for the enchanting variations of K. 453 (he taught his starling to whistle the tune). Several finales, including K. 459 and 467, adopt the $\frac{2}{4}$ of the contredanse, and the unique finale of K. 459 is a joyous piece blending of concerto form and fugue. First, the cheerful main theme is succeeded at bar 32 by a fugal exposition; then comes the second B theme. We might mistake bar 255 for the second entry of the rondo theme, but the big ritornello (from bar 288) is a double fugue combining the subject introduced at bar 32 with the insouciant rondo theme. What emerges from this belated development is the secondary theme, now in the tonic (bar 391; originally 203), followed by the last tutti and cadenza. Quite apart from the fugal element K. 459 is a rarity in having no rondo; a sonata-rondo finale such as K. 467 requires at least three entries of the rondo theme.

[5] The popularity of the movement, extracted from the rest of the concerto, owes something to its use in the film *Elvira Madigan*.

The concertos of 1785–86, Nos 22 and 23 in E♭ (K. 482) and A (K. 488, started in 1784) stand out because the orchestra includes clarinets but no oboes.[6] The third concerto in this *Figaro*-period group, No. 24 in C minor (K. 491), restores the oboes but keeps the clarinets, forming one of Mozart's largest orchestras, with trumpets and timpani. These three grandly conceived and serious works have four out of nine movements in minor keys (the slow movements of the first two, and the outer movements of K. 491). K. 482 is an example of Mozart's typical E♭ major opening, a sturdy gesture redolent of ceremonial (compare the wind serenade K. 375, and the piano concertos K. 271 and 449), followed by a quieter and contrapuntal response; the rhetoric is identical to Mozart's first symphony (see chap. 2, ex. 2.3), but the material, and instrumentation, transform routine into something magical. After entering with a new theme, the piano embellishes this response with a filigree of arpeggios; then, in its repetition, varied in register and instrumentation, with scalar *passaggi* (ex. 13.3). The sombre C-minor slow movement also has precedents in earlier E♭ concertos, K. 271 and the Sinfonia concertante (K. 364). Another retrospective element is that the finale, a hunting rondo, is interrupted to make way for an elegant passage in minuet tempo, a design reminiscent of the violin concertos and, again, of K. 271.

The A-major and C-minor concertos form one of Mozart's strikingly dissimilar pairs of adjacent masterpieces in major and minor, like K. 466 and 467, the string quintets K. 515 and 516, the piano quartets, and the last two symphonies. In K. 488 the unfailing melodic flow anticipates the later clarinet quintet and concerto; all three begin with the same melodic fall, e''–c#'', used again in the central episode of the concerto's slow movement (bar 35). This Adagio has a haunting melancholy attributable not simply to its key and instrumentation but to its limpid melodies, and the recurrent emphasis on the 'Neapolitan' G♮. The unison opening of the C minor (inverting the shape of K. 449) formed a model for Beethoven's concerto in the same key. The autograph of K. 491 suggests that Mozart rewrote the ritornello to change the order of themes.[7] The solo entry with a new theme attains a level of pathos

---

[6] The early leaves of K. 488 have oboes; Tyson, 'New Dates', 222.

[7] Facsimile edition, Kilkenny, 1979; John Irving, *Mozart's Piano Concertos*, 237.

Ex. 13.3 Piano concerto in E♭, K. 482, first movement, from bar 94

Allegro

matching that of K. 466, and the multiplicity of themes, exceptionally rich orchestration, and sinister quiet ending, with the piano settling down after the cadenza by accompanying the orchestra with arpeggios, make this one of Mozart's most original, indeed disturbing, movements. The Larghetto is a sublime example of the *Romanza*, with interludes differentiated by separating the clarinets and oboes, a pattern repeated in the two major-key variations of the finale. Unlike K. 466, K. 491 ends uncompromisingly with a movement which could claim to be Mozart's greatest set of variations. There is no relaxation into the major mode;

Ex. 13.3   *(continued)*

the coda, continuing a variation in $\frac{6}{8}$, persists in lamenting to the end despite its faster tempo.

Performance considerations

The cadenza is the main improvisatory space in a concerto, but at shorter pauses the piano should play an Eingang (lead-in). Mozart wrote down quite a few examples, and some cadenzas, well after composing the concertos themselves. He himself could have improvised such passages as the Eingang in the finale of K. 459 (bar 254), or indeed the formal cadenza, and notation of such passages reflects his roles as teacher and brother to Nannerl: the examples he provided, we must suppose, represent his own improvisatory style, in concertos he was prepared to let others play.[8] We cannot assume that these passages corresponded to what he may have improvised himself, and there is no reason to suppose that he wanted to fix the cadenzas as immutably as the harmony, instrumentation, or the order of themes.

It follows that he was unlikely to have confined himself strictly to the notated piano part, even within the body of the concerto. There are still pianists and scholars who maintain that every note must be played as written; yet the spirit, rather than the letter, might better be served by an element of fantasy. In the Andantino cantabile that interrupts the rondo finale to K. 482, each phrase of a luscious wind serenade is repeated by the soloist with string accompaniment, and in bar 231 the violins ornament the melody, while the piano does not. It is hardly credible that this notation was intended literally. More controversial is the slow movement of K. 488, sanctified by reception history for its haunting beauty and as Mozart's only important movement in F♯ minor. A few bars consisting of isolated notes in different registers (ex. 13.4) should not be appropriated as protomodern 'wide intervals', as they cannot be heard that way; there is none of the tension created by wide intervals for voice, a wind instrument, or even a violin. For piano, the passage as written is extremely easy to perform, and the notes may be intended as the poles of improvised figuration which should combine expressiveness with an element of fantasy, even of display.[9]

Chamber music with keyboard

Mozart's exploitation of the keyboard to please his public, and raise money through publication, was not an unmixed success, but it produced some of his most engaging music and some of the most innovative. Piano chamber music larger than a trio was comparatively rare until Mozart provided models balancing concertante elements with strong individual contributions from the melodic instruments: the difficulty of the keyboard writing never threatens their integrity as chamber music.

---

[8] However, there are no cadenzas for K. 466, which Heinrich Marchand is known to have played.

[9] For a sensitive résumé of this issue, see John Irving, *Mozart's Piano Concertos*, 151. Irving points out that the crudity of ornaments written by Barbara Ployer is not evidence that no ornaments are intended. It is also possible to get closer to Mozart's style than Hummel's elaborations for K. 491, or Beethoven's cadenzas for K. 466.

Ex. 13.4 Piano concerto in A, K. 488, second movement, from bar 80

The quintet in E♭ with oboe, clarinet, horn, and bassoon (K. 452) belongs in a cluster of fine works—the piano concertos K. 450, 451, 453, and 456, and the violin sonata K. 454—but remains unique. The blend and contrast of wind timbres, playing solos or forming a miniature orchestra, is perfectly integrated with the essentially percussive piano. After the tense grandeur of the introduction, there may be a temptation to start the allegro without regard to the qualifying moderato. The $\frac{4}{4}$ is, as more often in Haydn, in reality twice $\frac{2}{4}$, and the pianist has many

Ex. 13.4 (*continued*)

demisemiquavers ahead. In the short development, a wind echo dis-
places the theme by half a bar, producing quintuple metric units (bars
69–73): the disturbance to the atmosphere is slight, but, with the ascending modulations through minor keys, it is nevertheless palpable.
The harmonic development of the slow movement is of almost unprecedented richness; the rondo finale includes another composed cadenza and, after belatedly remembering its main theme, a characteristic
opera buffa coda.[10]

[10] A rich description of this piece, originally written as a programme note in 1900, is in D. F.
Tovey, *Essays in Musical Analysis: Chamber Music* (London, 1944), 106–20.

The following year Mozart wrote his first piano quartet (K. 478), also the first of the mature G-minor masterpieces which to the psychological or sentimental biographer become emblematic of his troubled years in Vienna. But Mozart composed to release aspects of his musical psyche, not to reflect real life; and tensions are dismissed by the sprightly rondo-finale in the major. The firm unisons of the opening form a topic to be contrasted with other material and provide clearly-defined motives for harmonisation (from bar 17), development in a more amiable mood when the relative major appears (as early as bar 23), and for imitation in the strings, as a foreground to glittering piano figuration (from bar 38). The last passage sounds more intense in the recapitulation (bar 157) when all the material appears in the tonic minor, and the dynamic off-beat accents and syncopations of the second theme acquire a new pathos (compare bars 57 and 178 in example 13.5: a theme that turns up in a friendlier manner in the rondo of the 'Kegelstatt' trio, K. 498). As in the great C-minor fugue for two pianos, the coda gathers, rather than re-solves, the intensity of the music into a string unison against piano figuration and a final unison of Baroque severity. The piano quartet in E♭ (K. 493), expansively laid out, introduces three distinct thematic ideas in its first movement, but the two-bar figure at bar 28 dominates the development, fully integrating the galant with the learned style of counterpoint. The slow movements of both quartets, in $\frac{3}{8}$, are milder cousins to

EX. 13.5 Piano quartet in G minor, K. 478, first movement, secondary theme
First movement, Allegro

a. From bar 57

b. From bar 178

Ex. 13.6 Piano trio in E, K. 542, first movement

K. 452, lacking such far-reaching harmonic exploration, perhaps because Mozart intended the works for sale.

Poor sales of the first piano quartet may have turned Mozart's, and
Hoffmeister's, mind to a more popular ensemble, the piano trio. In this,
Mozart's textural preferences were different from Haydn's, the finest of
whose trios were yet to be written. Mozart's conform more nearly to
the modern expectation (conditioned by Beethoven and Schubert), by
which the cello is an equal voice with the violin, rather than mainly

Ex. 13.6 (*continued*)

doubling the keyboard. On modern instruments, the cello in Haydn's trios seems dispensable; Mozart gives it bass lines unsupported by the piano, and provides it with rests and striking interventions. Such independence is barely discernible in K. 254, the only trio between the very early and the mature works, but even here, in the finale a minuet in rondo form, the cello makes its presence felt with a nicely timed pizzicatos. This trio is good for its date (1776) and was published six years later, when Mozart was already in Vienna.

Eleven years later, Mozart began his trio in G (K. 496) with seventeen bars of piano solo, yet in the development section his confidence in the cello allows it to dialogue with the piano's left hand; the violin part is correspondingly freer. The late trios may have been intended to appeal to an amateur market, but they are full of delights. Mozart wrote only a few pieces in E major. The trio in E (K. 542) is replete with melody. It is typical of later Mozart that he here coordinates ideas whose engaging surface may even disguise their real differences of character: the luscious chromaticism of the opening makes it a kindlier version of the isolated keyboard minuet in D (K. 355=576b, of uncertain date), for the trio does not risk such fierce scrunches as that curious work's middle section. The first theme (ex. 13.6) shows the independence of all three instruments; if the cello is left holding a pedal note, it frees the piano's left hand from doing so, and the violin vies with the right hand in passage-work. The melody of the second movement is enchanting, that of the rondo hardly less so: curious, therefore, that Mozart wrote so little music in this key, although it plays a special role within *Così fan tutte*. The trio in C (K. 548) has a particularly fine cello part, and in the slow movement it anticipates the tenor register cultivated in the quartets written soon afterwards for the king of Prussia. The trio in G (K. 564), like that in E, is tuneful to a fault, with a pastoral, opera buffa finale that never fails to lift the spirits—an achievement not to be despised and an effect of much of Mozart's chamber music, particularly when imprinted with the delicacy, subtlety, and variety of his own pianism.

CHAPTER 14

Vienna and Prague

1785–1788

LEOPOLD RETURNED TO SALZBURG AT THE END OF APRIL 1785 and never saw Wolfgang again. In June, he brought Nannerl home to deliver her child: 'little Leopold' remained with his grandfather, while Nannerl returned to her husband and unruly stepchildren in St Gilgen. Taking over Nannerl's baby was probably not done in the expectation of bringing up a new genius, a substitute for Wolfgang (after all, he knew the father), but to assure the child's health in a town with better facilities.[1]

In Vienna, Leopold's sharp nose may have scented imminent financial problems; as he wrote to Nannerl: 'If my son has no debts to pay, I think that he can now lodge two thousand gulden in the bank [. . .] the housekeeping is extremely economical'. Nevertheless the annual rent was 460 gulden, over three times the cost of Mozart's previous accommodation in the Trattnerhof, and more than the fee for writing a new opera.[2] The first known 'begging letter' from Mozart was addressed to Hoffmeister in November 1785, and amounts to a request for advance payment against work to be delivered; it implies that anything Mozart might have set aside was already exhausted. When Leopold was

---

[1] On this point I am less persuaded by Solomon, *Mozart, a Life*, 389–98, than by Halliwell, *Family*, 459.

[2] Leopold's letter of 19 March 1785. Halliwell is sceptical about this letter, of which the original is lost: *Family*, 476–77.

in Vienna, concert activities were at their height, and Mozart was earning well from performing and teaching. The more interesting students were not rich, but he could see them at home; wealthier pupils required him to go to their homes, wasting time and money. Mozart took pride in his appearance and was perhaps even a little vain, having a sharp eye for fashion. But it was necessary to be well dressed if he was to gain income as a freelance, for he was no less dependent than a Kapellmeister on the patronage of the wealthy. If he looked shabby, he would not be welcomed in the finer houses, in some of which he gave concerts. On 5 September 1781 he had written to Leopold that his shirts are coarse but his outer crust must be smart: 'I couldn't walk around Vienna like a tramp'. Hence his daily routine: rising early, working on a composition while awaiting a barber to arrange and powder his hair, and only then dressing and going out.

Too many unknowns prevent certainty in assessing Mozart's income and expenditure, or the extent to which one exceeded the other. For instance, there is no record of how much was paid by Attwood, whose studies were sponsored by the Prince of Wales (later George IV). In 1787, Mozart imitated his father by taking a prodigy, Johann Nepomuk Hummel, into his home. Again, the income (if any) derived from this arrangement is not recorded, but it is an example of Mozart's kindness, another being his assistance to Adalbert Gyrowetz, one of whose symphonies he presented at a subscription concert in 1785. Equally unknown is the extent to which he may have wasted money. Expenses such as a carriage, hairdressing, good clothes, and servants could be represented as necessary, as could expenditure on doctors, rent, food, and drink; but he indulged in luxuries, such as the billiard-table he owned for a time. There is no reason to suppose that he gambled heavily. But he was unable to make substantial savings, and when his income went down, expenses did not; so he had to borrow. His requests for short-term loans should not be overemphasised merely because we possess a few pathetic letters to Michael Puchberg. Mozart was generous when he could afford it and expected the same of his brother Masons; the evidence, or lack of demand upon his estate, suggests that he settled a good many of these debts quickly.

Certainly he was not idle. During 1785 he continued composing at the top of his bent. The Fantasia in C minor (K. 475), a masterpiece of carefully honed 'improvisation', was finished in May for publication with the C-minor sonata (K. 457). In the summer, he wrote a handful of Lieder including *Das Veilchen*, his best-known song and only setting of Goethe. In October, the piano quartet in G minor (K. 478) achieved mastery of a new medium at a stroke and launched an intermittent but masterful series of chamber works over the next few years. The quartet and a new violin sonata in E♭ (K. 481) were published by Hoffmeister in 1786. Probably early in the year Mozart composed two rondos for piano, K. 485 in D, and K. 494 in F which he later expanded as the finale to a sonata (K. 533).

During the winter season of 1785–86, Mozart continued the pattern of previous years by presenting three new concertos, Nos. 22–24 (K. 482, 488, and 491). What the Viennese made of these concertos we cannot know. In K. 491, Mozart's demands on a wider public, whose subscriptions he needed to solicit, may have been too heavy. Various reasons have been adduced for the apparent decline in his concert-giving. Part of the evidence is that the series of concertos peters out; he wrote only three more, their completion widely separated. Perhaps Mozart abandoned subscription concerts because he was no longer able to sustain public interest at a time of difficult economic circumstances in Austria, eventually exacerbated by the Turkish war. But in the absence of any newspaper of record, we only know about a number of his concerts through letters to Salzburg; thus it is possible that in his later years concerts may have taken place but left no trace.

Instead, Mozart reappeared in Vienna as a dramatic composer, a direction in which he had suffered frustration since *Die Entführung*. His persistence, after abandoning *L'oca del Cairo* and *Lo sposo deluso*, led him to Beaumarchais's comic masterpiece *La folle journée ou Le Mariage de Figaro*, and *Le nozze di Figaro* was eventually performed at the Burgtheater on 1 May 1786. The choice was affected by an opera based on the play to which *Le Mariage* is a sequel: *Le Barbier de Séville*. Paisiello's *Il barbiere di Siviglia* was written for St Petersburg in 1782. Joseph II was delighted by Paisiello's music and obtained material from Russia for a Vienna production by his new company, with Nancy Storace as Rosina, Stefano Mandini as the Count, Francesco Benucci as Dr Bartolo, and Francesco Bussani as Figaro. Vienna subsequently commissioned Paisiello's *Il re Teodoro in Venezia*, the major Burgtheater production of 1784. In 1785 the Burgtheater presented new operas by Stephen Storace (*Gli sposi malcontenti*) and Salieri (one of his most popular works, *La grotta di Trofonio*). Mozart must have been wondering whether he would ever get a foot in the door, but in November 1785 he contributed two ensembles to an opera imported from Venice, Francesco Bianchi's *La villanella rapita*. He may have derived satisfaction, if not income, from a revival of *Die Entführung* at the publicly funded Kärntnertortheater, where a German-language company presented translations from the French, revivals, and new works, including those of Dittersdorf.

By the winter of 1785–86, much of *Figaro* must have been written, but a more dangerous competitor appeared in Vicente Martín y Soler, who also worked with Da Ponte. *Il burbero di buon core* was given in January 1786; Da Ponte also provided the text for Giuseppe Gazzaniga's *Il finto cieco*, produced in February, and an early comedy by Salieri, *La fiera di Venezia* (1772), was revived.[3] Leopold had reported to Nannerl that Mozart was immersed in composing *Figaro*, this 'very tiresome play', and 'Count Rosenberg is prodding him [. . .]. God grant that the text may be a success. I have no doubt about the music' (11 Nov 1785). Mozart and Da Ponte were taking a risk with censorship; the play—brilliant and not at all tiresome—was banned because of its subversive implications. Da Ponte credits himself with persuading Joseph that the politically offensive matter had been removed, leaving only the sexual intrigue of the 'Droit de Seigneur', a lord's right to replace the husband on his wedding-night. Himself a model of rectitude, Joseph made no objection to a critique of aristocratic licentiousness, so long as Figaro did not denounce Count Almaviva (as he does in the play) for gaining power and wealth 'by taking the trouble to be born, nothing more'. Bussani sang Bartolo and may have resented not retaining the role of Figaro, but Benucci, the principal buffo, inevitably took the leading part. Perhaps from Bussani, Rosenberg learned that Da Ponte had introduced dances into the third act. Da Ponte reports that Rosenberg intervened because dancing was forbidden in operas, and that he foiled the plot by inviting the emperor to a rehearsal. At the relevant point the musicians fell silent, and action ceased except for the little mime, necessary to the plot and covered by dancing, in which Susanna passes a note of assignation to the count. Joseph saw the point and overruled Rosenberg.

[3] See the list of repertoire in Link, *Court Theatre*.

By a happy accident of operatic history, Mozart had found in Da Ponte a congenial collaborator, whose sophisticated command of language and sense of humour matched his musical gifts. But before *Figaro* was performed, Mozart laid down two further markers as a stage composer. *Der Schauspieldirektor* (The Impresario) is a short play by Stephanie, about theatrical rivalry, framing three arias and an ensemble and preceded by one of Mozart's best overtures. It was performed on 7 February 1786 in the Orangery at the palace of Schönbrunn, in tandem with Salieri's Italian satire on operatic words and music, *Prima la musica*. Salieri had the pick of the opera buffa troupe, but Mozart was surely content to write for Adamberger, Cavalieri, and Lange. Meanwhile, with a company of mainly amateur singers drawn from the minor nobility, there was a revival of *Idomeneo* on 13 March in the private theatre of the Auersperg palace. Ilia was sung by Countess Hatzfeld, whose singing was of professional standard. It must have been a moving occasion for Mozart if, as Constanze told the Novellos, he had been reduced to tears by a domestic rendering of the great quartet in Salzburg in 1783.[4] For this revival Mozart carried out one of the changes he had projected in 1781; Idamante was sung by a tenor (Baron Pulini), for whom he wrote a new scena at the start of act 2, including the rondò (see chap. 16, p 186) 'Non temer, amato bene', with violin obbligato for his friend Count Hatzfeld. He carefully recomposed the voice parts in the trio and quartet to accommodate this second tenor, and composed a new duet for Ilia and Idamante. The cuts made in Munich were not restored, and the Idomeneo (Giuseppe Bridi) required a simplified version of the central aria, 'Fuor del mar'.[5]

The reception of *Figaro* remains a favourite subject for controversy. With hindsight, the play has been read as presaging the French revolution.[6] From this it has been deduced that the opera offended the Viennese aristocracy, who thereafter boycotted Mozart's concerts. Yet *Figaro* was not precipitately withdrawn from repertoire. Kelly reported

---

[4] Medici and Hughes, *A Mozart Pilgrimage*, 114–15.

[5] The simpler version was not made to accommodate the aging Raaff in 1781, as is sometimes asserted.

[6] See William Weber, 'The Myth of Mozart, the Revolutionary', *Musical Quarterly* 78 (1994), 34–47.

its enthusiastic reception, and on 9 May, after the third performance, the emperor forbade the repetition of ensembles in what was already a long opera.[7] Many wealthy Viennese went to the theatre night after night; it follows that, as in spoken drama, repertoire had to be varied. During May 1786, Cimarosa's *L'italiana in Londra* (1779) was revived, and Anfossi's *Il trionfo delle donne* (1778) received a Vienna production; as the season progressed, other popular operas reappeared, including *Il barbiere*. Righini's new opera *Il demagorgone* (libretto by Da Ponte) did less well than *Figaro*, of which there were ten performances, spaced out into December. On 17 November, Martín, with the apparently indefatigable Da Ponte, produced his most popular work, *Una cosa rara*. Its relative brevity, lighter texture, and easy melodies, less challenging than Mozart, greatly appealed to the Viennese. The company had also to learn an opera as long and difficult as *Figaro*, Da Ponte and Storace's *Gli equivoci*, performed on 27 December.

To perform *Figaro* in 1787 would have required new casting, as Nancy Storace and Kelly had left Vienna. Its successful revival in 1789 puts paid to the idea that it offended its audience. It was not the success Mozart deserved, but nor was it a disaster. Martín (for whose triumph Mozart bore no ill will) obtained the next Vienna commission, while Mozart had to maintain his productivity in other fields. During the summer of 1786, he composed a new horn concerto for Leutgeb (K. 495) and the second piano quartet (K. 493), a piece of ample proportions and contrapuntal virtuosity. If it was offered to Hoffmeister, he declined it; perhaps sales of the G-minor quartet were poor (Artaria brought out K. 493 the following year). Mozart offered Hoffmeister two more saleable items, the piano trios in G (K. 496) and B♭ (K. 502), perhaps Mozart's masterpiece in this medium, as well as the fine string quartet in D (K. 499) that bears the publisher's name. Other pieces probably from this year, but not entered in Mozart's catalogue, include some horn duets (K. 487=496a), and a curious flute quartet in A (K. 298), a superior medley of other people's tunes.[8] Some of these pieces originated in the domestic circle of the von Jacquin family. Mozart was close to Gottfried von Jacquin and taught his

---

[7] The ban must have applied to all operas but was occasioned by *Figaro*; see *D-Doc*, 275; Kelly, *Reminiscences/Solo Recital*, 142.

[8] The Köchel number is misleading; see Tyson, 'Proposed New Dates', 215.

sister Francesca the piano. In the unique trio known as 'Kegelstatt' (K. 498, so called because he allegedly composed it while playing skittles), Francesca played piano with Mozart on viola and Stadler on clarinet. A work intended for private use, it consists of a delicately coloured andante, a minuet with minor-key trio in which clarinet and viola have contrasted material, and a leisurely rondo. The piano trios were also aimed at domestic music-making, as were the piano duets. Two masterpieces for that medium were composed in 1786, the sonata in F (K. 497), with a rapturous slow movement, where some of the more delicious scale passages are difficult for amateurs to piece together accurately, and an excellent set of variations in G (K. 501).

In February, after the last performance of *Figaro*, Nancy Storace gave a farewell concert for which Mozart had composed a second setting of the scena with rondò for Idamante, 'Ch'io mi scordi di te . . . Non temer, amato bene' (K. 505). A model of his ability to touch his listeners without alarming or offending the ear, it is marked as special through the piano obbligato (rather than the violin of the earlier setting). It combines two things Mozart did supremely well: writing for voice, and writing piano concertos. Small wonder that, without any other evidence, it has been assumed that Mozart was in love with Storace.

In November 1786, the Mozarts lost their third son, Johann Thomas Leopold, in a cot-death. There is no sense of bereavement in the new piano concerto in C, presented early in December (K. 503). If its slow movement is less haunting than its predecessor in that key (K. 467), its majestic opening movement and brilliant contredanse finale show no decline in inventiveness in this already well-exploited medium. Relative to the previous two years' piano concertos, we may sense the beginning of a later style-phase, exemplified in its two successors and in other types of composition: a move from challenging invention to a subtle harmoniousness and an assured mastery in which the complexity of the musical discourse is concealed by art. But it is still music calculated equally to delight the connoisseur and the amateur.[9]

Mozart's activities in the winter season 1786–87 departed from the pattern of previous years, but this is not necessarily a sign of public loss of interest in him as a performer. Early in 1787, while the Storaces, with

[9] See Joseph Kerman, *Mozart: Piano Concerto in C major, K. 503* (Norton Critical Score).

Kelly and Attwood, were shown around Salzburg by Leopold en route for England, Mozart went to Prague, summoned there to witness the triumph of *Figaro*. He wrote to Jacquin:

> I was very delighted to see everyone leaping about in sheer delight to the music of my Figaro, adapted as noisy contredanses and German dances [teitsche];–for here they talk of nothing but–Figaro; nothing is played, blown, sung, or whistled but–Figaro: no opera is enjoyed as much as–Figaro and eternally Figaro. . . . (15 Jan 1787)

To vary the available dance-tunes, he dashed off some German Dances (K. 509); and capitalising on applause amounting to adulation he gave a concert including a new symphony in D major (No. 38, K. 504, the 'Prague'). Perhaps he played his new concerto as well. But the most important outcome of Mozart's visit to Prague was a new opera commission. While awaiting the libretto, he composed more music for his friends, and for sale. In March 1787 he completed arias for Fischer and Jacquin (K. 512, 513), and composed perhaps his most beautiful piano work, the Rondo in A minor (K. 511). He renewed his chamber music campaign by returning to the string quintet, a medium already well known in Vienna. Perhaps he felt it wiser to add to an existing repertoire than create a new one, as with the piano quartets; the quintet of two violins, two violas, and cello had been exploited by, among others, Mysliveček, Hoffmeister, and Ignaz Pleyel. As usual, Mozart drafted a number of openings, and two potential quintets in B♭ and A minor never progressed beyond a few bars. But the great quintets in C (K. 515) and G minor (K. 516) are the unquestioned masterpieces of the genre; and to these, probably around this time, he added a quintet arrangement of the C-minor wind octet (K. 388 becoming 406), although this, and a third horn concerto (K. 447), were not entered in Mozart's catalogue. In May he composed his last piano duet sonata (K. 521) for Francesca von Jacquin, and in 1787 he composed more songs (eleven) than in any other year, mainly in June; they include *Abendempfindung*, perhaps his loveliest song, and *An Chloe*.

Perhaps he found songs, which he could finish in a day or less, a useful distraction. In April he heard that Leopold was seriously ill; he died on 28 May. The death of a once-dominating father marks an epoch for Mozart biographers, perhaps rather more than in his actual life, for the historian runs out of primary material in the form of Leopold's correspondence. They had not met for over two years, and Leopold had long ceased to cherish any hope that Wolfgang's genius would provide for a serene old age away from Salzburg. But in the ending of the family project, Nannerl's marriage was hardly less decisive. In his last known letter to his father (4 April), Mozart regrets that the Storaces' mother had stupidly failed to deliver an earlier letter; he also mentions a letter, also lost, that he sent from Prague. There is more discussion of recent musical events, but Mozart kept quiet about his own financial situation; instead, he turned to the consolations of death, to which he says he has already referred in connection with the premature death of Count Hatzfeld. Did Mozart really believe that 'Death [. . .] is the true and ultimate purpose of our life'? or are his sentiments recycled from contemporary philosophy? Wolfgang Hildesheimer attributes them to Moses Mendelssohn (the composer's grandfather), but that is not in itself a reason to suppose that they do not represent Mozart's feelings.[10]

Mozart's religion, like his political and class attitude, did not demand blind obedience to doctrine; as a Mason, he will have pondered the mysteries of life, death, and what may follow, as he knew Leopold had done. If Mozart's language struggles to articulate a philosophical position, that is because his astonishing intellect worked in sound, rather than in words. He did not go to Salzburg to see his father, but Leopold, unaware of the imminence of his own death, or perhaps out of pride, did not summon him. Mozart himself was not well, having a recurrence of what may have been his fatal weakness, a complaint of the kidneys. Was this connected to his habit, reported by Attwood, of working standing up, at a high desk?[11] The family was again moving house, to the Landstrasse. Leopold's last letter to Nannerl remarks that 'he doesn't say why he has moved. Not a word. But unfortunately I can guess the reason' (11 May 1787).

The death of another parent—Beethoven's mother—may have prevented the two composers meeting other than briefly during the younger prodigy's short visit to Vienna in April; reports from Beethoven's pupils are contradictory. The effect of Leopold's death is an

---

[10] Hildesheimer, *Mozart*, 192–93.

[11] Attwood's unpublished memoir, Landon, *Golden Years*, 156.

open field for speculation. It had little impact on his conditions of life. Writing to his brother-in-law on 29 September 1787, two days before leaving for Prague, he accepted 1,000 gulden as his modest inheritance, a suspiciously round sum that was probably less than his fair share, and which could not decisively relieve him of financial anxiety. He had not inherited Leopold's zest for correspondence, and his remaining letters to Nannerl are sporadic and perfunctory. The impact of Leopold's death on his music is harder to gauge; perhaps there was none. The next work entered into his catalogue (14 June) was his musical joke (*Ein Musikalisches Spass*, K. 522), but it had been started several months earlier.[12] Interpreting this piece as mockery of Leopold, or the powerful statue music in *Don Giovanni* as a sign of guilt towards a parent he had betrayed, is to force a psychological hypotheses upon facts susceptible of simpler explanation. The statue is not Don Juan's father; and the musical joke celebrates a sense of humour that Mozart shared with Leopold, who was no less inclined to castigate musical incompetence in performers and composers alike. Both come under Mozart's lash. K. 522 is a composition lesson in itself, a catalogue of what not to do, with its lame formal and contrapuntal procedures, including crude modulations and a particularly stupid fugato in the finale. Performers are guyed in the extravagant violin cadenza, which goes out of tune at the end, the split notes of the horns, and the enthusiastic ending in which all the players cadence in different keys.

Mozart's main concern during the rest of 1787 was *Don Giovanni*. Since he and Da Ponte both worked in Vienna, we have no letters to illuminate their collaboration, which was undoubtedly close. We should resist the temptation to attribute every strength of their collaboration to Mozart, and every weakness to Da Ponte. Perhaps the passage in Da Ponte's memoirs that speaks of dividing his time between Mozart (his 'Dante'), Martín (his 'Petrarch'), Salieri (his 'Tasso'), and his landlady's daughter is more fantasy than reality, but his productiveness in these years is astonishing and he did indeed adapt his muse to the qualities of his composers. For *Don Giovanni* he had a model, a one-act libretto by Giovanni Bertati, delivered from Venice where the setting by Gazzaniga had been performed in February. It may have been supplied by Guarda-

<hr>

[12] Tyson, *Autograph Scores*, 234–45.

soni, in which case Da Ponte did not choose it, as he claimed (but nor did Mozart, as the Freudian would desire). The Don Juan legend, drawn from popular traditions and seventeenth-century drama, had received numerous musical treatments including Righini's first opera, performed in Italian (Prague, 1776) and German (Vienna, 1777). Da Ponte, although he followed Bertati's structure for a few scenes, used hardly a word of his libretto, whose author he despised; the changes are all improvements, and Da Ponte devised new scenes, including the events leading to the first finale, and act 2 up to the cemetery scene. As with his Milan operas, Mozart composed a good deal before leaving home, perhaps including some arias. He had heard most of the singers in *Figaro* and could transfer the vocal qualities of the count (Luigi Bassi) to Giovanni, of Figaro (Felice Ponziani) to Leporello, and Susanna (Caterina Bondini) to Zerlina, while realising entirely different characterisations. The distribution of some roles is conjectural, but the only singer certainly not in the *Figaro* cast was the Ottavio (Antonio Baglioni), who had been singing the title role in Gazzaniga's *Don Giovanni*.

While preparing his opera, Mozart composed a serenade (K. 525), much simpler than the Finalmusik of the Salzburg years, and called it *Eine kleine Nachtmusik*. The purpose of one of Mozart's most popular compositions is unknown; perhaps it was written for entertainments in Prague. It has only four movements, but the *Verzeichnüss* mentions a second minuet. The other work completed before *Don Giovanni* was the violin sonata in A (K. 526), still designated 'Klavier Sonate mit Begleitung einer Violin', but treating the instruments with full equality: a work of effortless maturity, it was published by Hoffmeister later in the year.

Leaving for Prague on 1 October, Mozart and Constanze did not undergo the curious adventure described in Eduard Mörike's story *Mozart auf der Reise nach Prag* (1855) that fictionalizes Mozart as a man equivalent in charm and purity to his music. Constanze was again pregnant (a daughter, Theresia, was born on 27 December), and three-year-old Carl Thomas stayed behind. When time allowed, the Mozarts could relax in the Dušeks' Villa Bertramka. Josepha wanted a new aria in 'payment' and allegedly locked Mozart away until he had finished it; in revenge he filled the scena 'Bella mia fiamma . . . Resta, o cara' (K. 528) with difficult intervals, challenging Josepha to perform it at sight. Some of the opera remained to be composed, including the overture, which Mozart normally wrote last, since nobody had to memorise it. The orchestra sight-read splendidly, even if, as the story goes, 'a few notes fell under the desk'; but it is uncertain whether this was at the last rehearsal or at the performance. I hope it is not heretical to suggest that, perhaps owing to the circumstances of composition (Mozart allegedly kept going by a regular supply of coffee), the emphasis on the descending five-note theme in the development is excessive (a similar repetitiveness mars the overture to *Così fan tutte*). Mozart told Jacquin that the singers were slower to learn their parts than in Vienna, and the premiere was postponed more than once, finally taking place on 29 October, to great acclaim. The fourth performance, for Mozart's benefit, was on 3 November.[13]

Gluck died on 15 November, releasing his annual income. The court changed Salieri's job description and appointed Mozart chamber musician at a useful salary of 800 gulden, less than half Gluck's sinecure (2,000 gulden) and much less than Mozart's annual expenditure. But the court was making economies, and it was thus a mark of imperial favour that Mozart was appointed; there was no need to replace Gluck at all. Joseph must have wanted to help Mozart and retain him in Vienna.[14] His only duties were to dash off a few sets of dances for the Carnival balls in the Redoutensaal: 'too much for what I do; too little for what I could do', he is reported as saying.[15] Mozart hoped his English friends might procure an invitation to London, though Leopold had poured cold water on the idea, as Stephen Storace would hardly welcome so formidable a rival (Leopold to Nannerl, 2 Mar 1787).

Mozart no doubt hoped to make money by writing an opera every year, but over the next two years he had to be content with revivals. Nevertheless, 1788 was another year of outstanding productivity. In February, for Swieten, he directed an oratorio by C. P. E. Bach ('Christ's Resurrection and Ascension in Heaven'), composed in 1774. The same

---

[13] Mozart's reports to Jacquin on the preparations and success of *Don Giovanni* are in letters spread over several days (the first is 15–25 October), and are considerably more detailed than the perfunctory report sent to Nannerl. The letter of 4–9 November included a song (K. 530), later published under Jacquin's name.

[14] Dorothea Link, 'Mozart's Appointment to the Viennese Court', in Link, *Words about Mozart*, 153–78.

[15] *E-Doc*, 77.

month, he finished a new piano concerto (K. 537), presumably for a concert of which we have no record; it is unlikely that the premiere was delayed until the first known performance, at Dresden in 1789. He began another concerto, eventually finished in 1791 (K. 595), and was preparing the Vienna performance of *Don Giovanni*, which took place on 7 May.

Don Giovanni appealed less in Vienna than in Prague. There was fresh competition; Martín's erotically teasing *L'arbore di Diana* had been produced in October 1787 and remained in the repertoire into 1791, and in January 1788 Salieri's third French opera, *Tarare*, a strongly political affair to a libretto by Beaumarchais, appeared in Da Ponte's radical Italian adaptation as *Axur, re d'Ormus*; although no comedy, it was a success.[16] For *Don Giovanni* Mozart had to accommodate singers who had not performed in *Figaro*. The new tenor, Francesco Morella, required a less florid aria than 'Il mio tesoro', and Mozart substituted the more sensitive 'Dalla sua pace'. For Cavalieri (Donna Elvira), Mozart directed her 'flexible throat' to supremely dramatic ends in the superb scena 'In quali eccesse . . . Mi tradì', an impassioned song of love for the unredeemable Giovanni. Luisa Mombelli, the original countess, and Benucci received a comic duet for Zerlina and Leporello, 'Per queste tue manine', whose coarse humour was directed at Viennese taste. As if to compensate singers with no new music, Mozart completed an aria for Lange (who sang Anna) that he had probably started in Mannheim when they first met ('Ah se in ciel, benigne stelle', K. 538), and for Francesco Albertarelli, the baritone who sang Giovanni, Mozart wrote the engagingly cynical buffo aria 'Un bacio di mano' (K. 541).

A gap in performances was caused by Mombelli's advanced pregnancy; Therese Teyber took over Zerlina on 16 June. Joseph II's comment to Rosenberg, that Mozart's music was difficult for the singers, may have articulated a widespread perception.[17] Nevertheless, there

---

[16] Link, *Court Theatre*, 308–9 (note).

[17] Joseph was responding to Rosenberg's opinion; he himself did not hear *Don Giovanni*. The story that he called it 'tough meat for the Viennese', and Mozart replied 'Let them chew on it', comes from Da Ponte and can hardly be relied upon. The indefatigable diarist Count Zinzendorf found the music 'agréable et très variée' at the first performance, but on 12 May (the third performance) he reports one Madame de la Lippe as finding it learned, but not suitable for singing ('savante, peu propre au chant'). Link, *Court Theatre*, 315.

were more performances of *Don Giovanni* than *Figaro* had received in 1786. Viennese audiences probably enjoyed the walking statue and punishment of the wicked, even if Mozart's music brought them to life with alarming vividness, but the more decorous final scene, drawing the moral, was cut, the opera ending with Giovanni's death. It was not long before Mainz and Frankfurt, quickly followed by other German theatres, were presenting versions in German, albeit as Singspiel, with spoken dialogue.

For the rest of the year Mozart remained prolific, and his output diverse. Domestic music-making with the Jacquin family probably occasioned the delicious *Notturni* for voices and basset-horns (K. 436–439, 549), and a number of canons, mostly not entered into his catalogue. The piano sonata in F (K. 533) was published, including the earlier rondo (K. 494), somewhat extended, and he composed the well-known sonata in C (K. 545) and its companion-piece in F with violin (K. 547), both designated 'for beginners'.[18] The Mozarts' daughter died in June; the previous day Mozart had entered in his catalogue the Adagio introduction to the string version of his great C-minor fugue (K. 546). During the summer and early autumn he produced three more piano trios in E, C and G (K. 542, 548, 564), and the remarkable 'Divertimento' (K. 563), one of the few masterpieces that exist for string trio (violin, viola, cello); as with the quintets, there is a 'false start', an incomplete first movement in G major for the same combination. The divertimento was dedicated to Michael Puchberg in gratitude for several loans. While Mozart persisted in writing complex music, regardless of whether it was saleable, the piano trios may have been kept deliberately simpler; nevertheless they have a seductive melodic charm.[19] The isolated Adagio in B minor for piano (K. 540), composed at the time of the additions to *Don Giovanni*, is one of his most searching slow movements, in a key he practically never used; it is a full sonata form with coda, and thematic and harmonic development of outstanding richness.

[18] The last movement of K. 547, a set of variations, also exists in a version for piano alone; Köchel thought it was an early work (thus K. 54=547a-b).

[19] Mozart wrote substantial parts of three more piano trio movements in D minor, G major, and D major. Completed by Maximilian Stadler, they found their way into Köchel's catalogue as K. 442; the movements were, however, almost certainly not intended to form a single work. Tyson, 'New Dates', 220.

The last symphonies

The most remarkable event of 1788 is the rapid completion in June, July, and August of what proved to be Mozart's last three symphonies, in E♭ (K. 543), G minor (K. 550), and C (K. 551, the 'Jupiter'). Although the most obvious intention in writing such pieces was to supply works for performance, they may have been partly inspired by the recent publication of Haydn's 'Paris' symphonies, three of them in the same keys.[20] If so, as with the 'Haydn' quartets, the spirit of emulation, rather than of imitation, was what drove Mozart. It is only in retrospect that the symphonies appear as a triptych designed to show that Mozart, guided by his musical ambitions, could reshape the expectations of a genre familiar to all his audiences.

The slightly earlier 'Prague' symphony has Mozart's grandest slow introduction, but K. 543 runs it close. The 'Prague' uses a motif for the ceremonial call to attention that reappears to open the allegro of K. 551. In the 'Prague', majestic gestures related to the old-style French overture are dissolved by a passage of harmonic mystery in 'ombra' (shadow) vein. The playfulness and sinister undertones of *Don Giovanni* are not far away; the syncopations of the allegro are not those of Sturm und Drang but of anticipation, and shadows cast before the elegant lead-in to the flowing secondary theme, and within the slow movement, serve to brighten the sunshine.

K. 543 is Mozart's only symphony to displace oboes in favour of clarinets, effecting the sound-world as they do in the two piano concertos with this orchestration (K. 482 and 488). The introduction is only over-clouded in the last four bars before an allegro that jovially sublimates the early waltz, or Ländler. The emotional centre of this symphony is the slow movement, in A♭, based on the Romanza pattern: an innocent-sounding theme and a stormy episode which, through a piece of enharmonic wizardry, appears first in F minor, then in its polar opposite, B minor (compare bars 30 and 96). The lilting quality of the slow movement of the 'Prague' may compensate for the absence of a minuet, which in K. 543 seems faster, and less stately, than usual. The nerviness of the 'Prague' finale comes from its syncopated theme, and a certain

[20] See David Wyn Jones, 'Why did Mozart compose his last three Symphonies? Some new Hypotheses', *Music Review* 51 (1990), 280–89; and Zaslaw, *Symphonies*, 421–31.

brittleness in harmony (frequent recourse to minor inflections) and texture, notably the tiny passages for the woodwind groups. The contredanse finale of K. 543, like that of the later quintet K. 614, vies with Haydn for musical wit. The only theme of any importance is a seven-note motif, put through every harmonic and instrumental pace in music as intellectually stimulating as it is entertaining.

If the 'Prague' and K. 543 have much in common, the G-minor and C-major ('Jupiter') symphonies confirm Mozart's ability to deliver twins of opposite character, like the string quintets in the same keys; and also to confirm the danger of reading autobiography in the character of his music. These last two symphonies have been the subject of more intense scrutiny than any of Mozart's instrumental works.[21] Neither has any introduction, unless we count the first bar of the G-minor, a restless accompaniment before the entry of the theme. This theme sets and sustains a mood, moving almost seamlessly into the modulation; the second theme, although first presented in the major, is a chromatic sigh, and the pulsing first theme reasserts itself before the end of the exposition. By contrast, the 'Jupiter' exposition offers maximum contrast. The ceremonial opening is answered by the utmost suavity; the singing second theme, whose rising chromatic intervals are the opposite of a sigh, is succeeded by an explosion of Sturm und Drang, mocked in turn by an opera buffa melody—literally, for it is taken from Mozart's most recent insertion aria, 'Un bacio di mano' (K. 541).

The last symphonies come closest in their slow movements, ornate, expressive, periodically melancholy, but less astonishing than the equivalent in K. 543; and in the minuets, utterly contrasted in character—the G-minor stern, the 'Jupiter' flowing and courtly—but both exploring the contrapuntal possibilities of their themes in the reprise. One could argue, too, that both finales are all of a piece with the first movements, and that the strength of both symphonies lies in this rhetorical reinforcement of their principal topics. But the differences seem more imposing than ever. The G-minor finale exceeds its own first movement in agitation and harmonic daring; the 'Jupiter' finale begins innocently

---

[21] Nathan Broder (ed.), *Mozart: Symphony in G minor, K. 550* (Norton Critical Score), and Elaine Sisman, *Mozart: the 'Jupiter' Symphony* (Cambridge, 1993) gather critical opinions from the past as well as offering new insights.

enough, with a four-note motif Mozart used in several other works, but follows its galant beginnings with a display of contrapuntal wizardry. The grinding counterpoint of a secondary development, after the reprise (bars 233–62) should banish for ever thoughts that Mozart is invariably, or even usually, an easy composer, and in the immense coda, in a more festive spirit, no fewer than five motifs are combined. Unfortunately we have no knowledge of the reception of these works in his lifetime; after his death, they were soon established as a touchstone of symphonic mastery.

CHAPTER 15

Chamber Music

'the greatest composer I know'

IN THE MID-EIGHTEENTH CENTURY, CHAMBER MUSIC WITHOUT A keyboard was a comparatively modern idea and was epitomized by the rapid growth of the string quartet. Many such works were quite simple, or composed in a concertante style for a lively first violin accompanied by the other players. Joseph Haydn is usually credited with developing equal participation by all four instruments, while matching, indeed exceeding, simpler-minded galant quartets in popularity. In this Haydn unwittingly posed a challenge to the keyboard-orientated Mozart, who seems more comfortable, in his earlier output of chamber music without keyboard, with a participating wind instrument.

Mozart's string quartets divide into thirteen early works, and ten mature quartets: six dedicated to Haydn, one to Hoffmeister, and three intended for the king of Prussia. Apart from K. 80 (1770), the early quartets form two sets of six. The first set (K. 155–160), composed on the last Milan journey (1772–73), consists of slender three-movement works, in major keys organised by descending fifths (D, G, C, F, B♭, E♭); thematic interplay consists mainly of the violins taking turns with the melody. The second set (K. 168–173), composed only a few months later, marks a considerable advance in idiomatic layout and in equalising the upper parts, as in the short development of the first quartet, K. 168 in F (ex. 15.1). This is a fairly elementary egalitarianism, and the fifth quartet in B♭ is more typical, galant music that is almost entirely treble dominated except for a little dialogue with the viola in the minuet. In a

Ex. 15.1 String quartet in F, K. 168, first movement, from bar 42

curious experiment, the Allegro of the Eb quartet (K. 171) is framed by an Adagio, and both tempi contain uncomfortable contrasts: the Adagio between a sombre unison—the first bar apparently in C minor—and gentle sentiment, the Allegro between a quiet vocal style and galant material (ex. 15.2).

Although several movements are in a divertimento-like style calculated to appeal to Viennese amateurs, Mozart may have copied Haydn's op. 20

Ex. 15.2 String Quartet in E♭, K. 171

a. Opening

Adagio

quartets, which their composer called 'divertimenti', by including fugal
movements, in which the four players are more obviously equal; another
possible model is d'Ordonez. K. 168 goes one better than Haydn by including two fugues. The slow movement in F minor, a key Mozart rarely
used, deploys the four-note subject with diminished seventh heard in the
same key in Handel's *Messiah* ('And with his stripes'), which Mozart
probably did not yet know; more pertinently, it is used by Haydn in the
double fugue finale of op. 20 no. 5. The breathless fugal finale is more id-
iomatically conceived for strings, and includes an inversion of the subject.
The chromatic subject of the finale of the D-minor quartet (K. 173) is
treated so plainly that it could almost be performed by voices.

Ex. 15.2 *(continued)*

b. From bar 15

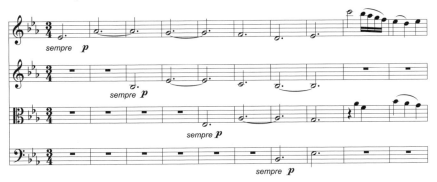

None of these quartets is as enjoyable as the string quintet in B♭ from late 1773 (K. 174). The texture is enriched by the second viola, liberating the first to sing duets with the violin. Mozart indulges his liking for broadly laid out thematic periods, achieved by repetition in different registers and instrumental colours (including various octave couplings). Where the quartets seem self-conscious, the outer movements of the quintet exude confidence, from the loose–limbed opening theme, a version of one of Mozart's favourite motifs (ex. 15.3a), to the virtuoso cut and thrust of the finale (ex. 15.3b).

The quartets with wind instruments are equally sure of themselves. The first of those written for Dejean, in D (K. 285), deserves its popularity for its melodious first movement, its eloquent slow movement in B minor (another key rare in Mozart), where the flute is poised in tensile

Ex. 15.3 String Quintet in B♭, K. 174

a. First movement, opening

Allegro moderato

elegance over pizzicato strings, and its kittenish finale. The later flute quartets have only two movements. The first movement of No. 2 in G (K. 285a) is an eloquent sonata-form Andante, followed by a simple Tempo di Minuetto. Mozart was evidently bored, and none of the flute quartets equals the oboe quartet of 1781 (K. 370=368b), written for an outstanding professional, Friedrich Ramm. There is pure chamber-music dialogue between oboe and violin, and also some giddy virtuosity, notably in the finale when the oboe, playing in $\frac{4}{4}$ against the persistent jogging $\frac{6}{8}$ of the strings, achieves a speed of sixteen semiquavers to the bar. The oboe signs off the outer movements with a note (f‴) higher than any in Dejean's flute

Ex. 15.3 (*continued*)

b. Last movement, coda, from bar 173

quartets. In the slow movement the theme, its diminished seventh reminiscent of K. 173, is taken over by the rhapsodic oboe, modulating unusually from D minor to B♭, an example of how Mozart's engagement with a
virtuoso performer could liberate his imagination (ex. 15.4).

Mozart's next chamber works without keyboard were the horn quintet
(K. 407) for the egregious Leutgeb, a delightfully witty piece in which the
string quartet has one violin and two violas, and the first of the six string
quartets dedicated to Haydn, finished at the end of 1782. Mozart composed
these quartets laboriously, and as the set proceeds his growing confidence is
almost palpable. No.1, in G (K. 387), accommodates a plethora of ideas in
a medium where Haydn cultivated the utmost economy, as if Mozart was
trying too hard to offer a rich musical experience entirely his own. The
basis of the first movement is an egalitarian textural complexity (ex. 15.5).

Ex. 15.3 (*continued*)

Notwithstanding a somewhat repetitive development, this is a remarkable
return to the medium, but Mozart may have been more at home in the
homophonic expressiveness of the slow movement. The minuet experiments with displaced accents, duple against the prevailing pulse, in a rising
chromatic motif, and it is with a sense of relief that the minor-mode trio
breaks from the private world of chamber music into a brief explosion of
passion. The finale is the first example, followed by the finales to the piano
concerto K. 459 and the 'Jupiter' symphony, in which Mozart integrates
fugue into a sonata form with galant themes. By contrast with the earlier
quartets, and perhaps through his study of Bach, Mozart can now refresh
his expressively neutral subject with new counterpoints, and by using it to
steer an enharmonic modulation that owes nothing to fugal techniques, before signing off with a closing theme that breathes the spirit of comedy.

Ex. 15.4   Oboe quartet, second movement

Adagio

The next quartet, in D minor (K. 421=417b), retains its tragic impetus to the end, a little mollified by the curiously hesitant Andante. The only variation finale of the set is based on melancholy Siciliano, but in the second variation Mozart reaches a rare level of textural complexity, with three conflicting rhythms ($\frac{6}{8}$, $\frac{3}{4}$, $\frac{6}{16}$) defined by *fp* markings. The light of the major-mode variation is extinguished by the faster coda in minor, whose dying fall recalls the opening of the first movement. Again, this work stands as the minor-mode contrast in a set of six, but the high level of chromatic exploration which Mozart loved to engage in, when writing connoisseurs' music, is reflected in the opening theme of the E♭ quartet (K. 428=421b), a serpentine unison taking in nine different pitches. Its subsequent harmonisation has a splendid resonance. The finale of K. 428 is the first of three in contredanse rhythm (a fast $\frac{2}{4}$), in this case sprightly but not too complicated, whereas the finales of the 'Hunt' quartet, in B♭

Ex. 15.4 *(continued)*

(K. 458), and the 'Dissonance', in C (K.465), combine the high spirits natural to this mood and metre with considerable contrapuntal ingenuity. None of the other quartets has an actual fugue, as Mozart developed his skill in manipulating a four-way conversation based on close imitation of characteristic themes. The apogee of this kind of fluent counterpoint, ingenious yet without the taint of being 'learned', is in the fast movements in the fifth quartet, in A (K. 464), whose overall mood is gently radiant. K. 464 is the only one of the set which has variations for its slow movement; that of K. 465 is the crowning example of the songlike andante used in K. 387 and K. 458, in what Charles Rosen calls a 'slow-movement sonata form'.[1] In these movements, the first violin takes on

---

[1] Charles Rosen, *Sonata Forms*, 104–10, basing part of the discussion on K. 465. A short transition rather than a development precedes the return of the opening.

Ex. 15.5 String quartet in G, K. 387, first movement

Allegro vivace assai

the role of a singer and begins the reprise by the kind of embellishment
familiar from the piano sonatas. But egalitarianism always reasserts itself,
and most of the variation in the reprises arises from Mozart's usual procedure of expanding material through contrasts of register, harmonic in-
tensification, and an additional coda.

Ex. 15.6 String quartet in C, K. 465, first movement

The only slow introduction of the set (ex. 15.6) gives K. 465 its nickname, the 'Dissonance', and invites questions about its purpose and meaning. The boldest dissonance (bar 2) appears in Mozart's autograph without the ♮ sign before the violin a″, though he cannot have intended anything else; clearly he didn't think it necessary in a passage otherwise, with dynamics and phrasing, notated so meticulously. The parallel major ninths between second violin and cello could be explained away by interpreting the second violin c♯' as an expressive chromatic neighbour to d', but the part-writing remains intriguingly unsynchronised. The progression is repeated a tone lower, the cello eventually completing a chromatic descent from tonic to dominant, a

Ex. 15.6 (*continued*)

universal symbol of mourning.[2] The remainder of the introduction continues introspective but with less cryptic syntax, and a third of it is governed by a prolonged dominant (from bar 16). Unlike Mozart's and Haydn's symphony, the chamber medium does not need to attract attention with a ceremonial gesture before beginning its progression from darkness to the light of the allegro. K. 465 is a direct ancestor to Beethoven's quartet op. 59 no. 3, in the same key, and symphonic slow introductions which give off an air of mystery from the start, like Beethoven's fourth symphony, are affected by its example. Given the difficulty of translating music into words, it may be pertinent to recall

[2] See Peter Williams, 'Some thoughts on Mozart's use of the chromatic fourth', in R. Larry Todd and Peter Williams (eds.), *Perspectives on Mozart Performance*, especially 225–27.

Mozart's stated principles, already quoted: 'Music must never offend the ear, even in the most horrid situations'; it should please both the connoisseur and the 'common listener'. In a quartet he could risk an adventure too dangerous for work intended for public performance; the 'Dissonance' is consistent with these principles.

The sale of Mozart's chamber music was generally a disappointment. Perhaps this is not surprising, given that there were no professional quartets, and amateurs had easier meat to chew upon. Although he did not risk another experiment like the start of K. 465, he could not resist exploring the limits of his musical language, even in a quartet specially written for a publisher (K. 499, the 'Hoffmeister'). It may seem pleasantly relaxed after its predecessors, but harmonic adventure arises even in a genially melodic context: the exposition cadences are prolonged by interruption, first by the natural third below the tonic, then the flattened third, keys totally unrelated but able to support an identical melodic pattern before resolving (ex. 15.7); this ingenious harmonic pun (the double meaning of the note D, as third of the chords of B minor and B♭ major) epitomises Mozart's progress since the simple repetition of interrupted cadences in the symphony K. 199 (ex. 10.2).

Mozart's next large chamber works were the great quintets of 1787, and most commentators have acknowledged their confidence, mastery, and grandeur of conception. But for the absence of an introduction, the design of the first quintet, in C (K. 515), is almost a replica of the 'Dissonance' quartet, with cantabile slow movement and contredanse finale. The slow harmonic pace of its first theme demands an expansive continuation, producing 'the largest "sonata-allegro" before Beethoven', according to Charles Rosen.[3] Well over fifty bars elapse before any move away from the tonic; at 151 bars, the exposition approaches that of the *Eroica*.[4] Aiming, perhaps, at maximum difference within a pair of compositions composed in tandem, the second quintet, in G minor (K. 516), poses formal and interpretative questions exceptional even for Mozart. Where K. 515 uses all five instruments with relatively few rests, the G-minor opens by exploiting contrasted groupings of three, so that the

[3] Rosen, *The Classical Style*, 268.

[4] In the *Eroica* first movement, however, Beethoven's development and coda are far longer than Mozart's.

Ex. 15.7   String quartet in D ('Hoffmeister'), K. 499, first movement, from bar 198

Allegretto

theme is played by two violins with viola 'bass', then by two violas with cello, a pattern much used in the quintets of 1790–91. As a result the first tutti has a sense of mass and also strain, with its yearning melodic line in octaves (bar 20). At bar 30, a more lyrical and symmetrical melodic idea, still in the tonic, begins the modulation; this is recapitulated in the normal way but returns to conclude the movement in a mood of melancholia. Mozart places the minuet second and defies the dance metre by explosive off-beat accents. A promise of consolation is offered when the trio shapes the cadence motif of the minuet into its own theme but in the major. Both quintets have richly textured slow movements, but contrast still obtains: the ornate Andante of K. 515 is cut from a fine piece of cloth left over from the 'Haydn' quartets, whereas K. 516, with even the cello muted, anticipates the hymnlike Adagios of the nineteenth century. But the note of worship cannot last;

Ex. 15.7 (*continued*)

a rapid dissolution into dialogued texture leads to a gathering of the tutti
for a note of despair, stretching the $\frac{4}{4}$ metre by sextuple units (from bar
18). Mozart's boldest stroke follows. A slow introduction to the finale is
exceptional even the nineteenth century, and this one overturns the textural norms of Mozart's chamber music, for it is an accompanied solo vi-

olin aria in the tragic mode of Konstanze's 'Traurigkeit'. With the utmost delicacy, Mozart introduces elements of the major mode in the last few bars and breaks through to a graceful, brilliant, and large-scale rondo. As with the 'Dissonance', no programmatic or biographical reason can be found for this enigma.

Before writing more quintets, Mozart composed his string trio ('Divertimento', K. 563) and returned to the string quartet. Despite its modest title and the small ensemble, the trio is a big work, and not only because, as a divertimento, it has six movements: between the sonata-form first and rondo-form finale come an Adagio in A♭, two minuets, and a variation movement, Andante. For most of the work's length, its wealth of thematic invention, contrapuntal play, and ornamental elaboration in the slow movements, mark the work as chamber music. If Mozart sometimes seems more at ease in composing with his largest group, the quintet, he seems no less comfortable with only three so long as they are virtuosi enough to manage the enriched texture of the adagio, through frequent double stopping (viola and violin), which liberates the cello to take a full share of melodic activity. Another strategy was to begin the variations in a two-part texture (violin and viola in octaves), from which artful simplicity grow the most fantastic elaborations. After a shorter minor-key variation, the return to the major is celebrated by the viola trumpeting out a simplified version of the theme against continual semiquaver arpeggios in the cello and scintillating demisemiquaver passagework for the violin. With such riches there seems no need for more instruments. The flavour of divertimento is restored in the second minuet, with its two dancing (Ländler) trios. But Mozart is rarely content to let us down gently, and the apparently innocent finale themes generate considerable complexity before order is restored and the main material lingered upon, as if reluctant to abandon its playful paradise.

The last quartets are known as 'Prussian' because Mozart planned them for the king of Prussia, and their texture is affected by the monarch's liking for melodies in the tenor register, on the A string of his cello. Accommodating this preference caused Mozart to reconsider the texture of the ensemble, which becomes airier than the 'Haydn' quartets when the viola plays bass to the singing cello; the modulations are less marked, and the texture flows with a seductive smoothness that almost conceals the music's originality. Mozart's practical sense of what would

Ex. 15.8 String quartet in B♭ ('Prussian'), K. 589, first movement

work with a soloistic cello part led him to incorporate more virtuosity in the first violin, without sacrificing near-equality of voices.

Both the first quartet, in D (K. 575) and the second, in B♭ (K. 589) develop their finale themes from their first movements, and in K. 589 the outer movements begin with the viola imitating the violin in the second bar. The opening (ex. 15.8) exemplifies Mozart's delicate balance between phrasing and instrumentation. The antecedent in the upper parts reaches its half-close at bar 6, with the matching 6-bar consequent led by the cello; but the latter enters a bar early with marking-time motive. This is passed through the viola to the violin; the viola's apparently acute clash with the cello hardly sounds dissonant. The cello plays a full melodic consequent (the viola imitating, then providing the bass), but before it is completed, the violin quavers somehow assume the role of primary voice. The egalitarian nature of the music is hardly different from K. 387 (see ex. 15.5), but the transparency of the texture could hardly be more different. In K. 589 most of the exposition consists of two-bar units, but, thanks to an elision, the closing part consists of seven plus eleven. The note-values, however, accelerate to triplets (including a near-citation from *Don Giovanni*).[5] The closing idea (bar 67) need have had no other function, but typically within the Mozartian economy, it is used to launch the development, a trick he had worked elegantly in the 'Hoffmeister' quartet (K. 499) and elsewhere.[6] Syntactical play with an ending that also functions as a point of departure frames the Allegro of another late masterpiece, the D-major string quintet (K. 593).

Perhaps the most original part of K. 589 is the Trio, nearly twice as long as the minuet. It seems to mock Mozart's youthful reliance on semiquaver figuration, here passed among the instruments to blossom in cadenza-like virtuosity (first violin from bar 53). The principle of contrast still holds: the rococo twirls of the melody, smoothly graded in dynamics, are fiercely interrupted after the double bar by gritty *sforzandi*, abrupt modulations foreshadowing Schubert, and a silent pause; this is no more a dance than the minuet of K. 516. The $\frac{6}{8}$ finale is a tour de force of tight but lucid counterpoint, with the theme frequently inverted. If Mozart found string quartets a labour to write, it no longer shows in this, nor its only successor, in F (K. 590).

Before finishing the 'Prussian' quartets Mozart had completed the clarinet quintet (K. 581), his last chamber work with a concertante wind instrument. Just as the middle-register horn was partnered by a string quartet with two violas, so the higher-pitched clarinet mixes with the orthodox group, with two violins. This leaves textural space for the low notes of the clarinet, which sets out its stall, as it were, by a luscious arpeggio response to the gentle opening theme on the strings.[7] The second theme is likewise introduced by the violin, but here the clarinet's response is a meditation on the same shapes, passing via the minor and its related keys; the version in the recapitulation is so much a variation

---

[5] The violin figure in bars 64–66 is an amplified sequence on Zerlina's 'Batti, batti', bars 68–69: Mozart probably did not know Bach's Overture in D (third orchestral suite, BWV 1068) where the whole shape appears in the Gigue.

[6] For example, the sonata K. 284 (see chap. 9), and the E♭ symphony K. 543.

[7] This opening makes nonsense of the transcription, made after Mozart's death, in which another viola replaces the clarinet.

that it amounts to a different melody. In the development, the clarinet takes over the violin's first theme, and the strings appropriate the arpeggio response, in a passage of fierce textural brilliance. The slow movement begins as a clarinet aria, turning into a duet with the violin. A minuet with two trios associates the work with the wind serenades, but the first is for strings only, while the clarinet leads the second in Ländler style. Having abandoned the draft of a rondo, Mozart settled on variations for the finale. The low 'chalumeau' register of the clarinet darkened the serene melodic line of the slow movement; here it provides accompaniment figurations. The viola takes centre stage in the minor-mode variation, and clarinet and violin share passagework and the interplay of ideas in the faster coda. The clarinet quintet provided later composers with a model worthy of emulation. The concertante-like Weber quintet and Brahms's introspective late masterpiece are only the best-known of its successors, making this perhaps Mozart's most influential chamber work.

Opera Buffa

'most important is that it must be really comic'[1]

MOZART'S CENTRAL PLACE IN THE OPERATIC CANON RESTS mainly on three works with libretti by Lorenzo da Ponte, thanks to which the privileged position of Viennese opera buffa among late eighteenth-century repertories remains unchallenged. When he began *Figaro*, Mozart had not finished an opera buffa for over ten years; his Viennese works belong to a different species. Given their sheer musical and dramatic fascination, their originality is hardly important; such as it is, it lies mainly in the ensembles for which even the quartets in *Zaide* and *Die Entführung* provide only a modest precedent. The multi-movement finales, among the glory of these operas, use a form older than Mozart himself. Mozart's originality lies more in method than in form, especially in his synchronisation of musical design and action; and his achievement proved surprisingly difficult for later composers to exploit.[2]

Approaching *Figaro*, 1: the aria

Figaro marked the climax of three years' preparation during which Mozart took every chance to compose for the Burgtheater singers, at the very time when his intense involvement with instrumental music

---

[1] Mozart's letter to Leopold, 7 May 1783, concerning *L'oca del Cairo*.

[2] See Joseph Kerman, 'Action and the Musical Continuity' and 'Mozart', in *Opera as Drama* (2nd edition), 58–108.

affected his perception of how different moods can be coordinated within a continuous tempo. He also composed fine Italian arias for concerts, to opera seria texts or for insertion into other composers' works. The scena 'Mia speranza adorata . . . Ah, non sai' (K. 416) for Lange begins with a carefully organised recitative: five tempo changes are ordered by a thematic repetition. The routine by which the orchestra falls silent for each vocal utterance, or holds a chord, is varied by plaintive oboe solos, adagio, entwined with the soprano; at the closing words of farewell, chromaticism controlled by a circle of fifths and a Neapolitan sixth before the cadence relate to the cluster of expressive elements detectable at dramatic high spots throughout his mature operas.[3] This scena might be heard more often had not the subsequent Rondo explored the stratospheric range (to f''') in which Lange specialised. The two arias Mozart wrote for her to sing in *Il curioso indiscreto* (K. 418, 419) make plentiful use of e''', in one case attacked after a rest; Mozart claimed to be bringing out 'the qualities of her voice' (2 Jul 1783).[4] The most beautiful of these arias, and dramatically the most interesting, is Adamberger's (K. 420), which recalls Mozart's description of Belmonte's aria, written for the same singer. The number is characteristic of the upper-class, potentially serious character so often found in *drama giocoso*, and the music embodies the contrasts with which Mozart liked to mark the complexities of such a person of 'middle character' (*mezzo carattere*; compare the count in *Figaro*, or Donna Elvira). These contrasts—solemn unison wind, galant strings—are fundamental to his musical language; they can even be compared to some of his sacred works, such as the Kyrie settings in examples 2.7 and 6.1, but are seldom so appropriate as in opera buffa. The voice begins ('I beg you, do not seek out the reason for my torment') in hymnlike vein; the tremolo accompanies a more broken, recitative-like utterance, then lyricism again blossoms into cantabile (ex. 16.1) as he suggests that it may be possible to assuage his apparent cruelty.

All these arias are in modern forms, which in turn depended on the

---

[3] See Julian Rushton, ' . . . hier wird es besser seyn . . . ein blosses Recitativ zu machen', in Sadie, *Wolfgang Amadè Mozart*, 436–48.

[4] Arpeggiated high notes, like the f''' required of Aloysia's sister Josepha in *Die Zauberflöte*, may be taken as harmonics, whereas tone quality has to be maintained over each note of a scale, covering a twelfth (b♭'–f''') in K. 416, and a sixteenth (d'–e''') in K. 419.

Ex. 16.1 'Per pietà', K. 420. Insertion aria for Adamberger, in Anfossi, *Il curioso indiscreto*

Ex. 16.1 (*continued*)

structure of the text. The modified Da Capo form useful for the older type of text has already been discussed (see chap. 4), but was itself becoming old-fashioned. In K. 419 (which Mozart says was encored), the ferociously difficult Allegro accelerates to Allegro assai for the second stanza, drawing the form near to that of 'Martern aller Arten'. Two arias (K. 416 and 420) he called, respectively, 'Rondeau' and 'Rondo' (now usually written Rondò). He had already used this form for Belmonte's 'Wenn der Freude Thränen fliessen'; it was a modern form, a version of the two-section aria defined by the return to the opening themes, both within the slow section and within the following allegro. In K. 416, there are three verse quatrains, the first and third confined to the andante and allegro, the second distributed between them, with an unusual return to the andante in the course of the allegro.[5] The Rondò form was mostly associated with a high point in a principal role, especially a prima donna's final aria. But Mozart used it elsewhere, as with K. 418 (not designated Rondò); 'Bester Jüngling' in *Der Schauspieldirektor*; and at the emotional heart of *Figaro*, the Countess's 'Dove sono i bei momenti', a touching example of how this form can summarise a movement from nostalgic sadness to an expression of hope.

Approaching *Figaro*, 2: the buffo ensemble and finale

Varesco's incomplete libretto for *L'oca del Cairo* shows signs of collapsing under its own leaden ingenuity, and Mozart's sharp critique put paid to the project (10 Feb 1784). The first Vienna run of *Il barbiere di Siviglia* took place during Mozart's visit to Salzburg, but he must have realised that Paisiello's opera had a similar plot, more deftly handled.[6] Nevertheless, he had drafted much of act 1. Given that, as Mozart put it, 'the Musique is the main thing in an opera' (21 Jun 1783), its fragmentary nature is regrettable; none of it is completely orchestrated, although voice and bass parts, and a few instrumental cues, make reconstruction feasible.[7] An important feature of the Da Ponte operas is the sharp characterisation of social class, and although this is apparent in parts of *La finta giardiniera*, the mature technique of *Figaro* was forged in *L'oca del Cairo*. The ensembles and finale to act 1 are trial runs for the later masterpiece and need only a little more dramatic focus to be worthy of their descendants. The finale builds up the number of characters on stage, adding a chorus, and

[5] In probably the last Rondò Mozart composed, Vitellia's 'Non più di fiori', the theme of the Larghetto returns in the Allegro, but adjusted in metre and note-values to the fast tempo.

[6] *Il barbiere* was first given on 15 August, and the last performance in 1783 was on 3 November, the day before Mozart gave his concert in Linz. It was revived in May 1784, after Mozart had abandoned *L'oca del Cairo*.

[7] A trio exists fully scored, but the MS is in a later hand and the orchestration may not be Mozart's.

getting faster at the end as the action freezes into a standoff. But Varesco had devised only a feeble sequence of events, and the characters expend too much effort merely dreading what may be going to happen.

Don Pippo's decisive entry, as in *Figaro* (act 2) and *Don Giovanni* (act 1), is marked by modulation down a minor third, from E♭ to C, after which Mozart descends by fifths to his starting-point, B♭. In *Figaro*, a similar tonal design is greatly extended. Since these finales move to the dominant in their early stages, an analogy to sonata form has been detected, spanning the successive sections: in *Figaro*, tonic (E♭) exposition (confrontation of the count and countess); dominant (the action develops: Susanna, rather than Cherubino, emerges from the closet); an abrupt change, from B♭ to G (Figaro enters); descent by fifths for his deception about the anonymous letter and the broken flowerpots, reaching B♭; back in E♭, the entry of the vengeful Marcellina and Bartolo, with Basilio. The various sections use different styles and metres, and accelerate according to the often-quoted precept of Da Ponte.[8] This brilliant and logical finale has been held up as a paradigm, but as John Platoff has observed, apart from its adumbration in *L'oca del Cairo*, it is unique; none of Mozart's later finales conforms to this pattern, and his later operas seem generally less connected than *Figaro* to instrumental sonata forms.[9]

With *Lo sposo deluso* the fragments are less extended, though more complete in texture.[10] His hopes rising, Mozart planned roles specifically for the Burgtheater singers.[11] Mozart's taste for experiment appears in a new way of linking the overture to the action. *Die Entführung* is his last opera to begin with a solo, in this case using the same theme as the slow central section of the overture. *Don Giovanni* and *Die Zauberflöte* begin with introductions in which characters are introduced successively; the first numbers of *L'oca del Cairo*, *Figaro*, and *La clemenza di Tito* are duets

[8] Da Ponte's prescription may be found in Tim Carter, *W. A. Mozart: Le nozze di Figaro*, 43–44.

[9] John Platoff, 'Tonal Organization in "Buffo" Finales and the Act II Finale of "Le nozze di Figaro"', *Music & Letters*, 72 (1991), 370–403, and 'Musical and Dramatic Structure in the Opera Buffa Finale', *Journal of Musicology* 7 (1989), 191–230.

[10] The overture and opening quartet were completed after Mozart's death for a performance in 1797; the trio was fully scored by Mozart. The arias are in the same condition as *L'oca del Cairo*.

[11] These include 'Signora Fischer' (Nancy Storace), Cavalieri, Teyber, Pugnetti, Benucci, Mandini, and Bussani. All but the tenor Pugnetti later performed in *Figaro* or *Don Giovanni*.

(the latter preceded by recitative); *Così* follows the overture with three short trios. *Lo sposo deluso* is the most radical; the quartet begins with the return of the overture's allegro, after a slow middle section, and is extended by its own dominant modulation and reprise. Mozart then abandoned the slow middle section in overtures; he began one for *Figaro*, but deleted it. He did not repeat the experiment of *Lo sposo deluso*, in which decidedly routine material is spread over more than 300 bars; only the brisk exchanges between the characters—three of them mocking old Bocconio's plan to take a young bride—make the piece tolerable. Even in the trio, a more confused dramatic situation remains unchanged at the end, whereas in *Figaro* the first-act trio and third-act sextet are notable for combining a secure musical form with a development in the plot.

Mozart next honed his skills with the ensembles added to *La villanella rapita*, in which the story (an immoral aristocrat trying to seduce a girl of lower social class) anticipates *Figaro*, *Don Giovanni*, and *Una cosa rara*. The trio 'Mandina amabile' (K. 480) is in A major, Mozart's favoured key for love and seduction, used twice again for the same singer, Calvesi, as Ferrando in *Così*. The count gives Mandina money to persuade her away from Pippo; the latter bursts in, with an abrupt change of tempo and mode, turning the scene into an imbroglio. Like Masetto in *Don Giovanni*, Pippo and Mandina's father, Biaggio, are spirited peasants, and they follow the abducted Mandina to the Count's palace. In the quartet 'Dite almeno in che mancai' (K. 479), they upbraid her for wearing the finery the count has given her; she protests her innocence. The change of tempo comes when the count enters. In a brief solo (ex. 16.2) Mandina pleads exquisitely ('if I haven't lost your love, my lord, have mercy': mark the augmented triad, not too common in Mozart), continuing to cry above the three male voices; the count's musical gestures match Don Giovanni's cowing of the lower classes with his sword; the two peasants are reduced to panic-stricken patter. As usual, the ensemble ends with a standoff, with everyone saying it would be wise to exit, and then doing so.

These insertion pieces are among the hidden treasures of Mozart; only partially effective in concert, they flourish in their true home, the theatre.[12] But they have still not reached the level of musical sophistication

---

[12] They were used, with the overture and quartet from *Lo sposo deluso* and several isolated arias, by Paul Griffiths in *The Jewel Box*, a 1991 tribute to Mozart staged by Opera North in Leeds.

Ex. 16.2 'Dite almeno,' K. 479. Insertion quartet for Bianchi, *La villanella rapita*, from bar 139

Allegro assai

resulting from the use of a sonata-like form. In *Figaro*, Mozart manages changes of dramatic situation without changing tempo. The act I trio springs into action when the count reveals his presence to Basilio. Susanna tries to end a dangerous conversation by throwing a faint (the music moves responsively to the dominant minor), only to revive when the succour unctuously offered by the men threatens to land her on top

Ex. 16.2 (*continued*)

of the hidden Cherubino. By way of development, the count tells of an occasion when he found Cherubino hidden in a compromising situation, under a cloth. Illustrating his story with action, he lifts the sheet; the boy is again revealed; and the melody goes into reverse. The musical requirements of recapitulation are fulfilled as the characters—except Cherubino, who remains silent—react to the situation. The act 3 sextet begins as a quintet as Marcellina embraces Figaro, revealed as her long-lost son. By way of development, Susanna enters, sees them embracing, and boxes

Ex. 16.2 *(continued)*

Figaro's ears; but when all is explained, these three and Bartolo (newly revealed as Figaro's father) dwell happily on the situation while the count and his lawyer intervene peevishly, with a slightly different text ('al fiero tormento' replacing 'di questo momento', ex. 16.3b). This reconciliation of modal and rhythmic contrast took instrumental form in the G-major piano concerto (K. 453), in the finale to the variations (ex. 16.3a). This passage, like many in Mozart's later ensembles, is built with repetition of substantial musical units (including the passage quoted).

Figaro and Don Giovanni

Despite the allure of *Figaro*'s ensembles and finales, the singers are admirably characterised by arias. Traditional comic styles, including patter-singing, bring Dr Bartolo to absurd life, and ironically infect the grimmest utterance of the opera, Figaro's aria of fury against women, 'Aprite un pò' quegl'occhi'. They find another use in Leporello's catalogue aria. A higher voice-type is used for the aristocrats, Count Almaviva and Don Giovanni himself.[13] Whether intending seduction, in his scenes with Susanna, expressing penitence, as in the central and last finale, or infuriated, in his aria 'Vedrò, mentr'io sospiro', Almaviva is transparent; his feelings have a real foundation in the arrogance of his

---

[13] Changed attitudes to voice-types today enable singers who have made a success of Figaro to move not, as did Benucci, to Leporello but to Giovanni, originally a completely different voice type and a role occasionally taken by tenors in the nineteenth century.

Ex. 16.3 a. Piano concerto in G, K. 453, finale, from bar 219

Presto

unquestioning sense of class superiority. Giovanni, no less selfish, adopts masks, which convince his interlocutors most of the time; he never reveals himself, even to the audience, perhaps because his pursuit of sexual gratification is the symptom of inner nullity. Mozart embodies this psychological distinction between the characters in his music.

Ex. 16.3 *(continued)*

b. *Le nozze di Figaro*, act 2, sextet, from bar 108 (voices are Susanna, Marcellina, Curzio, Count Almaviva, Figaro, Bartolo)

Andante

Ex. 16.3 (*continued*)

The hierarchy among female roles has its puzzles, because Nancy Storace sang Susanna rather than proceeding logically from Rosina in *Il barbiere* to the same person, now the countess, in *Figaro*. Susanna is the longer and more interesting role, but has no virtuoso showpiece. In the act 2 trio, the music of the countess and Susanna was exchanged by Mozart, so that Susanna sings the brilliant scales, one ascending to c‴. Dramatically his first thought was better, and modern editions restore the coloratura to the countess; after all, we are no longer constrained by the hierarchy within the Burgtheater personnel.[14] Perhaps, therefore, 'Dove sono' was composed when it was still assumed that the prima donna (Storace) would sing the countess. When the casting was established, Mozart began a rondò for Storace as Susanna, in prime position, just before the dénouement; it was fortunately abandoned in favour of 'Deh vieni, non tardar', a pastoral serenade to the hidden Figaro, who

[14] See Tyson, *Autograph Scores*, 304–7. Storace's amour propre seems a more likely explanation than that Luisa Laschi found the music difficult, and Mozart was merely helping her out.

assumes it is addressed to the count, and one of Mozart's most teasingly beautiful, and dramatically apposite, arias.

In *Don Giovanni* the rondò for Donna Anna is the last number before the finale, but the aria that projects her most powerfully is the succinct 'Or sai chi l'onore'. It retains the explosive energy of the D-minor duet in the first scene, where she is overtaken by weakness before making Ottavio swear an oath of vengeance. The D-major aria is focused, all weakness set aside, for she has recognised Giovanni as the man who attempted her honour and killed her father. In the preceding dialogue with Ottavio, Mozart's orchestral gestures, rather than having recourse to the conventional armoury of opera seria, return obsessively to the first, furiously syncopated idea; coming five times before she narrates the events of the previous night, it returns after 'grido' ('I screamed') and is heard three more times before the aria is launched, without ritornello, on a surge of tremolo strings. Her line is punctuated by martial rhythms in the woodwind; the word 'padre' ('father') brings a lyrical moment; the call for vengeance is enhanced by reference to the strict style, with imitation in the bass. The middle section (second stanza) projects the tonic minor, inflected towards F. The masterstroke of what might have been a rigid form is the interruption of the repeated first stanza by words from the second. She calls to mind her father's wounds, gasping phrases provoking a complementary modulation, to B minor (ex. 16.4); thus Mozart wounds his own musical symmetry, before completing the cadence and adding a coda with syncopation reminiscent of the preceding recitative.

Balancing the arias with their inspired representations of character are the ensembles, inimitably combining musical charm (and more) with dramatic movement. Susanna's arias embody action, in act 2, and deception, in act 4, rather than revealing her inner feelings; she is most her sharp-witted self when interacting with others, and she sings in every ensemble including six duets. Only when deceiving the count, who not only has power over his servants but is after her virginity, does she briefly lose control. Their duet begins, exceptionally within this brightly lit score, in the minor. Susanna, agreeing to an assignation which will be kept instead by the countess, confidently turns the music towards the relative major, but the count, gaining confidence, appears to take control of the faster section in the major. In his ardour he confuses Susanna, so

Ex. 16.4 *Don Giovanni,* act 1, aria, 'Or sai chi l'onore' (Anna), from bar 32

Andante

that she says 'yes' when she should say 'no' (and vice versa). This may seem like a verbal trick, although the music is exactly right, and she re-covers; but she has let down her guard. On leaving, she tells Figaro that they have won; the count overhears, and launches his scena, culminating in an aria of frustrated arrogance, 'Vedrò, mentr'io sospiro'.

To give credit where it is due, this smart piece of continuity comes unaltered from Beaumarchais' *Le Mariage de Figaro*. But Da Ponte's ingenuity in linking disparate scenes should not be underrated. *Don Giovanni* presented a completely different challenge, that of fleshing out a short opera into one of full length, while suppressing one female and one male role.[15] The scenes Da Ponte devised—the last part of act 1 and the first part of act 2—are as neatly plotted and less dependent on coincidence than the rest. Mozart's desire for an opera with three equal female roles was never better fulfilled, especially in the Vienna version when Anna's prima donna status is qualified by Elvira's extra scena (see chap. 14). The added duet for Zerlina and Leporello, although it caused the omission of a short aria for him, builds up the role of Giovanni's servant still more. Even without it Leporello, trying to snatch a bite from Don Giovanni's dinner, caustically identifying Mozart's own music played by the wind band on stage, howling and babbling in fright, and declining the statue's invitation to dinner ('Tempo non ha, scusate'), threatens to upstage his master.[16] Through both these operas, Mozart's delight in working with such singers, such situations, such a poet, shines through; a delight emphatically confirmed if we read between the lines of his letters to Jacquin from Prague.

A word is in order about versions of Mozart's operas. Those who work creatively in the theatre expect to make changes, even sacrificing favourite passages in the interests of effectiveness. From this truism it may be wise to conclude that the forms of Mozart's operas are not as stable as our handsome printed scores would suggest. While composers have every right to offer a definitive version to the public, to assume that they usually did so in the first 250 years of opera is to view the past through nineteenth-century romantic, even Wagnerian, spectacles.

That said, Mozart's operas are not particularly fluid in form if we understand that the basis of a performing text should be the traces left by a work's creators. The early operas had only a few performances, and there are no variants from revivals, unless Mozart had a hand in the

---

[15] Donna Ximena and a subordinate servant of Giovanni, neither of whom sings much in the Bertati-Gazzaniga opera.

[16] Giovanni's table-music includes numbers from Sarti, whom, contrary to his usual view of Italians, Mozart called 'a good, honest fellow', Martín, and 'Non più andrai' from *Figaro*.

German version of *La finta giardiniera*. The last three operas were only revived after his death. But with *Idomeneo*, even disregarding the Vienna version, still further cut, there are multiple possibilities; in Munich Mozart composed the music for act 3 and the act 1 recognition scene, before cutting them ruthlessly to their bare essentials, in the teeth of the librettist's objections, and removing most of the last-act arias. The dénouement is open season for hunting down a version that suits the conductor's, or nowadays probably the director's, preferences. But *Idomeneo* is exceptional, a glorious cornucopia of options like *Benvenuto Cellini* or *Carmen*. There is no comparable authorisation for changes in *Die Entführung*, though nowadays spoken dialogue is freely cut and perhaps Belmonte has one aria more than he needs. With *Figaro* and *Don Giovanni* there exist two authentic versions, but the minor alterations for *Figaro* in 1789 are a clear case of Mozart yielding to persuasion from the singer and her lover, Da Ponte. The act 4 arias for minor characters, Marcellina and Don Basilio, are routinely omitted; and while both have their defenders, in the theatre few lament their absence. With *Don Giovanni*, what is normally performed is a blend of the Prague and Vienna versions. Any sentimental attachment to first thoughts (Prague) comes into conflict with the excellence of Elvira's new scena, 'In quali eccessi . . . Mi tradì'. Ottavio is authorised to sing only one aria, but most tenors get away with two; perhaps Mozart was glad to jettison 'Il mio tesoro' in favour of 'Dalla sua pace'. As normally performed, the sequence of arias in act 2, for Leporello, Ottavio, Elvira, and Anna, is unrelieved by the Vienna duet. Any resultant sense that Ottavio's role is too long for a wimp who does little to avenge his beloved, even when she identifies her father's murderer, cannot be blamed on the authors.

CHAPTER 17

The Last Years

1788–1791

T HE PENULTIMATE ENTRY FOR 1788 IN MOZART'S CATALOGUE
reads 'NB: im Monath November Händels Acis und Galathée für
Baron Suiten bearbeitet'. Mozart had taken over from the ballet composer Joseph Starzer as musical director for Swieten's enterprise, and *Acis*
was the first Handel arrangement made to suit Viennese taste—one of
many activities for which we can only guess at how much Mozart was
paid. *Messiah* followed, for performances in March and April 1789 at the
house of Count Johann Baptist Esterházy; Lange and Adamberger were
among the soloists. In July 1790, he added arrangements of Dryden's St
Cecilia odes, 'From Harmony' and *Alexander's Feast.*[1]

Where Handel had to be elaborated for modern taste, Mozart's own
music was criticised for overelaborate orchestration. From his elevated
stance, some of the music he wrote in 1788 might be considered pot-
boiling, though the symphonies emphatically are not. The days of self-
promoted 'academies', at which the central attraction was Mozart the
pianist, had passed, and the lack of any new piano concerto indicates
that one avenue through which he had reached the hearts and wallets of
the Viennese had closed. But Mozart alluded to forthcoming concerts,

---

[1] The possibility that he began a version of *Judas Maccabaeus* has been raised by the discovery
of a full score with additional wind parts attributed to Mozart. See Rachel Cowgill, 'The
Halifax *Judas*: an unknown Handel arrangement by Mozart?', *Musical Times* 143 (Spring
2002), 19–36.

in a new hall or 'casino', and sent tickets to Puchberg.[2] He needed new symphonies as repertoire for the next winter season or for his hoped-for trip to London. In 1789 he tried to obtain subscriptions for a concert series, but only Swieten signed (letter to Puchberg, 12 Jul 1789).[3] Unidentified symphonies were performed when Mozart gave concerts outside Vienna, in which one would expect him to have presented his most recent works; and contemporary performing material survives. The oft-repeated notion that the last three symphonies were gratuitous displays of genius, written only to fulfil some inner compulsion, belongs to romantic legend.

Writing to Puchberg, Mozart claimed to expect income from the subscription sale of the immense and difficult string quintets of early 1787.[4] In June 1788 he asked for a loan of 1,000 (even 2,000) gulden, but the cautious Puchberg noted 'sent 200 gulden on 17 June 1788'. We cannot know whether similar letters to other Masonic brothers were also written, and how they were answered; Puchberg may have been unusual in keeping such documents. One such letter to Franz Hofdemel, from March 1789, alludes to his friend's forthcoming entry into a Masonic lodge. At this time Mozart was preparing to travel and needed funds in excess of what was required for housekeeping.

His problems may have been exacerbated by the deteriorating political situation, which caused economic hardship for those who could normally afford to support culture. Early in 1788, Joseph II took the Russian alliance a logical step further by declaring war on the Ottoman Empire. At first the Austrians prevailed, but even successful wars are costly; later things went badly, and after Joseph's death his brother and successor, Leopold II, was quick to conclude a treaty. Meanwhile the Viennese may have been less inclined to spend money on the arts. The German Singspiel had been temporarily restored but was disbanded again in August 1788. The Italian repertory later in 1788 was dominated

[2] This undated letter is usually assigned to June 1788. Landon suggests it should be earlier that year; Mozart would probably not plan summer concerts, when likely subscribers would be in the country.

[3] For a summary of the arguments concerning the symphonies, see Zaslaw, *Symphonies*, 421–42.

[4] The failure of the subscription for the quintets is indicated by their being taken over by Artaria and published in 1789 and 1790.

by *Axur* and Martín's *L'arbore di Diana*, but *Don Giovanni* had further performances in the autumn.[5] Threat of closure hung over the Italian opera itself, and about this time Mozart asked Nannerl to cajole Michael Haydn into sending some of his sacred music to Vienna. This request might have been connected with concert plans, but perhaps Mozart wanted to revive his own dormant skill in church music with a view to employment.

Mozart could not go on drifting into a circle of debts, repayments, and ever more meagre lodgings, while struggling to meet household and medical expenses. He therefore took the initiative of visiting Protestant North Germany, an area untouched by his childhood journeys. The principal magnet was Prussia, whose size and influence had been extended by the recently deceased Frederick the Great. Meanwhile Mozart's productivity was lower than usual. He finished his penultimate piano sonata (K. 570 in B♭) in February 1789; its immediate purpose is not apparent, but he was still teaching, one of his pupils being Magdalena Hofdemel. He wrote dances for Carnival entertainments in the Redoutensaal, but nothing new was needed for his tour because, in northern Germany, his recent instrumental works would not be known.

He left Vienna on 8 April. Travelling in Count Karl Lichnowsky's coach allowed a quick journey to Prague, whence he wrote to Constanze on 10 April. They arrived in Dresden on the twelfth, when he wrote again. The arrangement with Lichnowsky proved a false economy because, as was normal for his class, the count was serenely unaware that his companion could not afford the creature comforts he himself took for granted. Moreover Lichnowsky must have lent him money; in November 1791 he instituted a lawsuit against Mozart for over 1,400 gulden. Meanwhile Lichnowsky returned home early from this trip and, lacking ready cash, touched Mozart for 100 gulden: 'I couldn't very well refuse him, and you know why' (Mozart's letter from Berlin, 23 May 1789). Presumably Mozart, being indebted for a larger sum, made this repayment from his modest profits.

In Prague, Mozart met his old friends Ramm, who was returning from Berlin and reported that the king eagerly expected Mozart, and

---

[5] The exact total of performances at the Burgtheater in 1788 is not quite certain but is at least fifteen.

Josepha Dušek, who was also available in Dresden to sing arias from his operas at musical soirées. At one of these the string trio (K. 563) was played, but this was not activity calculated to generate much income. At a concert on 14 April he performed his most recent piano concerto (K. 537), and he may have been reminded of his youth when courtly compliments were accompanied by a snuffbox. Curiously, though he must have been aware that Constanze was pregnant, he ends his letter of 16 April with advice on conduct reminiscent of comments made during their engagement. He then proceeded to Berlin, and his next surviving letter, certainly not the next he wrote, is dated from Potsdam in June. In the meantime, apparently at Lichnowsky's urging, he had returned to Leipzig to give a concert, on 12 May. Dušek sang two items, one of them possibly K. 505 with piano obbligato; Mozart played two concertos (K. 456 and K. 503) and improvised; the symphony or symphonies framing the programme are not identified. He gave away too many free tickets, and told Constanze 'I made a 32-mile round-trip almost for nothing' (23 May).[6] The only new composition is the spiky little Gigue for piano (K. 574), one of Mozart's inventive responses to the style of J. S. Bach, whose name appears in letters and anecdotes concerning his time in Leipzig. Mozart is said to have studied a choral motet from the separate parts, exclaiming–despite his already long acquaintance with Bach through Swieten–that here at last was music he could learn from.[7]

He returned to Berlin and played before Friedrich Wilhelm II, writing down variations on a minuet by the king's cello teacher Jean-Pierre Duport. He was also able to see Die Entführung, which had at last reached Berlin. But the admiration of the king of Prussia and the elector of Saxony could not alleviate his financial problems. His letter of 23 May is disconcerting, and enigmatic. Suddenly Leopold's son, he counts up his letters to Constanze, and those received, concluding that some have been lost.[8] He holds out no hopes from Prussia: 'when I return,

---

[6] Spaethling points out that thirty-two German miles is a good approximation to the distance covered to give this concert (ca. 290 kilometres) (Mozart's Letters, Mozart's Life, 411).

[7] Maynard Solomon assesses these stories in 'The Rochlitz Anecdotes: Issues of Authenticity in Early Mozart Biography', in Eisen, Mozart Studies, 1–60; see 28–29.

[8] Of those acknowledged, Constanze's and some of Mozart's are not extant, including one from Leipzig which he says is 'in French'.

you'll have to put up with seeing just me rather than money'. He plans his route home meticulously and suddenly changes gear to describe his arousal at the thought of returning to his wife's 'little nest'.

There is a story that for the sake of Joseph II, Mozart turned down an offer to stay in Berlin. Although it appears in Nissen's biography, it rings false; Mozart really owed little to the Habsburgs, and if there were such an offer, it must have been insufficient to offset his estimate of future earnings in Vienna, not to mention the cost of uprooting his family. He also declined an invitation from London. Three eloquent letters to Puchberg in July confirm that the journey was largely wasted. He may have carried home a vague commission to write quartets for the king of Prussia, and easy piano sonatas for Princess Friederike; he told Puchberg, in the most agonised of his begging letters, that he was writing six of each (12 Jul 1789). This may have been disingenuous, and certainly he never completed them. His last piano sonata, in D (K. 576), composed in 1789, is far from easy, and the stern opening of an unfinished G-minor sonata, believed to be of this period, would hardly suit a young princess. The three 'Prussian' string quartets (K. 575, 589, 590) do, however, privilege the melodic possibilities of the cello's tenor register.

When he returned to Vienna, he was confronted with major expenses arising from Constanze's skin disease; she was so ill that on 17 July he told Puchberg that she might die. On the recommendation of Dr Closset, she went to bathe in the sulphurous waters of Baden. Mozart had to remain in Vienna, and in another reminiscence of their engagement period, he urges her not be jealous, and to behave herself modestly in the stylish company at the watering-place. Their fourth child, a daughter, was delivered in November but died the same day.

By Mozart's standards, the rest of 1789 was not surprisingly unproductive. In June, he completed the first 'Prussian' quartet, in D (K. 575), and K. 576 in July, and he probably began other works intended for sale. Then came the revival of *Figaro*, on 29 August. The new prima donna, Adriana Ferrarese, was a very different kind of singer from Storace, and intimate with Da Ponte; ever anxious to oblige, Mozart replaced Susanna's tricky action aria 'Venite, inginocchiatevi', during which the singer must dress Cherubino as a girl, while doubting whether Ferrarase could sing the replacement, 'Un moto di gioja' (K.577), artlessly enough

(19 Aug 1789).[9] Less accommodating than Storace, Ferrarese required a rondò, for which new words were supplied, rather than using those rejected in 1786. It is a shock to realise that most performances in Mozart's Vienna included this rondò, 'Al desio' (K. 579), well calculated to show off Ferrarese's range and coloratura; it was imitated by Salieri, in *La cifra* (premiered in December 1789), and capped by Mozart in *Così fan tutte*.[10] If it had not caused Mozart to abandon the much-loved 'Deh vieni, non tardar', we might appreciate 'Al desio' better; it is an effective piece coloured by a pair of basset-horns, instruments otherwise missing from the Da Ponte operas.

The clarinet and basset-horn of Anton Stadler also preoccupied Mozart at this period, although the only work completed, in September 1789, was the quintet in A (K. 581). His false starts included the beginnings of first movements for a clarinet quintet in Bb and a concerto for basset-horn in G, the latter eventually completed as the first movement of his clarinet concerto in A. Meanwhile at the Burgtheater, the revived form of *Figaro* remained in repertory, with nearly thirty performances extending into 1791, and it led to further work. Mozart must have admired the singing of Luisa Villeneuve, judging from the quality of the arias inserted into Cimarosa's *I due baroni* in September (K. 578), and Martín's *Il burbero di buon core* in November (K. 582–583). In the meantime, Da Ponte had prepared an original libretto, *La scuola degli amanti* (The School for Lovers) for Salieri, who abandoned it after tackling the first two numbers. Thus it came to Mozart, with the alternative title *Così fan tutte*.[11] The fragments composed by Salieri show that the libretto was altered for Mozart, and a curious flaw remains in the second finale, where four pieces are presented as quotations, but only three have been heard before.

The school is run by a 'philosopher' or cynic, Alfonso (sung by Bussani), who dominates much of the action without singing a full-length aria. The plot is a variation on an ancient literary trope: two officers pre-

[9] Other minor alterations to *Figaro* may have been made; see Tyson, *Autographs*, 290–327.

[10] 'Al desio' had a separate life in concerts, probably sung by Dušek and certainly by Constanze, as is testified by the manuscript vocal score (not autograph) that she presented to Vincent Novello, with an autograph cadenza.

[11] Another title difficult to translate, it means literally 'thus do all women', hence 'all women are inconstant'. On Salieri's settings, see Bruce Alan Brown, *W.A. Mozart: Così fan tutte*, 10–13.

tend to go to war, returning disguised to woo the other's partner. When the women fall, the men confront them, to be met with abject apologies and a restoration of the original pairings of chastened but wiser young people. The surpassing musical beauty of the opera enhances, rather than disguises, its disturbing moral qualities, and it has become a cliché of modern production to imply that the lovers are profoundly miserable at the end, despite the gaiety of the final ensemble.

Così fan tutte entered the repertory on 26 January 1790, with Ferrarase as Fiordiligi and Villeneuve as Dorabella. Their individual styles, as well as their ability to blend, were superbly exploited by Mozart. Ferrarese required no 'artlessness' to deliver her magnificent arias, the defiant 'Come scoglio', in which she proclaims her rocklike constancy, and 'Per pietà', in which she explores her own weakness. Villeneuve's arias are equally contrasted, the anguished, even hysterical 'Smanie implacabili' and the delicious 'È amore un ladroncello', in which she approves the maid Despina's philosophy of taking a lover at hand, rather than waiting for one who is absent. Despite its superb ensembles, the characterizations in Così and the asymmetry within a potentially symmetrical plot are articulated by these—and the men's—arias. An enormous aria for Guglielmo (Benucci), 'Rivolgete a lui lo sguardo', was completed but jettisoned, perhaps on grounds of excessive length and complexity, not least in the libretto, which is packed with literary allusions; the substitute ('Non siate ritrosi') is sharper dramatically and better comedy by far. Of the three arias for Ferrando (Calvesi), one ('Ah! lo veggio') is marked for omission and seldom performed.

In December 1789 Mozart invited Puchberg and Joseph Haydn to a rehearsal, and early in 1790, his operas vied in the repertory with Salieri and Martín, with two more performances of Figaro, and five of Così. But in mid-February Joseph II died, worn out by twenty-five years of power and the stress of the Turkish war. The Burgtheater was closed for two months; when it reopened after Easter, the repertory included Figaro and Così, the latter for only five more performances, and these were the last Mozart operas heard there until well after his death.

The new emperor, Leopold II, dismissed Ferrarese and Da Ponte; they left Vienna in June 1791. Mozart must have feared for his own stipend, but Leopold, who like most of his family had a good musical education, probably knew his value. During his long rule in Tuscany, he and his Spanish wife, Maria Luisa, had developed a strong partiality for Italian music. Mozart had to find other ways to gain favour. He drafted a letter to Leopold's son and heir Archduke Franz, asking for promotion to second Kapellmeister, emphasising that his experience in church music exceeded Salieri's; this style, neglected in the circumstances he found himself in during the 1780s, was one 'I have thoroughly acquainted myself with [. . .] since my youth'. The petition may not have been sent.

At some point during 1790, Mozart became informally involved with the latest enterprise of an old acquaintance, the touring actor, director, playwright, and occasional singer Emanuel Schikaneder. He had a lease on a new theatre outside the city walls, the Freihaus-Theater auf der Wieden. There he mounted a variety of shows, specialising in magical operas and attracting an audience by beautiful sets and cunning stage machinery. It is uncertain exactly how much Mozart contributed to *Der Stein der Weisen* ('The Philosopher's Stone'), produced on 11 September. A duet ('Nun liebes Weibchen', K. 625=592a) exists partly in his hand. It was calculated to appeal to Mozart; Lubano (Schikaneder) questions his wife, but because of the evil magician's spell she can only meow. A secondary source attributes most of the music to the young director Johann Baptist Henneberg, and other passages to the tenor Benedikt Schack, the bass Franz Xaver Gerl, Schikaneder himself, and Mozart, including part of the second-act finale.[12]

During 1790, Mozart's productivity was at its lowest, partly because he, as well as Constanze, seems to have been ill. Along with the Handel odes, only two original works, the second and third 'Prussian' quartets (K. 589 and 590) were entered into his catalogue between January and December, when he registered completion of the string quintet in D (K. 593). Mozart's return to the quintet may have been encouraged by Artaria's publication of K. 516, but it is possible he was responding to a commission from the violinist and merchant Johann Tost, who commissioned a dozen quartets from Joseph Haydn. Mozart's last quintet, in E♭ (K. 614), followed in April 1791.

Mozart's health recovered sufficiently for another venture abroad late

---

[12] See David J. Buch, '*Der Stein der Weisen*. Mozart and collaborative Singspiels at Emanuel Schikaneder's Theater auf der Wieden', *Mozart Jahrbuch* 2000, 91–126; for a sceptical review of the evidence, Faye Ferguson, 'Interpreting the source tradition of *Der Stein der Weisen*', *Mozart Jahrbuch* 2000, 127–44.

in 1790. Leopold II was crowned Holy Roman Emperor in Frankfurt-am-Main on 9 October, reaffirming tradition and perhaps intending to impress the revolutionary French government, which was holding his sister, Marie Antoinette, and her husband, Louis XVI, as virtual prisoners. There is nothing about events in France in Mozart's correspondence, and his dependence on imperial favour makes it unlikely that he harboured revolutionary sentiments. No doubt he hoped to impress Leopold by his attendance in Frankfurt, where he had no official function, although his Mass in C of 1779 (K. 317), ever since known as the 'Coronation', was included in the ceremony, directed by Salieri. Mozart left Vienna on 23 September, having pawned his silver to buy a coach (it was not redeemed). In company with Constanze's brother-in-law Franz Hofer, he travelled quickly to Frankfurt, writing home on the twenty-eighth. The surviving letters mingle a little optimism with palpable anxiety about Constanze's health and their financial situation; during his absence, she handled negotiations for a loan of 1,000 gulden from a merchant, Lackenbacher, probably with a guarantee from Hoffmeister.

Frankfurt was filled with the kind of people who supported high culture, but Mozart received more acclamation than money for his concert on 15 October. He played his most recent concerto (K. 537: hence its nickname 'Coronation'), and perhaps the concerto in F (K. 459). Ceccarelli sang and Mozart improvised. The diary of an admirer, Count Ludwig von Bentheim-Steinfurt, alludes to 'that beautiful Symphony [. . .] which I've had for a long time', but adds that a new symphony (unidentified, but supposedly one of the last three) was planned but not played, as the concert had already lasted three hours.[13] The journey home went more slowly. Mozart gave another concert in Mainz, and spent a few days in Mannheim helping rehearse *Figaro*. In Munich, he visited old friends and his father's student, Marchand, and was delayed because Carl Theodor invited him to perform for visiting royalty: 'what an honour for the court of Vienna that the King of Naples [the emperor's brother-in-law] has to hear me in a foreign country' (c. 4 Nov 1790).

During his absence, Constanze had removed to the Rauhensteingasse, where the rent, 330 gulden, was lower than the Domgasse, but hardly

[13] Landon, *1791*, 13–15.

cheap.[14] Late in 1790 there came two invitations from London. In October, Robert May O'Reilly asked him write operas for the Pantheon; in December Johann Peter Salomon invited Mozart to participate in concerts he promoted in the Hanover Square Rooms. But Salomon's real quarry was Haydn (whose Esterházy pension considerably exceeded Mozart's court salary). Perhaps health, perhaps debt, or perhaps new possibilities sensed in Vienna, led Mozart to decline, as in the summer of 1791 he declined an invitation to Russia from Count Razumovsky, a son-in-law of Countess Thun and later one of Beethoven's patrons.

A rosier future in Vienna was certainly possible in 1791. In April, Mozart was preappointed without salary to help the ailing Leopold Hoffmann as organist of St Stephan's cathedral and eventually succeed him (Hoffmann survived until 1793, to be succeeded by Albrechtsberger). In her petition for a pension, Constanze referred to an income guaranteed by patrons in Hungary and Holland, in exchange for new compositions; perhaps he received an instalment, which could explain why Constanze had fewer debts than might have been expected after his death.[15] During his last twelve months, Mozart's fortunes waxed, and his output was restored to its normal level. He produced over forty dances for the Redoutensaal, and sold them in piano arrangements to publishers (one uses 'Non più andrai' from *Figaro*). There was no point in trying to organise concerts, but he completed his last piano concerto (K. 595), performing it on 4 March at a benefit for the clarinettist Joseph Bähr (or Beer). In March, he composed keyboard variations on 'Ein Weib ist das herrlichste Ding' (K. 613; the title may have appealed to the uxorious composer), from a comic opera popular at the Freihaus-Theater, *Der dumme Gärtner* by Schack and Gerl. The following month, Salieri directed a 'a new grand symphony by Mozart' at a Tonkünstler-Societät concert, the Vienna premiere of one of the last three, possibly the G-minor symphony in its second version, with added clarinets.[16]

---

[14] For the description of the apartment and inventory of Mozart's property, see Landon *1791*, 27–30.

[15] *D-Doc*, 421–22.

[16] The Tonkünstler Societät, or Society of Musicians, like Britain's Royal Society of Musicians, offered financial support to musicians in cases of hardship; it might have offered support to him, or subsequently to Constanze, if only Mozart had presented his birth certificate and become a member.

Another commission, complained about in a letter from Frankfurt, was for pieces for a clockwork organ to provide background music for a display of art in wax and plaster in the gallery of 'Herr Müller' (Count Joseph von Deym). This sort of thing Mozart would only do for ready money, and as with other such commissions, it became a chore. He completed one piece in December 1790 (Adagio and Allegro, K. 594) and two more by the following May, by which time he had also finished the last quintet, K. 614. Then in May he composed two pieces for the blind virtuoso on the glass harmonica, Marianne Kirchgässner. The short solo Adagio (K. 356=617a) is not in his catalogue, and was perhaps experimental; the Adagio and Rondo for quintet (K. 617) was played in the Kärntnertortheater on 19 August.

The summer months are briefly illuminated by the last letters from Mozart to Constanze. She was again pregnant, and spending time in Baden for the cure. In a touch inherited from Leopold, Mozart apparently considered himself fit to pronounce on her health regime and that of little Carl ('give him some rhubarb'). He visited her when he could and enjoyed the mixed society which included one relatively new acquaintance, the young composer Franz Xaver Süssmayr. He was more a disciple than a pupil of Mozart, and he was useful in conveying messages and scores between Vienna and Baden; he was also the butt of Mozart's humour. Mozart entered nothing in his catalogue for nearly a month after K. 617, when he noted the beginning of another unique piece, the beautiful motet *Ave verum corpus* for chorus, strings, and organ, composed in Baden for the local choirmaster Anton Stoll. But he was hard at work on *Die Zauberflöte*, some of which he composed in a summerhouse attached to Schikaneder's theatre.

The sources and authorship, not to mention the meaning, of this opera's libretto are too complicated—and disputed—to be discussed here.[17] Schikaneder supplied all or most of the words, but the collaborative practices typical of his theatre make it likely that others contributed ideas and possibly lines.[18] Mozart, whether by invitation or because he insisted, composed all the music, which was essentially finished by the

---

[17] For a succinct account, see Peter Branscombe, *W. A. Mozart: Die Zauberflöte.*

[18] A minor actor, Ludwig Gieseke, later a distinguished mineralogist, claimed to have written the libretto; he may have contributed, but the whole design is characteristic of Schikaneder.

end of July. Two instrumental pieces (overture and march) are entered separately in his catalogue, and dated two days before the first performance. (The entry for *Die Zauberflöte* under July includes the date of the first performance, which Mozart cannot have known then; presumably this was a retrospective entry.) One would never guess it from the music, but he complains on 7 July that he cannot enjoy his work without taking a break for a little chat with Constanze, and he feels empty and lost, recalling their merry time together in Baden.

In this summer of 1791, Mozart was much in demand and working overtime. A little cantata for voice and piano on a Masonic text ('Die ihr des unermesslichen Weltalls Schöpfer ehrt', K. 619) was written in July, and he received two further commissions, for an opera and for a Requiem. The opera had to be attended to at once, as it was required for another coronation of Leopold II, this time as king of Bohemia. Salieri had decided against taking on this contract through pressure of work; he was in charge of musical arrangements for the coronation, in which he again programmed Mozart's music. Since the commission came via Guardasoni from the Bohemian Estates and for performance in Prague, Mozart must have felt confident of his reception, even for an opera quite unlike those the Bohemian capital had already taken to its heart. Given the occasion and the preferences of their Imperial majesties, it had to be opera seria; there was no time to commission a new libretto, and the choice of the Estates fell upon Metastasio's hackneyed *La clemenza di Tito*, first produced with music by Caldara in 1734.

Joseph II, once a model of an enlightened absolutism, had clamped down on the Freemasons and retracted many of his own reforms. Leopold II was not to blame for the problems created by his brother's overreaching ambition, such as the Turkish war. *La clemenza di Tito* was a flattering, but not altogether an inappropriate, choice. There is no reason to suppose that Mozart undertook it reluctantly and merely because he needed the money. Composing it was part of his campaign to cultivate fields neglected since his Salzburg years, but appealing to the new regime, like church music. He may have welcomed the chance to revive memories of his Italian campaign of the early 1770s by tackling another serious opera. Apart from one performance of *Idomeneo*, the nearest he had come to it since *Il re pastore* was in composing scenas for singers such as Lange and Dušek (this circumstance has misled historians into supposing that serious opera by this time was a dead form: it was not).

If the emperor had paid no attention to him in Frankfurt, surely he could not ignore the composer of a new opera seria: preferment, and more commissions, should follow. The Requiem could wait a little longer, though the fee was generous and—exceptionally—included advance payment. The commission was offered anonymously through an intermediary by Count Franz Walsegg-Stuppach, an amateur musician and patron whose wife had recently died. He wished to commemorate her while indulging his customary whim (which deceived nobody) of passing off the commissioned music as his own. Puchberg had been living in the count's Vienna house, and conceivably steered the commission towards Mozart, rather than a composer the count might more plausibly be supposed to have imitated.

Constanze returned to Vienna before the Mozarts' second surviving son, Franz Xaver Wolfgang, was born on 26 July. Work on *La clemenza* must have occupied Mozart before he went to Prague, with Constanze, arriving on 28 August. The company which had created *Don Giovanni* having largely dispersed, Mozart was not well acquainted with the singers other than Baglioni, in the title role. In Vienna, he wrote choruses, ensembles, and two arias for Baglioni, but the rest was reportedly written once he met the performers in Prague. Since the first performance took place on 6 September, this is barely credible, and he must have laid down most of his ideas before leaving home. The opera was swiftly put into rehearsal but was surely underprepared. As in *Idomeneo*, the young male lead (Sesto) was a castrato, but this time middle-aged and experienced; Domenico Bedini was declared 'wretched' by Mozart's Prague-based biographer, Franz Xaver Niemetschek, but his music is more sophisticated and expressive than what Mozart had composed for young Dal Prato. The prima donna, the twenty-four-year-old soprano Maria Marchetti-Fantozzi (Vitellia), possessed a remarkable range (g to d'''), carefully exploited by Mozart. Some simplification of his language, and a great deal of ornate beauty, may be attributed to his desire to seduce the Imperial couple into thinking they were hearing Italian music. If so, they failed. At the premiere Leopold was enthused by Marchetti, but the empress told a friend that she was bored and the music was bad.[19]

---

[19] The empress probably did not say, as later reported, that it was German hogwash. Zinzendorf reports Leopold being 'entousiasmé', adding that it was difficult to get out of the theatre, because of the press of public. Link, *Court Theatre*, 382.

Once the coronation party was dispersed, the opera increasingly pleased the Prague public. Mozart relayed to Constanze, in Baden, reports of a triumphant last performance on 30 September, coinciding with the brilliantly successful premiere of *Die Zauberflöte*. By the time he wrote (8 October), his Singspiel was well launched into a run of performances; Schikaneder could not rotate a large repertory like the Burgtheater. Mozart's three letters of early to mid-October suggest that he was in the highest spirits, relishing his achievement, no doubt anticipating further commissions, and finishing 'Stadler's rondo', the finale of the clarinet concerto (K. 622). The essence of the first movement dated from two or three years before, but the slow movement and finale were presumably new. Mozart may also have been working on a horn concerto in D (K. 412/386b) for Lentgeb, which he left unfinished.[20] Having handed over the direction of *Die Zauberflöte* to Henneberg, he continued to attend performances, delighting in his son Carl's enjoyment of the opera. Once he went backstage and played the glockenspiel to trip up Schikaneder (Papageno) and encourage a bit of ad-libbing. But he took the symbolic aspects of the opera seriously; earlier that evening in Joseph Goldhahn's box he was infuriated when his host laughed even at religious scenes; to Constanze, he called him 'Bavarian' and 'nitwit', but to his face only 'Papageno' (luckily Goldhahn could not take the hint). In his last letter to Constanze, Mozart describes fetching Caterina Cavalieri and Salieri to a performance as his guests; both admired it, Salieri calling it an 'operone'.

Work on the Requiem was delayed by the last work entered in his catalogue, the Masonic cantata 'Laut verkünde unsre Freude' (K. 623), but it then absorbed his remaining compositional energies. Constanze remembered taking the score away to force him to rest. She alleged that, six months before his death, on an outing in the Prater (in Vienna), Mozart spoke of being poisoned; but at the relevant period Constanze was in Baden. Perhaps the conversation took place six weeks, rather than months, before Mozart's death, but that would be a surprisingly large-scale error; she could as well have recalled something from the previous year. There is no reason, in any case, to trust Mozart's own diagnosis,

[20] There is no slow movement; the rondo finale was elaborated by Süssmayr for a Lenten concert in 1792, including a plainchant that Mozart would surely not have included.

and by the autumn of his last year, he had evidently recovered from whatever illness brought on this curious bout of paranoia. In November 1791 there was an epidemic of 'military fever' in Vienna, which he may have contracted at the Lodge meeting on 17 November, when he directed the first performance of his cantata.[21] The fever was not always fatal, but his constitution was not robust and earlier episodes of illness may have contributed to his condition rapidly becoming critical, and pushing him beyond the point at which mere resting, or medical attention, could save him. His body was swollen—there were surely problems with its fluids—while his mind mostly remained clear; but it is not likely that he went on composing. The coup-de-grace was delivered by the well-meaning Dr Closset.[22] The drastic application of a cold compress caused Mozart to lose consciousness, and death followed in the first hour of 5 December. His burial two days later, on a day of mild, damp weather, followed the austere custom of the time for one neither a pauper, nor rich: a simple ceremony and rapid disposal of the remains.

---

[21] The date usually given, 18 November, appears to be wrong; *E-Doc*, 71.

[22] See the report by Constanze's youngest sister Sophie Haibel; *D-Doc*, 524–27.

The Last Works

'a rich possession, but even fairer hopes'[1]

MOZART'S LAST WORKS ARE NOT THE FRUIT OF GREAT AGE, BUT of great experience nevertheless. It is possible to detect a 'late style' characterized, as with Beethoven, by a new directness, and unlike Beethoven, by an exceptional surface smoothness coupled, in some works, with greater thematic economy. But such evidence should be considered alongside his memory of his father's advice about being sure to please his public, as he unquestionably did with *Die Zauberflöte*. The 'Prussian' quartets and the clarinet quintet derive their lucidity of texture from his handling of instrumentation and, in certain passages, his way of threading ideas together so that, if he does change key, it hardly seems to matter. This style is already taking shape in *Don Giovanni*, for instance in Zerlina's second aria, 'Vedrai, carino', and prevails in *Die Zauberflöte* and *La clemenza di Tito*.

The last instrumental works

Although Mozart no longer had a royal cellist in mind, the D-major string quintet (K. 593) shares the luminous quality of the 'Prussian' quartets. It begins with a slow introduction, rare in chamber music. Rarer still is its reappearance before the end of the allegro, as if to prepare one of Mozart's most melancholy slow movements, where a blue sky is soon overclouded,

---

[1] Franz Grillparzer's epitaph for Schubert (trans. John Reed, *The Master Musicians: Schubert*, London, 1987, 212).

Ex. 18.1   String quintet in D, K. 593, second movement

and never quite cleared (ex. 18.1). The shadows are dispersed in a sunny minuet and trio. The finale's main theme is impudently chromatic, and the second theme is its diatonic foil. In a late reprise, both are involved in an exercise of five-part contrapuntal interplay. The diatonic motif (first viola, then first violin in ex. 18.2) is a close relative of one in the 'Jupiter' finale. While it acts out its role as second theme, it is metamorphosed into the epitome of calm (bars 73, 219), a moment of Mozartian poetry to treasure.

The E♭ quintet (K. 614) makes superficially easier listening, and might have been composed in order to confound our expectations of Mozart in this key (he is more likely to have intended a contrast with K. 593). Rather than a military fanfare in $\frac{4}{4}$, the first movement adopts

Ex. 18.1 (*continued*)

the hunting $\frac{6}{8}$ metre, the violas imitating horns. The compound metre offers less scope for rhythmic, and thus thematic, contrast, and Mozart directs our attention to this fact by starting both main themes with repeated notes; the first theme then reenters quite naturally as a sequel to the second. The slow movement is of disarming simplicity, harking back to the 'Romanza' type used in piano concertos, with no minor-mode episode, instead weaving enchantment by textural variation. This quintet seems to transmute the divertimento into 'serious chamber music'; the trio to the minuet is a Ländler, like those Mozart turned out so deftly to earn his stipend from the court, and the finale confirms this generic transgression by taking a cheerful contredanse and forming out of its materials one of Mozart's most adventurous developments, including a double fugato and some radically modulating sequences. To-

Ex. 18.1 *(continued)*

wards the end the insouciant main theme reappears with a variety of new counterpoints. This tour de force could be a tribute to Joseph Haydn, to whom Mozart had supposedly bidden a tearful farewell on his departure for London. But the nearest equivalent in Haydn is the finale of his symphony No. 99, still some years in the future.

The last two concertos have been interpreted as examples of a purified late style, almost as if Mozart were aware of his impending death. In their exhaustive chronological account of his works, Wyzewa and Saint Foix devote particular attention to the last piano concerto, in B♭ (K. 595). The absence of heroics, or storm and stress, superficially suggest a backward look; the 'master' renounces virtuosity; 'there is scarcely any work where we sense, with such consistency, feelings of melancholy, resigned sorrow'. They add the curious speculation that if Mozart had

Ex. 18.2   String quintet in D, K. 593, finale, from bar 197

Allegro

composed a symphony in 1791, it would have been elegiac in spirit, making no gesture to encourage applause.[2] Their interpretation is founded on the essentially lyrical qualities apparent from the opening of the concerto. The discovery that the material of the first movements of K. 595 and the clarinet concerto had been shaped up to three years earlier, however, ensures that the qualities of these works will no longer be confused with Mozart's alleged feelings of impending doom during 1791. Moreover the finales of both concertos, in $\frac{6}{8}$, refresh the joyously

[2] Wyzewa and Saint-Foix, *W.-A. Mozart: sa vie musical et son oeuvre*, ii, 990, 1026.

springy style associated with this metre, without the hunting implications: occasional shadows, such as the minor-key episode in the clarinet concerto from bar 138, never threaten the friendly, conversational qualities of the main themes. Mozart used the main idea of the finale of K. 595 in a song welcoming the return of spring (K. 596). It need not follow from this that the first movement represents autumn, or the slow movement winter, despite the passing shiver still sometimes heard within the latter; an eerie sonority results from the theme being harmonised in parallel triads, but doubled at a lower octave, and thus filled with consecutive fifths (bars 104–6). This was a mistake in notating the piano part, and Mozart is unlikely to have gone so far as to perform it this way.[3] A less fanciful view of K. 595 is that it embodies tendencies apparent in the two previous concertos, and in other genres including chamber music (the 'Prussian' quartets, the piano trios) and the last operas. If we postulate a 'late style', it is one prone to limpid textures, free of what Mozart's contemporaries might have condemned as learned, or 'tough meat'; overflowing with melody; the surface serene, as if compositional difficulties no longer existed; complex passages (which do exist) seductively packaged so that 'the ordinary listener will also find them satisfying, without knowing why'.

The imposing and adventurous Fantasia in F minor (K. 608), the most remarkable of the three 'OrgelStücke für ein Uhr', could hardly be used in any definition of 'late style'. Mozart disliked the timbre of the mechanical instrument: ('little pipes . . . too high and childish') he wrote when at work on K. 594 (3 Oct 1790). Perhaps out of cussedness he produced a piece that mingles powerful rhetorical gestures with counterpoint, as energetic in expression as it is ingenious, and with a modulation of some violence to bring back the opening idea in the alien key of F♯ minor (bar 59). The form is that of the overture as interrupted sonata, like *Die Entführung* or the symphony in G (K. 318). The beautiful andante, almost extravagantly ornate, is cut from older cloth; the return to the opening material brings a new flowing countersubject to the fugue, and as with the great C-minor fugue for two pianos, counterpoint yields at the last to emphatic, homophonic cadential activity. Whatever Mozart felt about the original instrumentation, the appeal of

---

[3] See NMA, series V, Werkgruppe 15, viii, foreword, xxv–xxvi.

this music is strong enough for it to be drawn into the repertories, necessarily in arrangements, of organists, piano duettists, and wind quintets,
the latter an ensemble Mozart never used. The Adagio and Rondo (K.
617), or 'Konzertquintet' for glass harmonica, with flute, oboe, viola,
and cello is almost excessively transparent in texture. But this too has no
intrinsic connection with a 'late style', being the inevitable outcome of
the instrumentation, with cello the only bass instrument. The harmonica part, written on two staves like a piano, is mostly above c'; its lower
limit was f, and perhaps Mozart found these pitches ineffective. The
rondo includes extended passages for the unusually formed quartet, with
the solo resting; its charms are made more apparent by transferring the
solo part to an early piano than by reviving the etiolated moans of the
harmonica.

Anton Stadler had devised a clarinet with the extended downward
compass normal on a basset-horn, to make what is nowadays dubbed the
'basset-clarinet'.[4] The autographs of the quintet and concerto are lost,
and the versions published after Mozart's death reduce the clarinet part
to its normal range. Scholars and performers have reconstructed something like the original texts, aided in the concerto by an earlier incomplete draft for basset-horn in G.[5] Exploitation of the lowest register
makes sense of passages like the minor-key variation in the finale of the
quintet, and the otherwise unplayable passage (bars 311–13) in the concerto finale. The mellowness perceived in the concerto, despite the
supremely well-crafted virtuosity of the solo part, may result from an orchestration that excludes oboes, using flutes, bassoons, and horns. Some
tightening of the listener's throat, even a spasm of nostalgia, is to be expected in the late stages of the slow movement, where the harmonic in-
tensification of the theme, touching the minor relatives of D major (E
and F♯ minor) and an inflection from D minor (the B♭) is a rich mixture,
even for Mozart (ex. 18.3).

---

[4] He must have had basset-clarinets in B♭, for the obbligato in *La clemenza di Tito* and the second clarinet part in *Così fan tutte*, as well as the A needed for the quintet and concerto. The
lowest written pitch of the basset-clarinet and basset-horn is c, a third below the bottom of
the normal clarinet.

[5] Tyson suggests this may have been as early as 1787 ('New Dates', 226). The basset-horn is
usually in F.

Ex. 18.3 Clarinet concerto, K. 622, second movement, from bar 76

Adagio (tutti, horns omitted)

The last operas

While essentially original, the libretto of *Die Zauberflöte* capitalised on, or even plagiarised, a popular tradition of magical operas such as *Kaspar der Fagottist* and *Der Stein der Weisen*, where adventure, comedy, and moral posturing rub shoulders, and magic can be worked by musical instruments. The Singspiel form, severely discontinuous with extended scenes both comic and serious in spoken dialogue, made it easier for Mozart to match the free-ranging fantasy of the libretto by a liberal mixing of the musical styles appropriate to each situation. The genre already accommodated finales of comparable length to those of opera buffa, and the libretto was designed to bring out the strengths of the performers: Mozart's sister-in-law Josepha Hofer (Queen of Night) in fiery coloratura, Schack (Tamino) the lyrical tenor, Gerl (Sarastro) with his fine low notes, and the impulsive pathos of seventeen-year-old Anna Gottlieb (Pamina).[6] Parallel to the serious plot of self-discovery and initiation, the figure of Schikaneder as the bird-man Papageno provides comic relief and a refreshingly earthy view of the religious and symbolic activities within the temples of wisdom.

As to the meaning of the opera, opinions differ, as they do on its value as musical theatre (questioned even by some who admire Mozart). Is it an allegory of politics, religion, and Freemasonry, as is widely believed? Is Sarastro the enlightened Ignaz von Born, and the Queen of Night the Catholic Empress Maria Theresia (if so, a cruel libel on an autocratic but far from unenlightened monarch)?[7] The opera's alleged misogyny could be interpreted as supporting Catholic, rather than Masonic, views on women's place in society, or as opposing either of them; Mozart subverts the most misogynistic sung text (the duet for two priests) with buffa music, and in the end Pamina is crowned alongside Tamino, as joint ruler of the order.

Even if the existence of Masonic symbols, and especially numerology, within Mozart's work has been exaggerated, Freemasonry cannot be dismissed as an influence on the opera, if only because of the visual element, based on Egyptian models, in the first productions. Tamino's quest leads him into an ancient priestly order, the natural stage metaphor for the craft.[8] The opera cannot have been considered subversive, as it remained in repertory when the Viennese lodges were closed and Leopold II's successor was establishing what eventually became the Austrian police state. Its moral story, in which jealousy and possessiveness are defeated, transcends social, political, or philosophical frameworks. One of its aspects, as with *Die Entführung*, is a hymn to marriage, as nearly between equals as the period could envisage. Pamina, legally the

---

[6] It is unlikely that Schack himself played the 'magic' flute. Gottlieb had appeared as Barbarina in *Figaro*, at the age of twelve.

[7] On Masonic interpretations, see Jacques Chailley, *La flute enchantée: Opéra maçonnique* (Paris, 1968); Katharine Thomson, *The Masonic Thread in Mozart* (London, 1977).

[8] David Buch argues that the fairy-tale tradition is a sufficient explanation of the plot. '*Die Zauberflöte*, Masonic Opera, and Other Fairy Tales', *Acta musicologica* 76 (2004), 193–219.

owner of the magic flute itself, passes with Tamino through the ordeals of fire and water, after which Papageno, redeemed by his willingness to die, is allowed his Papagena. The positive role of these women may be part of the enlightened message, one that was set back by the male ferocity (Mme Defarge notwithstanding) of the French revolution and the Romantic and Imperial phase of European culture that followed.

As for the music, it hangs like a series of mixed jewels upon the brittle thread of the plot, illuminating the situations, deepening the paste-board characterizations, and gathering, in two immense finales, all the dramatic threads into a labyrinthine musical organization. The late style discussed in connection with instrumental music informs the arias of Tamino and Pamina: 'Dies Bildnis' makes more convincing than usual the dramatic trope of falling in love with a portrait, and 'Ach, ich fühl's' is the last distillation of Mozart's use of G minor for despairing women. The luminous simplicity and rightness of Mozart's late music is nowhere more apparent than in the unearthly choral responses to Sarastro's solemn invocation, 'O Isis und Osiris'. But Mozart was writing for a theatre of the present, and without thought of transcending his circumstances; he reached for weapons in an unmatched armoury of musical devices to suit each situation; the antic coloratura of the Queen of Night, popping up to f''' in each of her arias, suited both singer and situation, like the low notes of Osmin and the incessant flow of Elvira's 'Mi tradì'; the learned counterpoint against a chorale sung in octaves by two armed men in octaves prefaces the ritual of the trials; the sound of the Viennese suburbs befits the boisterous, pusillanimous Papageno. It is not surprising that Papageno, originally played by the author-actor-manager, sometimes steals the show; and it is not entirely wrong that he should do so, for his own journey to fulfilment is closer to normal human experience than Tamino's.

From what is surely a humanistic vision, masked by the trappings of a coronation in the final scene, it is a far cry to Metastasio's *La clemenza di Tito*. Fortunately that is not what Mozart had to set, for it would have been impossible in so short a time. Presumably with the agreement of Guardasoni, he worked with Caterino Mazzolà, Da Ponte's temporary successor as court poet, to make it into a 'real opera'.[9] Pressure of time

---

[9] Mozart entered it in his catalogue as 'ridotta á vera opera dal Sigre Mazzolà'.

prevented him from composing the finger-breaking simple recitatives, which were assigned to an assistant, possibly Süssmayr. Thus *La clemenza* could be considered unfinished, and it may be in response to this perception that so many variants were introduced in the fifteen or so years after Mozart's death when it was one of his most often performed works. It then sank into neglect, and until the later twentieth century was dismissed condescendingly as inferior work by a sick man in a hurry; and remembering that he died not long afterwards, witnesses conveniently remembered him as already ill, when he could simply have been mortally tired. Sickness, as Weber's *Oberon* shows, is not necessarily an obstacle to artistic excellence, and the other work composed before and after *La clemenza* suggests that the arias, ensembles, and choruses are exactly as Mozart wanted them. Nevertheless, in act 2 there are signs of a lack of planning, in that some recitatives end in keys remote from that of the following number.[10] Had he lived, Mozart would surely have tried to get this opera produced elsewhere, having first tidied up points of this kind and perhaps increased the amount of orchestral recitative, of which there is considerably less than in *Così*, never mind *Idomeneo*.

Mazzolà compressed the libretto into the more fashionable two acts, the first ending in a concerted finale with chorus. Part of the plot was painlessly removed, scenes were shortened, some aria and recitative texts were rearranged to make ensembles, and where necessary new words were written. Tito's motives are analysed in three arias without making his ultimate clemency anything less than predictable; he remains a stiff figure at home in an opera seria, partly, no doubt, because he was sung by Baglioni, the original Don Ottavio. The characterizations of Vitellia and Sesto are more interesting, and moving. They both sing rondòs in act 2 to articulate their willingness to submit to fate—death for Sesto ('Deh, per questo istante solo'), disgrace for Vitellia ('Non più di fiori', for which new words were written). Sesto's first-act aria ('Parto, parto') and Vitellia's 'Non più di fiori' engage in dialogue with obbligatos played by Anton Stadler. The matching virtuosity of the basset-clarinet supports Sesto's plea to Vitellia to show gratitude for the sacrifice he is

---

[10] The first act 2 recitative ends in E♭, followed by Annio's aria in G; more drastically, the trio in E♭ is preceded by a cadence in D; other recitatives end in the subdominant or tonic of the following number rather than the more logical dominant favoured in act 1—and before Tito's last aria, which was composed in Vienna.

making (she is sending him off to murder his friend and patron, the emperor). For Vitellia, the darker sounding basset-horn is like the voice of conscience, and Mozart boldly drives the music through an orchestral coda into the next scene, depriving the singer of the applause which is her due—not least because of her final descent into the contralto register (to g). The whole aria lies lower than the rest of her role, as if the defeat of all her hopes has changed her irrevocably: we can believe in her penitence and the self-sacrifice which brings her, just before Tito has uttered words of forgiveness for Sesto, to take the blame on herself. It is the most convincing of Mozart's dénouements by forgiveness.

All this Mozart might have achieved within the conventional framework of opera seria, but he again took the risk of mixing styles. The two short duets in act 1 have a directness and melodic charm reminiscent of *Die Zauberflöte*. Tito's escape from death is celebrated in a kind of minuet. The ensembles are clearly affected by Mozart's skill in opera buffa. The first duet and the trios expand on conflicting states of feeling without embodying any dramatic development, but they are too short for this to be considered a defect. When Vitellia hears she is to be empress, immediately after launching the attack upon the emperor, this hitherto iron lady is thrown into, and humanized by, panic, delivered to the audience in the act 1 trio in which she rises to d'''. This number leads directly into Sesto's obbligato recitative, exploring his horror at the murder he is about to commit for her. He launches into an aria but is immediately overtaken by events, and the number turns out to be the finale; this in turn comes to a standstill, in a slower tempo (the opposite of opera buffa practice), in a broad lament over the emperor's supposed death. This is indeed a 'vera opera', and its position in the repertoire, while never likely to rival that of Mozart's comedies, should now be secure.

The Requiem

Analysis of surviving manuscripts has established beyond reasonable doubt how much of the Requiem Mozart actually wrote.[11] There were sketches, of which two have survived; then Mozart began laying out his

---

[11] The manuscripts have been published in facsimile (introduction by Günter Brosche, Graz and Kassel, 1990). See also Richard Maunder, *Mozart's Requiem. On Preparing a New Edition* (Oxford, 1988); Christoph Wolff, *Mozart's Requiem: Historical and Analytical Studies* (Berkeley and Los Angeles, 1994).

full score by completing the voice parts, and where necessary the orchestral first violin and bass, and main features of the accompaniment. Nothing indicates feverish haste, and rather than drive to the end, he took time to orchestrate most of the first movement (Requiem, Te decet, Kyrie). He designed the whole of the Sequence, from Dies irae to Lacrimosa, but broke off the latter after eight bars; however, the next main section, the Offertory (Domine Jesu), was also fully drafted. No music in Mozart's hand survives for the last three sections (Sanctus, Benedictus, Agnus Dei), for which the texts are almost the same as for the Ordinary of the Mass. A sketch for an Amen fugue survives, presumed to be meant to follow the Lacrimosa; the subject is a version of material used elsewhere in the Requiem, and related to the 'Tonus peregrinus' plainsong.

The overall design, had it been realised, would have contrasted grand contrapuntal statements with more dramatic sections (Dies irae, Confutatis) and passages of prayer, which are not necessarily all as sombre as the opening movement. The Introit is partly derived from Handel's funeral anthem 'The ways of Zion do mourn'; but this is no mere modernization of Handel's sparse orchestration but a recomposition that raises the material onto a higher expressive plane. An aural memory of Michael Haydn's Requiem in C minor of 1773 seems to affect the design of this movement, but the orchestral colouring is Mozart's, with basset-horns and bassoons the only woodwind, and trumpets cutting through the sober texture unimpeded by horns. Trombones mainly double the chorus, as in the Salzburg Masses. The double fugue (Kyrie) revisits the descending diminished seventh, while adopting a Handel countersubject from the same anthem; but Handel's double fugue is in the major.

The setting of the Sequence divides into several contrasting movements, a design more like the C-minor mass than those composed for Salzburg, and is completely drafted except for the closing Lacrimosa. The Offertory, also completely drafted, consists of four sections, of which the second and fourth are identical fugues on 'Quam olim Abrahae'. Mozart left all the voice parts and indications of what the orchestra should be doing, so there is enough information to realise most of these sections better than Süssmayr did, and it is surprising that new versions did not appear before about 1970. Some scholars feel it is enough to improve the

Ex. 18.4 Requiem, 'Hostias', closing bars

style and layout of the orchestration, and otherwise leave Süssmayr's work intact, on the grounds that at least he knew Mozart and composed as best he could in the same ambience.[12] Others point out that his counterpoint is defective and his orchestration crude, and take what little remains from the other composers to whom Constanze first entrusted the score: Joseph Eybler's two-bar continuation of the Lacrimosa tails off pathetically on a page otherwise in Mozart's hand. For more radical scholars, there is the Lacrimosa to finish, with the Amen fugue; and there is the question of whether Mozart had any hand in the Sanctus, Benedictus, Hosanna, and Agnus Dei.[13] Whether or not Mozart really told Süssmayr to finish the work by repeating the end of the Introit and the Kyrie fugue to the words 'Cum sanctis tuis in aeternum', it at least means that his and every subsequent version ends with music substantially by Mozart.

The Lacrimosa fragment is not necessarily the last music Mozart set down; he may have moved on to the Offertory, intending to turn back to the Lacrimosa. In that case, his musical life ended with the instruction to the performers to repeat 'Quam olim Abrahae', following an exquisitely sensitive harmonic exploration (ex. 18.4 includes only what Mozart himself wrote down) that illuminates the prayer to the Lord, to make those we remember pass from death into life—'. . . de morte transire ad vitam'.

---

[12] Those who have been content to revise Süssmayr's version include Franz Beyer (1971) and H. C. Robbins Landon (1991).

[13] Richard Maunder rejects these movements as there is no evidence of Mozart's participation (his edition: Oxford, 1988). The possibility exists that Mozart had made sketches; Süssmayr claimed as much, and his openings are developed by Duncan Druce (1984, London, 1993) and Robert Levin (Neuhausen-Stuttgart, 1994).

CHAPTER 19

Aftermath

'. . . de morte transire ad vitam'

OZART WAS A FAMOUS COMPOSER IN HIS OWN LIFETIME. This simple assertion needs to be made from time to time, as the story is still told of the hopelessly misunderstood genius, dying in poverty and obscurity, whose reputation soared after his death. The last part is true, and in the romantic nineteenth century it did him no posthumous harm to have died young. Other than in England, where the honour goes to Handel, Mozart was the first composer to remain permanently lodged in the minds not only of practising musicians but also of the musical public. Individual works have been forgotten and required revival, including masterpieces like *Idomeneo*, little known before its sesquicentenary in 1931. The nineteenth century was selective in its admiration. *Figaro* had its place in the repertoire, but *Così*, frivolous, immoral, was considered in need of apology. But for the romantics, *Don Giovanni* was the quintessential opera, followed by *Die Zauberflöte*—both of them, however, subject to manipulation to suit local tastes in London and Paris. In Germany, the Singspiel version *Don Juan* had as much currency as the Italian original, whereas England rejected Singspiel in favour of *Il seraglio* and *Il flauto magico*. Mozart was hardly known as a composer of opera seria, but *Don Giovanni* was promoted to grander status, with Donna Anna as prototype suffering heroine and avenging angel—an attention focused by E.T.A. Hoffmann's curious short story of 1813. Hoffmann's fantastical deductions about her relationship to Giovanni have influenced interpretation ever since, both in the study and on the stage. *Die Zauberflöte* became the official fountainhead of German Romantic opera; its potent blend of magic, adventure, and religion, and its conflict of good and evil, passed from such epigones as Eberl's *Die Königin der schwarzen Inseln* (Vienna, 1801) to Weber's *Der Freischütz* and *Oberon*, and thence to Marschner and Wagner himself. Although Beethoven deplored the immorality of the Da Ponte operas, *Fidelio*, despite its immediate French ancestry, shows his understanding and admiration of Mozart's dramatic music, shared by many composers outside Germany, including Rossini, Berlioz, and Gounod.

The unique position occupied by Beethoven in instrumental music, whether piano and violin sonatas, piano trios, string quartets, piano concertos, and symphonies, for many years overshadowed the achievements of Mozart. The minor-key concertos (K. 466 and 491) could be appropriated by romanticism, as could the G-minor symphony, while the 'Jupiter' remained a paragon of compositional virtuosity. But in these fields Mozart quickly receded from the status of 'romantic' offered him by Hoffmann, to that of remote classic, a model of purity, rather like Palestrina in Catholic church music and in musical pedagogy more generally. Nevertheless his reputation, and the possibility of talking to people who knew him, stimulated a remarkable amount of biographical and scholarly study. Vincent and Mary Novello took a gift of money to the elderly Nannerl and talked at length to Constanze.[1] Their friend Edward Holmes was Mozart's first English biographer (1845), preceded by Alexander Ulibishev (Oulibicheff), a Russian whose more thoroughly researched study (1843) was composed in French.[2] The extensive biographical sources were not an unmixed blessing: the necrologies, reminiscences, and even the biography prepared by Georg Nikolaus Nissen, Constanze's Danish second husband, perpetrate a mixture of anecdotes of variable credibility. It is a truth which should, reluctantly, be generally acknowledged that even the widows of great men sometimes validate legends, exaggerations, or even downright falsehoods. In the mid-nineteenth century, three major undertakings in Germany began the

---

[1] Nerina Medici and Rosemary Hughes (eds.), *A Mozart Pilgrimage*.

[2] Both books were republished in Mozart's bicentenary. Edward Holmes, *The Life of Mozart* (ed. Christopher Hogwood; London, 1991); Alexandre Oulibicheff, *Mozart* (ed. Jean-Victor Hocquard; Paris, 1991).

task of sifting truth from fiction: the biography by Otto Jahn, published in 1856, the catalogue of Ludwig Köchel (1862), and the Breitkopf und Härtel collected edition (1877–1905). The twentieth century continued the musicological projects of the nineteenth, with the revision of Jahn by Hermann Abert, the various revisions of Köchel, and the new collected edition (NMA). To these may be added the monumental labours of those who have produced bibliographies of Mozart, and of Otto Erich Deutsch, who in association with the NMA took a role in editing the family letters and documents, many of which have not yet been published in English, and in sorting the iconographical wheat from some curious chaff—although when there is a 'Mozart story' in the press, the accompanying portrait is still usually one of those that are posthumous and idealised into a terrible blandness.

Scholars continue to research Mozart's life, analyse his music, and try to gain insight into his personality, but the twentieth-century response to Mozart may best be measured through his rising popularity. I would not want to diminish the work of pioneering critics, for instance Abert, Wyzewa and Saint-Foix, and Edward J. Dent (whose book on the operas is still readable with profit).[3] But if Mozart has emerged from being Beethoven's agreeably pomaded predecessor, to becoming an iconic figure in his own right, it is through the efforts of promoters (saliently at the festival in his home town) and performing musicians, both amateur and professional. Tracing this development is a task for whole books longer than this one, and has so far mostly been attempted in relation to operas, where the documentation and iconography are more plentiful.[4] But it is no less important that the twentieth century recognised the quality of the chamber and orchestral music, and not only revived the mature works comprehensively but visited the early music, there to find a number of treasures as well as, to be frank, music one only spends time with because, in a Mozart, one desires completeness.

The sea-change that came over performance in the later twentieth century has most affected the orchestral music (including concertos and operas), although it touches everything about Mozart. Itself thoroughly

[3] Wyzewa and Saint-Foix, *W.-A. Mozart: sa vie musical et son oeuvre*; E. J. Dent, *Mozart's Operas, a Critical Study*.

[4] See for instance the beautifully illustrated book by Rudolf Angermüller, *Mozart's Operas*.

modern, if not modernist, in its aims, the 'early music' movement has revived the instruments and as far as possible instrumental techniques of Mozart's time. The shift towards historically informed performance has brought fortepianos into frequent use; orchestras and chamber ensembles play on replicas of late eighteenth-century instruments, the strings made of gut, the wind with narrower bores, woodwind with cross-fingerings, the valveless horns unable to avoid variation of tone colour between adjacent notes. To suppose we are hearing what his listeners heard would be naïve, and not only because our listening is conditioned by all the music written since. There will always be areas of disagreement, for instance on articulation, vibrato, and ornamentation; and some questions, such as the size of orchestras which varied from one centre to another, have no definitive answer. Moreover, our concert programmes are differently planned; few mingle instrumental and vocal items, and fewer still split a symphony by using the first movements to start, and the finale to close, the entertainment. Pieces designed for liturgical performance, such as the Requiem, are performed in concerts, without interruption; sonatas never intended for public performance are offered from a recital platform. We listen in modern halls more often than in surroundings typical of the eighteenth century; indeed, and far more, we listen to recordings.

It would be entirely wrong for the revival of historic practices to inhibit performances of Mozart (or Bach, or anybody) on modern instruments. But it has changed our perception of what is acceptable, even in a concert on a grand piano or symphony orchestra, and in a programme otherwise devoted to Liszt or Strauss. Crisp articulation, faster tempi, the tendency (not always historically informed) to avoid ritardandi and accelerandi not marked by the composer—such things we now take for granted, as we do a high standard of accuracy and togetherness in the ensemble, conveniently disregarding the probably scrappy rehearsal system of Mozart's time. Not that I suggest that Mozart heard only poor performances; I have no doubt most of those he directed were excellent. All music played outside the Swieten circle was modern anyway; performers knew the style and did not need to be taught the difference between playing Mozart and Brahms. Mozart was apparently not worried that his overtures might be sight-read at the last rehearsal or performance; otherwise, he would have written them earlier. Meanwhile the revival of early Mozart recordings, even those as recent as the 1950s, becomes an extension of the movement to bring all the past, as far as possible, into our cultured present.

Mozart's musical personality

Mozart's style shared so many features with his contemporaries that he can appear the least original of the great European masters. He could assimilate any type of music and make it his own; his muse was fed by Italian, German, and even French opera, German symphonic and chamber music, Italian and German counterpoint, Catholic and Protestant music (German and English), dance music, and folk music. Because he survived when the music of his contemporaries fell out of use, we thoughtlessly apply the epithet 'Mozartian' to, for example, J. C. Bach or Cimarosa, though it would be better suited to those composers he influenced such as Süssmayr, Eybler, or early Schubert. Early completions of several works were taken to be entirely by him, for example a beautiful and ornate sonata-form movement in C minor for piano and violin, completed by Maximilian Stadler and disseminated as a fantasia for piano solo (K. 396=385f). Not all the Mozartian pieces that have been attributed to him were forgeries, or dishonestly marketed to take advantage of his fame; people may sincerely have believed that something apparently Mozartian could only be Mozart. The Benedictus of the Requiem and the spurious 'Twelfth Mass' published by Novello came to be appreciated alongside the 'Coronation Mass' and other genuine works, and the former was especially admired. Where there is a chance the music may be Mozart's, it appears in the Neue Mozart Ausgabe in volumes of 'Werke zweifelhafter Echtheit' (works of doubtful authenticity). One such includes the wind sinfonia concertante (see chap. 7); another contains three wind divertimenti, seven keyboard and violin sonatas, sonatas for piano duet and piano alone, and various piano pieces.[5]

---

[5] NMA series 10, vol. 29. The wind divertimenti are K. 289=Anh.226 and two authenticated by Einstein (K3) and removed by the editors of K6 (K3.196e=Anh.C17.01; K3.196f = Anh.C.17.02). The violin sonatas are K. 55–60=Anh.C23.01–06 and one K deest. The piano music includes fourteen variations on 'Come un'agnello' from Sarti's *Fra i due litiganti*, the tune Mozart quoted in *Don Giovanni*, and a sonata in B♭ K. Anh.136=498a which the author remembers playing from the edition published in London (Associated Board of the Royal Schools of Music), now superseded by the publication edited by Stanley Sadie and Denis Matthews (2 vols.; London, ca. 1982).

Mozart was sometimes content to base music on good models, but his quartets and symphonies are strikingly unlike Haydn's. Modelling, or borrowing, occurs more often when the source was either not modern, as with Handel and Bach, or when, to a Mozart, it seemed to deserve better treatment. Hence his models for the Requiem are Handel, and Michael rather than Joseph Haydn; and if he borrowed the main theme of the *Zauberflöte* overture, it was because he saw in it possibilities left unexplored by Clementi. What differentiates Mozart from his stylistically similar contemporaries is partly his richer assimilation of Baroque models: his bolder use of idioms such as the French overture or his daring counterpoints. But there was no mere pastiche; the old style is brought up to date. In the unfinished piano suite (K. 399=385i) Mozart departed from Baroque practice by adopting a progressive key-scheme: the overture begins grandly in C, but its fugue ends on the dominant of C minor, the key of the following Allemande; the Courante is in Eb, and the incomplete Sarabande begins in G minor (perhaps it would have ended on G major, ready for a Gigue in C). Even in a piece presumably written for his own instruction, he breaks stylistic boundaries in the first bars of the overture (ex. 19.1a); grand major triads unrelated to the tonic lead to deliquescent chromaticism, reminiscent of *Idomeneo*, and anticipating the eloquent clarinet additions to 'The people that walked in darkness have seen a great light' in *Messiah* (ex. 19.1b).

Conventional fugue subjects were also modernised by their Mozartian context, and treated partly according to genre and the likely audience. The fugue subject with a diminished seventh leap sounds old-fashioned in the early string quartet (K. 168) and Vespers of 1780 ('Laudate pueri'), where despite its inversion and stretto, the counterpoint is securely based on the consonances of the minor mode. A similar subject is used in the relentlessly gritty C-minor fugue for two pianos (K. 426) and is handled quite differently again in the Requiem's Kyrie, there adapting Handel's countersubject as well. Given the quantity and quality of counterpoint in later Mozart, culminating in his last symphony, our debt to Swieten's Sunday afternoons is hard to overestimate.

To divide Mozart from the galant models which remained the basis of his musical language, it may be enough to say 'genius', but the sceptical may want some demonstration that this opinion is founded in the musical facts. The centre of any case for Mozart is to recognise his skill in

Ex. 19.1 a. Suite in C, K. 399, Overture

Grave

musical combinations of all kinds: harmonic, thematic, stylistic, and formal. No one moved as he does, above all in his later instrumental music,
with such swiftness, serenity, and sleight of hand to create a musical argument combining his greatest loves—counterpoint, chromaticism,
comedy. Few if any could so effectively set off lyricism against storm
and stress, richness of sound against textures of the utmost economy, so
that his string duets and trio (K. 563) have an amplitude of sound that
belies the sparsity of their instrumental forces; but better still are the
quintets and the orchestral works, where small groups can contrast with
the tutti.

Mozart's music usually flows with such conviction that it is easy to
overlook questions of rhythm and proportion. His skill in keeping the
listener in touch by repetition, albeit with variation, before moving on,
is a lesson in compositional rhetoric, but it would require large-scale examples to make any sense and a theoretical framework in need of its own
exposition. The matter of rhythm, as a means of distinguishing Mozart
from his contemporaries who worked in the same style, was broached in

Ex. 19.1 (*continued*)

b. Handel, *Messiah* ('The people that walked in darkness'), from bar 24 (wind parts by Mozart)

an article published in the bicentenary of Mozart's birth, in which Edward E. Lowinsky drew a telling contrast with a musician Mozart admired, J. C. Bach.[6] Others have also drawn attention to Mozart's uneven phrase-lengths. Stravinsky sighed that he would tolerate Cimarosa's four-by-four if only there had been no Mozart.[7] Schoenberg listed what

[6] Edward E. Lowinsky, 'On Mozart's Rhythm', *Musical Quarterly* 42 (1956), 162–86, reprinted in Paul Henry Lang (ed.) *The Creative World of Mozart* (New York, 1963), 31–55.

[7] Igor Stravinsky and Robert Craft, *Conversations with Igor Stravinsky* (London, 1959), 76.

he had learned from his primary teachers, Bach and Mozart: from the latter, inequality of phrase-length, coordination of heterogeneous characters to form a thematic unity, deviation from even-numbered construction in the theme and its component parts, the art of forming subsidiary ideas, the art of introduction and transition.[8]

Mozart did indeed use uneven phrasings at times, a good example being the original theme for the variation finale of an early piano sonata in D (K. 284), a piece he thought well enough of to publish in Vienna in 1784 (ex. 19.2). The theme contains seventeen bars, rather than the expected sixteen. Its first part consists of the standard four plus four bars, modulating to the dominant; the second part begins with a four-bar 'middle', ready for a reprise. But the cadence is slowed and followed by rests, so that the reprise comes in a bar late. The rests are subsequently filled in by figuration appropriate to each variation. (The theme is not without other subtleties: note Mozart's scrupulous care in dynamic markings, with the sudden *p* near the end, and his imaginative use of the 'Alberti' figuration in the left hand.) But one cannot equate using so-called irrational numbers with genius. In one of the early piano concertos arranged from various composers (K. 40), the second movement is based on Eckard; surely Mozart did not choose it because of its seven-bar phrases, which are as stiff as a board. And the adult Mozart is a better composer than Cimarosa, Clementi, or Cherubini, even when every phrase falls into the symmetrical even-numbered groupings of bars typical of the period.

Other manifestations of Mozart's mental quality may be identified, but not explained or measured. The material he invents is more striking, less dependent upon formula, than his contemporaries' ideas. The openings of the A major, 'Haffner', and late G-minor symphonies are well-known examples of immediately striking thematic ideas which imprint the music as unique; in the first two, the ideas are based on rising and falling octaves; in the more complex theme of the G-minor, the persistent rhythm characterises a repeated semitone and a simple falling scale. The fluency of Mozart's melody, and his occasional preference for melody in the central part of a sonata form, which we have become ac-

---

[8] The third and fourth seem to replicate the first two. Schoenberg, 'National Music', reprinted in *Style and Idea* (London, 1975, 173); see also the analyses in 'Brahms the Progressive', ibid., 409–16.

customed to call, and hence expect, 'development', might even be held against him. Most of us, however, will simply relish such pieces (arbitrarily chosen from a legion of possible examples) as the 'Kegelstatt' trio's rondo, the duet of Annio and Servilia in *La clemenza di Tito*, or the Hostias of the Requiem. As for development, it is no less a sign of genius to retain the thread of a musical argument and propel the music forward with a new melody, than with a *Durchführung* or 'working out' of themes in counterpoint. Mozart could do that superbly and often did. His occasional choice of a melodic centre to a sonata-form movement is not a soft option; it is not a criticism to say that his choice may have been affected by the nature of a solo instrument, as in the horn quintet, or partly by his experience in writing arias in which new words practically compelled him to produce new melodic shapes.

Mozart's distinction appears no less marked when he is deploying conventional material, including ideas he used more than once. The opening of the 'Rondo' in D (K. 485) could not be more straightforwardly balanced (ex. 19.3a). The melody begins with a favourite tag of Mozart's, one he may have used even more than the often-discussed four-note motif of the 'Jupiter' finale; the descending fifth arpeggio made into a scale by grace-notes opens two of the Milan quartets (in the major, K. 169, and minor, K. 173), and the early string quintet (K. 174; see ex. 15.3). The minor version reappears in an episode, led by the viola, in the 'Kegelstatt' rondo. For the piano piece Mozart picked out the theme note for note from the finale of the G-minor piano quartet (ex. 19.3b). The full version with dominant to tonic response may have been taken from the first movement of J. C. Bach's quintet op.11, no.6, published in 1774. Accordingly Einstein, relating the development of K. 485 to 'the manner of the rondos' of C.P.E. Bach, called the piece a 'reconciliation of the Bach brothers', although Mozart surely had no such agenda (J. C. Bach was already dead).[9] Like C.P.E. Bach, Mozart does bring in the theme in unrelated keys, but despite the received title, the piece is not really a rondo but a monothematic sonata form with repeated exposition, the dominant key being established by a reworking of the opening theme. Einstein follows Wyzewa and Saint-Foix in considering K. 485 to lie outside Mozart's norms, an experiment in wearing

---

[9] Alfred Einstein, *Mozart, His Character, His Work*, 118.

Ex. 19.2 Piano sonata in D, K. 284, finale

THEMA
Andante

others' clothes, even if they were not entirely fashionable.[10] But experimentation was itself entirely typical of Mozart, and if he did not repeat his experiments, it may sometimes be because they succeeded; to this writer, at least, the piece seems quintessentially Mozartian.

An aspect of Mozart's distinction that is rightly singled out is that he

[10] Einstein, loc. cit.; Wyzewa and Saint-Foix, *W.-A. Mozart: sa vie musical et son oeuvre*, ii, 570.

Ex. 19.3 Mozart's favorite tag

a. 'Rondo' in D, K. 485

Allegro

b. Piano quartet in G, K. 478, finale, from bar 60 (strings omitted)

Allegro moderato

was capable of magnificent work in nearly every available musical form. Even the handful of songs includes a number of pieces more worthy to be considered the predecessors of the romantic Lied than the lesser figures on whose shoulders Schubert stood. Where Haydn's operas remained at Eszterháza, Mozart's travelled Europe; yet he could match Haydn in sonata, quartet, and symphony, in quality if not in quantity. In comparing such incomparable masters, we must recall that although Haydn was the senior by nearly a quarter of a century, much of his great music was composed after Mozart's death: not only two oratorios and six masses but several symphonies, quartets, and piano trios, and the English-language songs. Mozart paid tribute to Haydn by styling his quartets differently; Haydn paid tribute to Mozart by ceasing to write operas for Eszterháza once he knew *Figaro*. Mozart's all-round competence is, however, partly the result of circumstances. Had he been called to serve the Habsburg princes in Italy, he would have written more operas, and less chamber music. Had he not settled in the 'Land of the Clavier', he might not have written his greatest concertos.

Mozart and Constanze

It is Mozart's present misfortune that the popularity of his music, in an age of intrusive journalism, has led not only to fictional constructions such as Peter Shaffer's *Amadeus* but to speculations about his character and health that go well beyond the accessible data, sometimes in order to fit a preconceived theory. In terms of modern reception history, the anecdotage of the years following his death, sometimes from people who barely knew him, like Friedrich Rochlitz, remains in the historical record and cannot be wished away.[11] This is not the place to raise and dismiss the often contradictory ideas that have been formulated, even in recent years, and maintained within the literature. The sober fact is that Mozart lived a busy, often difficult but by no means an extraordinary life, except in the quantity and quality of his productivity; and that despite frequent ill health, he lived perhaps longer than might have been expected, and longer than some close friends including his doctor Sigmund Barisani, in an age when early death was not uncommon.

Mozart was above all a musician; he had other interests, but the need

[11] Nevertheless anyone interested in Mozart should read William Stafford, *Mozart's Death*.

to exercise his profession for profit means that we have little idea of the intellectual range of which he may have been capable in other spheres. There can be no doubt of his intelligence, but its greatest potential was in mathematics, which he presumably abandoned at an early age, languages, in which he was an agile learner but had no need to exercise discipline, and, of course, music. Words he handled uneasily, but in music he exercised all the professional self-discipline that was needed (whatever his father sometimes implied), and also a sense of obligation which led him to explore possibilities untouched by his contemporaries.

Mozart knew he was exceptional and may unwisely have allowed his justified self-esteem to communicate itself. He suffered because he was no intriguer; most of the time he seems to have been as frank as he occasionally claimed to be in letters to Leopold. His personality was always admitted to be amiable, his nature obliging, even yielding, and this too Leopold found a problem, as his son may indeed have been prone to waste time and skill on an unworthy, or more importantly a nonpaying, cause. Generous, witty, if perhaps sometimes malicious, he retained a wide circle of friends among his social equals and to an extent his social superiors. For friends like Jacquin, Schikaneder, Schack, and Gerl, he would do almost anything, and in some cases maybe for no gulden at all. Mozart was not tolerant of what he considered to be weak or facile musicianship, even from a Clementi; but he was a committed teacher of singing, piano, and composition. His effect on his sister-in-law Aloysia cannot be quantified, but it must have been considerable; some of his piano students were among the best female players of the age; and besides his composition students, such as Attwood, he had an immediate affect on such associates as Storace, Eybler, and Süssmayr.

Constanze has now been cleared, one hopes definitively (*Amadeus* notwithstanding), from the accusation that she was unworthy, profligate, or incompetent in housekeeping. Even if the debts were not as bad as all that, at the end of 1791 her situation, as a widowed mother with no profession, was desperate, more so than if Mozart had died a few years earlier or, probably, later. She coped, brought up her children, and undertook a sober second marriage (without issue) largely devoted to securing Mozart's legacy for the world. If she profited from this, it was her right to do so. One of the less endearing aspects of their relationship, surely deriving from Mozart's own treatment by his father, is the strength of his reproof for her occasionally indiscreet behaviour; when she allowed a young gentleman to measure her calf, it nearly ended their engagement. Yet such a reaction is a sign of love—the kind of love strongly mingled with dependence. Mozart enjoyed mixing with professional cronies, and he was a seasoned traveller; but his misery when parted from her, in his last fruitless journeys to Frankfurt and Berlin, is palpably clear from the letters.

A Mozart for our time is a Mozart about whom 'discoveries' are reported in the national press, discoveries on a level of interest which, with anyone outside a handful of canonical masters, would be confined to specialist publications. Even since the start of the twenty-first century there has been found what may prove to be a 'new' symphony of his youth, and a 'new' portrait from 1790; new investigations into the skull dug up in Vienna and housed for years in the Salzburg Mozarteum threaten the posthumous peace of his relations for a scrap of DNA, to determine whether the skull's owner was male or female, entirely unrelated to Mozart, or, just conceivably, was him. What we would learn if the skull proves 'authentic' is not clear; what mattered was the brain it once housed, now lost beyond recall. If Mozart seems fated to be the topic of gossip, the victim of misrepresentation, and the subject of investigations with no useful purpose, that is yet another measure of his hold over the contemporary imagination.

Calendar

Dates of musical works refer to first performances unless otherwise indicated. Cities/ theatres for opera performance: B Berlin, Mi Milan, Mu Munich, N Naples, PO Paris Opéra, PC Paris Comédie italienne or other opéra comique theatre, Pr Prague, R Rome, WB Vienna Burgtheater, WK Vienna Kärntnertortheater, WW, Vienna Theater auf der Wieden.

Other abbreviations: comp composed; pub publication date of the work named; unf unfinished work.

Year	Age	Life	Contemporary Musicians and Events
1756		Johannes Chrysostomus Wolfgangus Theophilus Mozart born 27 Jan in Salzburg, son of Leopold (36) and Maria Anna (35), and brother to Maria Anna ('Nannerl', 6). Christened 28 Jan	Abel aged 32, Albrechtsberger 19, Anfossi 28, Arne 45, C. P. E. Bach 41, J. C. Bach 20, W. F. Bach 45, František Benda 46, Jiří Benda 33, Bonno 44, Boyce 44, Burney 29, Cannabich 24, Cimarosa 6, Clementi 4, Dalayrac 2, Da Ponte 6, Dittersdorf 16, Duni 47, Eberlin 53, Eckard 21, Edelmann 6, Gassmann 26, Gazzaniga 12, Gluck 41, Gossec 22, Grétry 14, Handel 70, Hasse 56, Joseph Haydn 23, Michael Haydn 18, Hoffmeister 1, Holzbauer 44, Jommelli 41, Kozeluch 8, Majo 23, Padre Martini 49, Martín y Soler 1, Metastasio

			58, Monsigny 26, Mysliveček 20, Ordonez 21, Paisiello 15, Philidor 29, Piccinni 28, Rameau 72, Rousseau 43, Sacchini 25, Salieri 5, Sammartini 55, Sarti 26, Schobert ?20, Stamitz 38, Schikaneder 4, Schweitzer 20, Starzer 32, Traetta 28, Umlauf 10, Vanhal 16, Wagenseil 40, Peter Winter 1, Righini born 22 Jan, Linley born 5 May, Kraus born 20 Jun, Vogel born ?17 Mar, Wranitzky born 30 Dec. Seven Years' War begins
1757	1		Stamitz (39) dies ?27 Mar, Scarlatti (71) dies 23 Jul
1758	2	Maria Anna Thekla Mozart ('Bäsle') born 25 Sep	Schack born, 7 Feb
1759	3		Handel (74) dies 14 Apr
1760	4	First compositions (allegedly)	Death of George II: George III king of England. J. L. Dussek born 12 Feb, Piccinni *La Cecchina* (R) 6 Feb, Aloysia Weber born
1761	5		Freystädtler born 13 Sep
1762	6	Visits Munich, Jan; Vienna and Schönbrunn, Sep	Constanze Weber born 5 Jan, Stephen Storace born 4 Apr, Eberlin (60) dies 19 Jun. Gluck *Orfeo ed Euridice* (WB), 5 Oct
1763	7	Return to Salzburg, 5 Jan. Depart 9 Jun, visiting Munich, Augsburg, Frankfurt, Brussels, arriving Paris 18 Nov	Gyrowetz born 19/20 Feb, Mayr born 14 Jun. End of Seven Years' War
1764	8	Op. 1 and 2 pub Versailles, Jan; London from 23 Apr. Leopold ill, summer. Singing lessons with Manzuoli; meets J. C. Bach; writes first symphony	Gluck *La Rencontre imprévue* (WB) 7 Jan, Rameau (80) dies 12 Sep, Gerl born 30 Nov
1765	9	Travel to The Hague, Jul; Nannerl and Wolfgang seriously ill (Nov). Composes aria, symphony, *Gallimathias musicum*. Trios op. 3 pub	Eybler born 8 Feb, Philidor *Tom Jones* (PC) 27 Feb, Eberl born 13 Jun, Nancy Storace born 27 Oct, Attwood born 23 Nov

1766	10	Sonatas op. 4 pub. Travel to Paris, May; Switzerland, Aug–Oct; Munich 8 Nov, Salzburg 29 Nov	Süssmayr born, Weigl born 28 Mar
1767	11	*Die Schuldigkeit des ersten Gebots* 12 Mar; *Grabmusik*; *Apollo et Hyacinthus* 13 May. Visits Vienna, Olomouc, and Brno (Moravia). Nannerl and Wolfgang ill with smallpox	Schobert (ca.32) dies 28 Aug, Philidor *Ernelinde* (PO) 24 Nov, Gluck *Alceste* (WB) 26 Dec
1768	12	Return to Vienna, 19 Jan. Composes *La finta semplice*. *Bastien und Bastienne* and 'Waisenhausmesse' perf, autumn (Vienna)	Grétry *Le Huron* (PC) 20 Aug, Henneberg born 17 Dec
1769	13	*La finta semplice* (Salzburg) 1 May. Leaves for Italy, 13 Dec	Gluck, *Alceste*, pub
1770	14	Visits Verona, Milan, Bologna (meets Padre Martini), Florence (meets Thomas Linley), Rome, Naples (May–Jun). Returns to Rome, knighted by the pope. Bologna, admitted to Accademia filharmonica, 10 Oct. Milan, 18 Oct. *Mitridate, re di Ponto* (Mi) 26 Dec	Reicha born 26 Feb. Dr Burney visits France and Italy. Jommelli *Armida abandonnata* (N) 30 May, Gluck *Paride ed Elena* (WB) 3 Nov, Majo dies 17 Nov, Beethoven born 16 Dec
1771	15	Venice, Feb; returns to Salzburg, Mar. Second visit to Milan, Aug; *Ascanio in Alba* (Mi) 17 Oct; *Betulia liberata* comp. Return to Salzburg, 15 Dec	Paer born 1 Jun, Salieri *Armida* (WB) 2 Jun, Hasse *Ruggero* (Mi) 16 Oct, Archbishop Schrattenbach (73) dies 16 Dec
1772	16	Hieronymus Colleredo becomes Archbishop of Salzburg, Mar. *Il sogno di Scipione*, May. Appointed Konzertmeister, Aug. Third visit to Milan, leaving 24 Oct; 6 string quartets comp. *Lucio Silla* (Mi) 26 Dec	Dr Burney visits Germany and Austria. Haydn's op. 20 quartets pub. Wilms born ?29 Mar
1773	17	Returns to Salzburg, Mar. Visits Vienna, Jul–Sep. Family moves to Hannibal-Platz	
1774	18	Apr, *Thamos, König in Aegypten*? Leaves for Munich, 6 Dec	Gluck *Iphigénie en Aulide* (PO) 19 Apr, *Orphée* (PO) 2 Aug. France: Death of Louis XV: accession of Louis XVI. Gassmann (44) dies 20 Jan, Jommelli (59) dies 25 Aug, Spontini born 14 Nov

1775	19	*La finta giardiniera* (Mu) 13 Jan. Returns home in Mar; *Il re pastore* 23 Apr; violin concertos	Sammartini dies 15 Jan, Duni (67) dies 11 Jun, J. C. Bach *Lucio Silla* (Mannheim) 5 Nov
1776	20	Salzburg. 'Haffner' serenade Jul, 'Credo' Mass Nov	Gluck *Alceste* (PO) 23 Apr, Declaration of American Independence
1777	21	Leaves Salzburg with mother, Sep. Munich, Augsburg (Oct), meets cousin; 30 Oct, Mannheim. Meets Cannabich, Dejean, Raaff, Weber family, Wendling family. Falls in love with Aloysia Weber. Comp sonatas, flute concertos, and quartets	Wagenseil (62) dies 1 Mar, Gluck *Armide* (PO) 23 Sep, Adlgasser (48) dies in Salzburg, Dec
1778	22	Proposes taking Aloysia to Italy. Leaves for Paris, arriving 23 Mar. Composes lost Sinfonia concertante for wind; 'Paris' Symphony 17 Jun. Maria Anna Mozart (57) dies 3 Jul. Leaves Paris, 26 Sep, returning via Strasbourg, Mannheim, Munich	Piccinni *Roland* (PO) 27 Jan, Arne (67) dies 5 Mar, Rousseau (66) dies 2 Jul, Hummel born, 14 Nov. Linley (22) dies 5 Aug
1779	23	Returns to Salzburg, Jan. Appointed court organist. Mass in C, K. 317 ('Coronation'). Sinfonia concertante K. 364. *Zaide* comp (unf)	Boyce (67) dies 7 Feb, Traetta (52) dies 6 Apr; Gluck *Iphigénie en Tauride* (PO) 18 May, J. C. Bach *Amadis de Gaule* (PO) 14 Dec
1780	24	Mass in C, K. 337, *Vesperae solennes de confessore*. Schikaneder's company in Salzburg. Goes to Munich, Nov	Aloysia Weber marries Joseph Lange, 31 Oct; Empress Maria Theresia (63) dies 17 Nov
1781	25	*Idomeneo* (Mu) 29 Jan. Summoned to Vienna, Mar; lodges with Webers. Dismissed by Colleredo. Falls in love with Constanze. Begins work on *Die Entführung*. Sonatas etc. published by Artaria, Nov. 'Contest' with Clementi 24 Dec	Mysliveček (43) dies 4 Feb, Vincent Novello born 6 Sep, Grand Duke Paul visits Vienna, Gluck *Iphigenie auf Tauris* (WB) 23 Oct, Haydn's op. 33 quartets pub
1782	26	Attends Swieten's house on Sundays, to perform Handel and Bach. Composes fugues, some unfinished. *Die Entführung* perf 16 Jul. Marries Constanze, 4 Aug. Starts work on 'Haydn' quartets with K. 387, and series of piano concertos with K. 414	J. C. Bach (46) dies 1 Jan, Metastasio (84) dies 12 Apr, Paisiello *Il barbiere di Siviglia* (St Petersburg) 15/26 Sep. Haydn *Orlando paladino* (Eszterháza) 6 Dec

1783	27	Gives Lenten concerts in Mar. Italian opera company in Vienna; seeks a libretto. Birth of Raimund Leopold 17 Jun. 2nd. 'Haydn' quartet, K. 421. Jul–Nov, visits Salzburg with Constanze; C-minor Mass (unf). Raimund Leopold dies in Vienna, 19 Aug. Work on *L'oca del Cairo* (unf), quartet K. 428. Returns via Linz: Symphony in C, K.425 ('Linz'), 4 Nov	Holzbauer (71) dies 7 Apr; Piccinni *Didon* (Fontainebleau) 16 Oct; Hasse (84) dies 16 Dec
1784	28	More Lenten concerts. Begins *Verzeichnüss* with piano concerto K. 449. Work on *Lo sposo deluso* (unf.). Piano concertos (to K. 459), quintet with wind K. 452. Nannerl marries, 23 Aug; Carl Thomas born 21 Sep. Mozart admitted to Freemasons Lodge 'Zur Wohltätigkeit', Dec	Haydn *Armida* (Eszterháza) 26 Feb; Spohr born 5 Apr, Salieri *Les Danaïdes* (PO) 26 Apr, W. F. Bach (73) dies 1 Jul, Onslow born 27 Jul, Padre Martini (78) dies 3 Aug, Paisiello *Il re Teodoro in Venezia* (WB) 23 Aug; Ries born 28 Nov
1785	29	'Haydn' quartets (K. 458, 464, 465). Piano concertos K. 466, 467, 482. Leopold Mozart visits Vienna Feb–Apr, meets Haydn. *Davidde penitente* (WB) 13 Mar. Masonic compositions. Begins *Le nozze di Figaro*	Pinto born 25 Sep, Salieri *La grotta di Trofonio* (WB) 12 Oct, Kalkbrenner born Nov
1786	30	*Der Schauspieldirektor* (Schönbrunn Orangerie) 7 Feb; Piano concertos K. 488, 491; *Idomeneo* (W Auersperg), one perf; *Le nozze di Figaro* (WB) 1 May. Johann Thomas Leopold born Oct, dies Nov. Piano concerto K. 503	Martín y Soler *Il burbero di buon core* (WB) 4 Jan, Sacchini *Oedipe à Colone* (Versailles) 4 Jan; František Benda (76) dies 7 Mar, Salieri *Prima la musica* 7 Feb, Ordonez (52) dies 6 Sept, Sacchini (56) dies 26 Oct; Martín *Una cosa rara* (WB) 17 Nov, Storace *Gli equivoci* (WB) 27 Dec
1787	31	Jan–Feb, in Prague for performances of *Figaro*; Symphony K. 504 ('Prague'). String quintets K. 515, 516. Leopold Mozart (67) dies 28 May. *Ein musikalische Spass*, *Eine kleine Nachtmusik*, last violin sonata K. 526. Prague, 1 Oct; *Don Giovanni* (Pr) 29 Oct;	Storaces, Kelly, Attwood leave Vienna, Feb; Beethoven visits Vienna, Apr; Starzer (59) dies 22 Apr; Salieri *Tarare* (PO) 8 Jun, Abel (63) dies 20 Jun; Martín *L'arbore di Diana* (WB) 1 Oct; Gluck (73) dies 15 Nov, Schweitzer (52) dies

1788	32	returns to Vienna, 7 Dec; appointed Imperial Kammermusikus. Theresia born 27 Dec

1788 32 *Don Giovanni* (WB) 7 May. Piano concerto K.537. Theresia dies 29 Jun. Jun–Aug, symphonies K. 543, 550, 551. Arranges Handel, *Acis and Galatea*, Nov

1789 33 Arranges Handel, *Messiah*, Jan Visits Prague, leaving 8 Apr, Dresden, Leipzig, Berlin, leaving there 28 May. *Figaro* revived (WB) 29 Aug; Anna Maria born and dies, 16 Nov; Clarinet quintet 22 Dec

1790 34 *Così fan tutte* (WB) 26 Jan; 'Prussian' quartets K. 589, 590 comp. 23 Sep–10 Nov, to Frankfurt for coronation of Leopold II: gives concerts, returns via Mainz, Mannheim, Augsburg, Munich. String quintet K. 593

1791 35 Piano concerto (K. 595) 4 Mar, String quintet K. 614; *Die Zauberflöte* comp, Jul. Commission for *La clemenza di Tito* and Requiem. Franz Xaver Wolfgang born 26 Jul. *La clemenza di Tito* (Pr) 6 Sep, *Die Zauberflöte* (WW) 30 Sep. Clarinet concerto comp, Oct; cantata K. 623 18 Nov; works on Requiem, but taken ill and dies 5 Dec; buried, 7 Dec

23 Nov; Haydn, Quartets op. 50 pub

Salieri *Axur, re d'Ormus* (WB) 8 Jan, Bonno (77) dies 15 Apr, Vogel (32) dies 28 Jun, C. P. E. Bach (74) dies 14 Dec. Joseph II declares war on Turkey

14 Jul, Paris, Bastille stormed. Salieri *La cifra* (WB) 11 Dec

Joseph II (49) dies 20 Feb, Beethoven Cantata on the death of Joseph II, Mar. Henneberg and others *Der Stein der Weisen* (WW) 11 Sep, Haydn leaves for London, Dec

Haydn in London: first 'London' symphonies. Albrechtsberger 55, Anfossi 64, Attwood 26, Beethoven 20, Jiří Benda 69, Burney 65, Cannabich 59, Cherubini 31, Clementi 39, Dalayrac 38, Da Ponte 42, Dittersdorf 52, Dussek 31, Eckard 56, Edelmann 41, Eybler 27, Freystädtler 30, Gazzaniga 48, Gerl 27, Gossec 57, Grétry 50, Gyrowetz 30, Joseph Haydn 58, Michael Haydn 54, Henneberg 31, Hoffmeister 37, Hummel 13, Kozeluch 44, Kraus 35, Martín y Soler 37, Mayr 27, Onslow 7, Paer 20, Paisiello 51, Philidor 65, Piccinni 63, Pinto 6, Reicha 21, Ries 7, Righini 35, Salieri 41, Sarti 63, Schikaneder 40, Spohr 7, Spontini 17, Storace 29, Süssmayr 25, Umlauf 45, Vanhal 52, Weber 15, Weigl 25, Winter 37, Wranitzky 35

List of Works

Key:
1. Stage works
   1.1 Operas; 1.2 Other stage works; 1.3 Music inserted into stage works by others
2. Other secular vocal works
   2.1 Concert scenas and arias; 2.2 Songs; 2.3 Ensembles; 2.4 Canons
3. Sacred works
   3.1 Masses, Requiem, sections of the Ordinary of the Mass; 3.2 Other liturgical music; 3.3 Shorter sacred works; 3.4 Masonic works; 3.5 Handel arrangements
4. Orchestral works
   4.1 Symphonies; 4.2 Concertos (a piano, b string, c wind); 4.3 Other orchestral (a Serenades, Divertimenti, Finalmusik, b Social dances, c Liturgical ('Epistle sonatas')
5. Chamber music
   5.1 Chamber music with piano (a Including wind instruments, b Strings and piano, c Keyboard and violin); 5.2 Chamber and ensemble music without piano (a Wind, b Wind and strings, c Strings only, d Bach arrangements)
6. Keyboard music
   6.1 Duets; 6.2 Solo piano (a Sonatas, b Variations, fantasias, smaller pieces, c Other instruments)

Note: While some unfinished works are included, lost and spurious works, fragments, sketches, and arrangements by other hands are omitted. The list is, as far as possible, chronological within each category. The date of completion is given if a work straddles two or more years. Köchel numbers are from the first and sixth editions in the form 51 = 46a; if one number appears, it was unchanged in the sixth edition; Anh. (Anhang) signifies appendix; [deest] means not in Köchel. More comprehensive lists in *The New Grove* and Landon (ed.), *Mozart Compendium* include the reasons for assigning dates. The most reliable sources are dated autographs and the catalogue (*Verzeichnüss*) kept by Mozart from 1784 (beginning with K. 449). Other factors—paper types, handwriting, ink studies—have been brought into play by recent scholarship and are referred to where appropriate.

Within each entry, different categories of work are allowed a different level of detail. The design of entries is indicated, unless it is unchanged from the previous section.

1. Stage music

1.1 Operas

Year	K. number	Title. Genre, no. of acts (librettist), place of premiere, date
1767	38	*Apollo et Hyacinthus.* Intermezzo, 3 (Widl), Salzburg, Benedictine University, 13 May
1768	51 = 46a	*La finta semplice.* Opera buffa, 3 (Goldoni, rev. Coltellini), planned for Vienna, perf. Salzburg, Archbishop's palace ?1 May 1769
	50 = 46b	*Bastien und Bastienne.* Singspiel, 1 (Weiskern and Müller, rev. Schachtner, after Favart), Vienna, Mesmer's theatre, Sep/Oct
1770	87 = 74a	*Mitridate, re di Ponto.* Opera seria, 3 (Cigna-Santi), Milan, Regio Ducal, 26 Dec
1771	111	*Ascanio in Alba.* Festa teatrale, 2 (Parini), Milan, Regio Ducal, 17 Oct, with ballet music K. Anh. 207 = Anh. C 27.06
1772	126	*Il sogno di Scipione.* Azione teatrale, 1 (Metastasio), Salzburg, Archbishop's palace, May
	135	*Lucio Silla.* Opera seria, 3 (De Gamerra), Milan, Regio Ducal, 26 Dec, with ballet *Le gelosie del seraglio* K. Anh. 109 = 135a
1775	196	*La finta giardiniera.* Opera buffa, 3 (?), Munich, Salvator, 13 Jan
	208	*Il re pastore.* Serenata, 2 (Metastasio), Salzburg, Archbishop's palace, 23 Apr
1779	344	Untitled: known as *Zaide.* Singspiel, ?3: unfinished (Schachtner, after Sebastiani). First perf. Frankfurt, 1866
1781	366	*Idomeneo, re di Creta.* Dramma per musica, 3 (Varesco, after Danchet), Munich, Rezidenztheater, 29 Jan (with ballet music, K. 367); Vienna version, 13 Mar. 1786, Auersperg palace, with duet K. 489, aria K. 490
1782	384	*Die Entführung aus dem Serail.* Singspiel, 3 (Stephanie, after Bretzner), Vienna, Burgtheater, 16 Jul
1783	422	*L'oca del Cairo.* Opera buffa, unf (Varesco)
1784	430 = 424a	*Lo sposo deluso.* Opera buffa, unf (? after Petrosellini)

1786	492	*Le nozze di Figaro*. Opera buffa, 4 (Da Ponte, after Beaumarchais), Vienna, Burgtheater, 1 May. Revived 29 Aug 1789, with arias K. 577, 579
1787	527	*Il dissoluto punito, ossia Il Don Giovanni*. Opera buffa, 2 (Da Ponte), Prague, National Theatre, 29 Oct. Vienna version, 7 May 1788, with arias K. 540a, b, and duet K. 540c
1790	588	*Così fan tutte, ossia La scuola degli amanti*. Opera buffa, 2 (Da Ponte), Vienna, Burgtheater, 26 Jan
1791	621	*La clemenza di Tito*. Opera seria, 2 (Mazzolà, after Metastasio), Prague, National Theatre, 6 Sep
	620	*Die Zauberflöte*. Singspiel, 2 (Schikaneder), Vienna, Theater auf der Wieden, 30 Sep

1.2 Other theatre works

ca. 1774–79?	345=336a	*Thamos, König in Aegypten*, incidental music, 5 (play by Gebler), ?Vienna; enlarged for Salzburg revivals ?1776, 1779
1778	Anh 10=299b	*Les petits riens*. Ballet (choreography Noverre), Paris, Académie royale de musique, 11 Jun[1]
	300	Gavotte, possibly intended for *Les petits riens*
1783	446=416d	Pantomime (commedia dell'arte), for strings, Vienna, Hofburg, 3 Mar; five mvts survive
1786	486	*Der Schauspieldirektor*, comedy (Stephanie) with musical numbers, Schönbrunn Orangery, 7 Feb

1.3 Numbers inserted into operas by other composers

Year	K. number	First line (work for which composed), voice type (singer) for whom composed; place[2]
1767?	70=61c	A Berenice . . . Sol nascente (?, Sarti, *Vologeso*), S; Salzburg ?or 1769
1775	209	Si mostra la sorte (for an *opera buffa*), T; Salzburg, 19 May
	210	Con ossequio, con rispetto (?Petrosellini, for Piccinni, *L'astratto*), T; Salzburg, May
	217	Voi avete un cor fedele (Goldoni, ?for Galuppi, *Le nozze di Dorina*), S; Salzburg, 26 Oct
1776	256	Clarice cara mia sposa (as K. 210), T; Salzburg, Sep
1783	418	Vorrei spiegarvi, oh Dio (Anfossi, *Il curioso indiscreto*), S (Aloysia Lange); Vienna, Burgtheater, 30 Jun

[1] Overture and thirteen numbers by Mozart.

[2] Texts separated by ellipses imply a scena, consisting of recitative . . . aria. Voice types: S, soprano (either female or castrato); A, alto; T, tenor; B, baritone/bass.

	419	No, che non sei capace (as 418)
	420	Per pieta, non ricercate (*Il curioso indiscreto*), T (Adamberger); as 418, but not performed
1785	479	Dite almeno in che mancai (quartet, Bertati, for Bianchi, *La villanella rapita*), S, T, B, B; Vienna, Burgtheater, 28 Nov
	480	Mandina amabile (trio), S, T, B, as K. 479
1788	541	Un bacio di mano (?Da Ponte, for Anfossi, *Le gelosio fortunate*), B (Francesco Albertarelli); Vienna, Burgtheater, 2 Jun
1789	578	Alma grande e nobil core (Palomba, for Cimarosa, *I due baroni*), S (Luisa Villeneuve), Burgtheater, Sep
	580	Schon lacht der holde Frühling (for German version of Paisiello, *Il barbiere*), S (Josepha Hofer), Vienna, 17 Sep, not used
	582	Chi sà qual sia (?Da Ponte, for Martín y Soler, *Il burbero di buon core*), S (Villeneuve); Burgtheater, 9 Nov
	583	Vado, ma dove? (as 582)
1790	[deest]	No caro fà corraggio (recitativo obbligato for aria by Cimarosa inserted in Guglielmi, *La Quakera spiritosa*), S; Vienna, Burgtheater, 13 Aug
	625=592a	Nun liebes Weibchen (duet, Schikaneder, for Henneberg et al., *Der Stein der Weisen*), S, B; Vienna, Theater auf der Wieden, Aug[3]

2. Other secular vocal works

2.1 *Arias and concert scenas*

Year	K. number	First line (librettist Metastasio unless otherwise stated, source of text), voice type (singer for whom composed if known); other information
1765	21=19c	Va, dal furor portata (*Ezio*), T; London
	23	Conservati fedele (*Artaserse*), S; The Hague
1766	36=33i	Or che il dover . . . Tali e cotanti sono (?), T; Salzburg, 21 Dec
	78=73b	Per pietà, bell'idol mio (*Artaserse*), S; The Hague
	79=73d	O temerario Arbace . . . Per quel paterno amplesso (*Artaserse*), S
1767/9?	[deest]	Cara, se le mie pene (?*Alessandro nell'Indie*), S; ?Olomouc/Salzburg

[3] On the possibility that Mozart wrote other sections of *Der Stein der Weisen* see p. 208; K. 625 is the only passage partly in Mozart's autograph.

1770	885 73c	Fra cento affanni (*Artaserse*), S; Milan, Mar?
	775 73e	Misero me . . . Misero pargoletto (*Demofoonte*), S; Milan, Mar
	825 73o	Se ardire, e speranza (*Demofoonte*), S; ?Rome, Apr
	835 73p	Se tutti i mali miei (*Demofoonte*), S; ?Milan or Rome, May[4]
1771	[deest]5 74b	Non curo l'affetto (*Demofoonte*), S; Milan or Pavia
1776	255	Ombra felice . . . Io ti lascio (?de Gamerra, *Arsace*), A (Francesco Fortini); Salzburg, Sep (the only aria for alto)
1777	272	Ah, lo previdi . . . Ah, t'invola agl'occhi miei (Cigna-Santi, *Andromeda*), S (Josepha Dušek); Salzburg
1778	294	Alcandro, lo confesso . . . Non sò d'onde viene (*L'olimpiade*), S (Aloysia Weber); Mannheim, 24 Feb
	295	Se al labbro mio non credi (?Salvi, for *Artaserse*), T (Anton Raaff); Mannheim, 27 Feb
	[deest]5 295a	Basta vincesti . . . Ah, non lasciarmi (*Didone abbandonata*), S (Dorothea Wendling); Mannheim, 27 Feb
1779	3165 300b	Popoli di Tessaglia . . . Io non chiedo (Calzabigi, *Alceste*), S (Weber); begun Paris, Jul 1778, finished Munich, 8 Jan
1780	368	Ma che vi fece . . . Sperai vicino (*Demofoonte*), S; Salzburg
1781	369	Misera, dove son! . . . Ah! Non son io (*Ezio*), S (Josepha, Countess Paumgarten); Munich, 8 Mar
	374	A questo seno . . . Or che il cielo (De Gamerra, *Sismano*), S (Francesco Ceccarelli); Vienna, 8 Apr
?1782	1195 382h	Der Liebe himmlisches Gefühl, S; Vienna[6]
1782	383	Nehmt meinen Dank, S (Aloysia Lange); Vienna, 10 Apr
	416	Mia speranza adorata . . . Ah, non sai (Sertor, *Zemira*), S (Lange); Vienna, Mehlgrube, 11 Jan
1783	4325 421a	Così dunque tradisci . . . Aspri rimorsi atroci (*Temistocle*), B (?Ludwig Fischer)
	4315 425b	Misero! O sogno . . . Aura, che intorno spiri (Mazzolà: *L'isola capricciosa*), T (Adamberger), Vienna, Dec

[4] For alternative dates see Anthony Pryer, 'Mozart's Operatic Audition. The Milan Concert, 12 March 1770: a Reappraisal and Revision', *Eighteenth-Century Music* I/2 (2004), 265–88.

[5] K1 deest. K2: 486a; corrected to 295a in K3.

[6] Only piano reduction of orchestra survives and no fully authenticated sources.

1786	505	Chi'io mi scordi di te . . . Non temer, amato bene (?, from Vienna *Idomeneo* revision, K. 490), S (Nancy Storace), with piano obbligato (Mozart); Vienna, 23 Feb 1787
1787	512	Alcandro, lo confesso . . . Non sò, d'onde viene (*L'olimpiade*), B (Fischer), Vienna, 19 Mar
	513	Mentre ti lascio (Angioli-Morbilli, *La disfatta di Dario*), B (Gottfried von Jacquin), Vienna, 23 Mar
	528	Bella mia fiamma . . . Resta, o cara (Scarcone, *Cenere placata*), S (Dušek), Prague, 3 Nov
	538	Ah se in ciel, benigne stele (*L'eroe cinese*), S (Lange); Vienna, 4 Mar, begun in 1778
1788	539	Ich möchte wohl der Kaiser sein (war song, Gleim), B (Friedrich Baumann), Vienna, 5 Mar
1789	584	Rivolgete a lui lo sguardo (Da Ponte), B (Francesco Benucci); Dec, for *Così fan tutte*; replaced by 'Non siate ritrosi'
1791	612	Per questa bella mano (?), B (Franz Gerl); Vienna, 8 Mar, with obbligato contrabass (Friedrich Pischelberger)

2.2 *Songs (voice and keyboard unless otherwise indicated)*

Year	K. number	Title ('first words': poet) or 'First words' (poet), place and time of composition; other information
1768	53 = 47e	*An die Freude* ('Freude, Königin der Weisen': Uz), with unfigured bass, Vienna (autumn)
1778	307 = 284d, 308 = 295b	'Oiseaux, si tous les ans' (Ferrand), 'Dans un bois solitaire' (de la Motte), Mannheim (early); for Elisabeth Augusta Wendling
1781	349 = 367a, 351 = 367b	*Die Zufriedenheit* ('Was frag' ich viel nach Geld und Gut': Miller), 'Komm, liebe Zither' (?), Munich (early); for Herr Lang (mandolin accompaniment)
1782	390 = 340c, 391 = 340b, 392 = 340a	'Ich würd' auf meinem Pfad mit Tränen', 'Sei du mein Trost', 'Verdankt sei es dem Glanz' (Hermes), Vienna (early, or 1781)
1785	472, 473, 474	*Der Zauberer* ('Ihr Mädchen, flieht Damöten ja!'), *Die Zufriedenheit* ('Wie sanft, wie ruhig'), *Die betrogene Welt* ('Der reiche Tor, mit Gold') (Weisse), Vienna (May)
	476	*Das Veilchen* ('Ein Veilchen auf der Wiese stand': Goethe), Vienna (Jun)
	506	*Lied der Freiheit* ('Wer unter eines Mädchens Hand': Blumenauer), Vienna (?late)

1787	517, 518, 519, 520	*Die Alte* ('Zu meiner Zeit': Hagedorn); *Die Verschweigung* ('Sobald Damötas Chloen sieht': Weisse), *Das Lied der Trennung* ('Die Engel Gottes weinen': Schmidt), *Als Luise die Briefe* ('Erzeugt von heisser Phantasie': von Baumberg), Vienna (May)
	523, 524	*Abendempfindung an Laura* ('Abend ist's': Campe), *An Chloe* ('Wenn die Lieb'': Jacobi), Vienna (24 Jun)
	529, 530	*Des kleinen Friedrichs Geburtstag* ('Es war einmal, ihr Leutchen': Schall), *Das Traumbild* ('Wo bist du, Bild': Hölty); the latter published as by Jacquin, Prague (6 Nov)
	531	*Die kleine Spinnerin* ('Was spinnst du?': in part Jäger), Vienna (11 Dec); children's song
1788	552	*Lied beim Auszug in das Feld* ('Dem hohen Kaiser-Worte treu': ?), Vienna (11 Aug)
1791	596, 597, 598	*Sehnsucht nach dem Frühling* ('Komm, lieber Mai': Overbeck), *Im Frühlingsanfang* ('Erwacht zum neuen Leben': Sturm), *Das Kinderspiel* ('Wir Kinder, wir schmecken der Freuden': Overbeck), Vienna (14 Jan)

2.3 *Vocal ensembles*

| 1786 | 441 | 'Liebes Mandel, wo ist's Bandel?' (S, T, B, strings), comic trio (?Mozart) |
| 1788[7] | 436, 437, 438, 439, 346/ 439a, 549 | Notturni (S, S, B, 3 b.-hns or 2 cl, b-hn; texts Metastasio or unknown): 'Ecco quell fiero istante' (*Canzonette*), 'Mi lagnerò tacendo' (*Siroe*), 'Se lontan, ben mio' (*Strofe per musica*); 'Due pupille amabile', 'Luci care, luci belle' (?), 'Più non si trovano' (*L'olimpiade*) |

2.4 *Canons*

1772	89=73i, k, r, x	Canons on sacred texts
1782	229–231, 233–4, 347–8=382a–g	Seven canons on various texts, some mildly obscene, Vienna
1786	508	Eleven canons (no texts), Vienna, after 3 Jun
1787	283=515b	Canon 4 in 2, Vienna, 24 Apr
	232=509a	Canon 'Lieber Freistädtler, lieber Gaulimauli' (Mozart), after 4 Jul

[7] Only K. 549 is entered in the Verzeichnüss with the date 16 Jul 1788.

| 1788 | 553–560 (560=559a), 561–562, 562a | 'Ave Maria', 'Alleluia', 'Lacrimoso son'io', 'Gre-chtelt's enk', 'Nascoso e il mio sol', 'Gehn wir im Prater', 'Difficile lectu mihi mars', 'O du eselhaf-ter Peierl', 'Bona nox! bist a rechta Ox', 'Caro bel idol mio'; untexted (German texts Mozart), Vienna, 2 Sep |
| ? | Anh. 191 | Canon a 4 in C (instrumental) |

3. Sacred works

3.1 Masses, Requiem, and texts from the Ordinary of the Mass

Year	K	Title (place: Salzburg unless otherwise indicated, date of composition if removed from performance date), performance
1766	33	Kyrie in F (Paris, 12 Jun)
1768	139=47a	Missa solemnis in c ('Waisenhausmesse'), (Vienna), 7 Dec (see also K. 34)
	49=47d	Missa brevis in G (Vienna, Nov)
1769	65=61a	Missa brevis in d (Salzburg, 14 Jan), 5 Feb
	66	Missa in C ('Dominicus'), Salzburg 15 Oct
1772	89=73k	Kyrie in G
	90	Kyrie in d
1773	140 [8]	Missa brevis in G
	167	Missa in C ('in honorem Sanctissimae Trinitatis', Jun)
1774	192=186f	Missa brevis in F, 22 Jun
	194=186h	Missa brevis in D, 8 Aug
1775	220=196b	Missa brevis in G ('Spatzenmesse')
	262=246a	Missa 'longa' in C (Jun–Jul)
1776	257	Missa in C ('Credo', Nov)
	258	Missa brevis in C ('Spaur' or 'Piccolominimesse', Dec, also dated 1775)
	259	Missa brevis in C ('Organ solo', Dec)
1777	275=272b	Missa brevis in B♭, 21 Dec
1779	317	Missa in C ('Coronation'), 23 Mar
1780	337	Missa solemnis in C, Mar
	341=368a	Kyrie in d (?Munich) [9]
1783	427=417a	Missa in c, unfinished (see also Davidde penitente), 26 Oct
1791	626	Requiem, d, unfinished

[8] Authenticity disputed; K3 235d; K6 Anh. C1.12.

[9] Alternative dating to ca.1788 is hypothetical. See pp. 83–84.

3.2 Other liturgical music

1771	109=74e	*Litaniae Lauretanae BVM in B♭ (May)*
1772	125	*Litaniae de venerabili altaris sacramento in B♭ (Mar)*
1774	195=186d	*Litaniae Lauretanae BVM in D (May)*
	193=186g	Dixit Dominus and Magnificat in C (Jul)
1776	243	*Litaniae de venerabili altaris sacramento in E♭ (Mar)*
1779	321	*Vesperae de Dominica*
1780	339	*Vesperae solennes de confessore*

3.3 Short sacred works: choral unless otherwise indicated

1765	20	Motet ('Chorus'), 'God is our refuge' (London)
1767	34	Offertory 'Scande coeli limina' (Kloster Seeon, Bavaria)[10]
?1768	47	Veni Sancte Spiritus in C
1768	117=66a	Offertory 'Benedictus sit Deus' (Vienna, 7 Dec)
1769	141=66b	Te Deum in C
1770	85=73s	Miserere in a (Bologna, Jul–Aug)
	86=73v	Antiphon 'Quaerite primum' (Bologna, 9–10 Oct)[11]
1771	108=74d	Antiphon 'Regina coeli' in C (May)
?1771	72=74f	Offertory 'Inter natos mulierum' (24 Jun)
1772	127[12]	Antiphon 'Regina coeli' in B♭ (May)
?1772	197	Tantum ergo in D
1772	143=73a	Motet 'Ergo interest' (S solo)
1773	165=158a	Motet 'Exsultate, jubilate' (S solo (Vincenzo Rauzzini), Milan, 17 Jan)
1774	198[13]	Offertory 'Sub tuum praesidium' (S, T)
1775	222=205a	Offertory 'Misericordias Domini' (Munich)
1776	260=248a	Offertory 'Venite populi'
1777	277	Offertory 'Alma Dei creatoris'
	273	Gradual 'Sancta Maria, mater Dei' (9 Sep)
?1779	146=317b	Aria 'Kommet her, ihr frechen Sünder'
?1779	276=321b	Antiphon Regina coeli in C
1787	343	Two German sacred songs 'O Gottes Lamm', 'Als aus Ägypten' (Prague/Vienna?)
1791	618	Motet 'Ave verum corpus' (Baden, 17 Jun)

[10] Authenticity doubtful, but possibly the same as the 'grand offertory' perf. Vienna, Waisenhaus (orphanage), with Mass K. 139/47a.

[11] Exercise for admission to Accademia Filarmonica, Bologna.

[12] Authenticity disputed; K3, Anh.186e; K6 Anh. C3.05.

[13] Authenticity disputed; K3, Anh.158be; K6 Anh. C3.08.

3.4 Other sacred vocal music

1767	35	*Die Schuldigkeit des ersten Gebotes*, Sacred drama, Part 1 (I.A. Weiser. Part 2 by J.M. Haydn, Part 3 by Adlgasser), 12 Mar
	42	*Grabmusik*, cantata, 7 Apr?;1 additional recitative and chorus, ca. 1772)
1771	118	*La Betulia liberata*, oratorio (Metastasio), for Padua, not performed
1785	469	*Davidde penitente*, oratorio (?Da Ponte), Vienna, Burgtheater, 13 Mar; music from C minor Mass K. 427, with two new arias

3.5 Masonic vocal music

1784[14]	147, 148	Two masonic songs, 'Wie unglücklich bin ich nit' (author unknown) and 'O heiliges Band' (Lenz)
1785	468	*Lied zur Gesellenreise* ('Die ihr einem neuen Grad') (von Ratschky), Vienna (Mar), voice and piano
	471	Cantata, *Die Maurerfreude* (Petran), Vienna, 24 Apr
	483, 484	Two masonic songs, with male chorus, 'Zerfliesset heut', geliebte Brüder', 'Ihr unsre neuen Leiter' (Schloissnig), Vienna, end of year
1791	619	Cantata, 'Die ihr des unermesslichen Weltalls Schöpfer ehrt' (S solo, piano), Vienna, Jul
	623	Cantata, 'Laut verkünde unsre Freude' (?Giesecke), Vienna, 15 Nov

3.6 Arrangements of choral works by Handel

1788	566	*Acis and Galatea*, Vienna, Nov
1789	572	*Messiah, Vienna*, Mar
1790	591, 592	*Alexander's Feast* and *Ode for St Cecilia's Day*, Vienna, Jul

4. Orchestral music

In symphonies and concertos, a standard orchestration is assumed of 2 oboes, 2 horns, a single bassoon (assumed even if a separate part is not included), and strings. Variants are indicated after + or − signs (+ bn(s) means a separate part is notated for bassoon(s)); [timp] means that timpani may be intended in symphonies including trumpets, although the part is not notated.

Abbreviations for instruments: fl, ob, c.a., cl, b-hn, bn, hn, tpt, timp, vn, vla, cello, db

---

[14] Handwriting studies have suggested a date up to twelve years earlier, but it is not clear why Mozart should have composed Masonic texts at that time.

4.1 Symphonies[15]

Year	K=K6	Key *= in three movements (number in Breitkopf edition).[16] Place Salzburg unless otherwise indicated, time of year if known; orchestration if not standard; other information
1764	16	E♭* (No.1) London, Oct–Dec
?	17=Anh.C11.02	B♭ (No.2); probably by Leopold
1765	Anh.223=19a	F* (deest) ?London, Feb–Apr
	19	D* (No.3) ?Holland
	22	B♭* (No.5) The Hague, Dec
1766	Anh.221=45a	G (deest) The Hague; ?revised Lambach, 1767[17]
?1767	Anh.214=45b	B♭* (deest) ?Salzburg
	95=73n	D (24.5). ?Salzburg
	76=42a	F (24.3) ?Vienna; perhaps spurious
1767	43	F (No. 6) Vienna/Olomouc, Oct–Dec
1768	45	D (No. 7) Vienna, Jan; + tpts, timp; reworked as sinfonia to *La finta semplice*
	48	D (No. 8) Vienna, 13 Dec
1769	deest	G (deest) ?Vienna late 1768 or Lambach, Jan; by Leopold?
	Anh.216=Anh.C.11.03	B♭ (24.63); of doubtful authorship
?1769	73	C (No.9) ?Salzburg or Italy; + tpts, timp; fl in slow mvt (sometimes dated ca. 1771–72)
	81=73l	D* (24.4); probably by Leopold
1770	97=73m	D (24.7), ?Rome; + tpts, timp. Possibly spurious
	84=73q	D* (No. 11), ?Milan, Bologna. Authenticity queried
	74	G* (No. 10), Rome. Italian overture form[18]

[15] The authorship of several symphonies attributed to Mozart is doubtful. A Symphony in A minor, identified as 'Mozart' in the Breitkopf catalogue, was 16a in K3 on the basis of the incipit. A complete copy (not autograph) appeared in Odense, Denmark, in 1986. Zaslaw concludes that it cannot definitely be attributed to either of the Mozarts (*Symphonies*, from 265).

[16] The traditional numbering is from the Breitkopf and Härtel Complete Edition, series 8. Works in that edition but registered within series 24 are not in the traditional numbering; these are indicated (e.g.) 24.3. Works not in the Breitkopf edition are marked (deest).

[17] Formerly known through the MS at Lambach and sometimes attributed to Leopold. See Zaslaw, *Symphonies*, 127–45.

[18] Italian overture form: no clear break after the first movement, which flows into the second.

?1771	96=111b	C (24.6), ?; + tpts, timp; uncertain date[19]
1771	75	F (24.2), ?Salzburg, summer; slow movement follows Minuet
	110 =75b	G (No. 12), Jul; fl in slow mvt
	111a	D★ Milan, Oct; + tpts, timp; finale (K. 120) added to sinfonia *Ascanio in Alba*
	112	F (No. 13) Milan, Nov
	114	A (No. 14) Dec; fl for ob in mvts 1, 3, 4
1772	124	G (No. 15) 21 Feb
	128	C★ (No. 16) May
	129	G★ (No. 17) May
	130	B♭★ (No. 18) May; 4 hns
	132	E♭ (No.19) Jul; 4 hns
	133	D (No. 20) Jul; + tpts, ?timp
	134	A (No. 21) Aug; fls not obs
	126/161 =141a	D★ date?; + fls, tpts, timp; finale (K.161) added to sinfonia *Il sogno di Scipione*
1773	184=161a	E♭★ (No. 26) 30 Mar; + fls, tpts, [timp]
	199=161b	G★ (No. 27) mid-Apr; fls not obs
	162	C★ (No. 22) late Apr; + tpts, [timp]
	181=162b	D★ (No. 19) 19 May; + tpts, [timp]
	182=173dA	B♭★ (No. 24) 3 Oct; fl for ob in slow mvt
	183=173dB	g (No. 25) 5 Oct; + bns, 4 hns
1774	201=186a	A (No. 29) 6 Apr
	202=186b	D (No. 30) 5 May; + tpts, [timp]
	200=189k	C (No. 28) mid-Nov; + tpts, timp
1778	297=300a, 'Paris'	D★ (No. 31) Paris, 18 Jun (perf.); + fls, cls, tpts, timp; alternative slow movements
1779	318	G (No. 32) 26 Apr; + fls, bns, 4 hns, tpts, timp
	319	B♭ (No. 33) 9 Jul; + bns
	320	D; symphony extracted from 'Posthorn' serenade
1780	338	C★ (No. 34) 29 Aug; + bns, tpts, timp
1782	385, 'Haffner'	D (No. 35), Vienna, Jul–Aug; + bns, tpts, timp; comp for Salzburg; second version (Vienna) + fls, cls
1783	425, 'Linz'	C (No. 36), Linz, Nov; + bns, tpts, timp
1784	444=425a = Anh.A.53	G (No. 37); slow introduction to a symphony by Michael Haydn
1786	504, 'Prague'	D★ (No. 38) Vienna, 6 Dec; + fls, bns, tpts, timp
1788	543	E♭ (No. 39) Vienna, 26 Jun; + fl, cls, no obs, bns, tpts, timp
	550	g (No. 40) Vienna, 25 Jul; + fl, bns; second version also + cls
	551, 'Jupiter'	C (No. 41) Vienna, 10 Aug; + fl, bns, tpts, timp

[19] Zaslaw suggests perhaps 1775.

4.2 Concertos

4.2a Piano concertos (comp Vienna and for Mozart's own performance unless otherwise indicated)

Year	K	Key (No. after Breitkopf edition), Place, time of year; orchestration
1767	37, 39, 40, 41	Four concertos adapted from movements by H. F. Raupach, J. Schobert, J. Honauer, G. Eckard, C.P.E. Bach
1772	107	Three concertos in D, G, E♭, adapted from sonatas by J. C. Bach (op. 5 Nos. 2–4)
1773	175	D (No. 5), Salzburg, Dec; + tpts, timp
1776	238	B♭ (No. 6), Salzburg, Jan; fls, 2nd mvt
	242	F, for three pianos (No. 7), Salzburg, Feb
	246	C (No. 8), Salzburg, Apr
1777	271	E♭ (No. 9), Salzburg, Jan; for Jenamy
1779	365	E♭, for two pianos (No. 10), Salzburg, ?early 1779; ?to perf. with Nannerl, later perf. by Mozart and Josepha Auernhammer, Vienna, 23 Nov 1781; later + cls, tpts, timp, of uncertain authenticity
1782	382	Rondo in D, ?Feb, substitute finale for K. 175; + fl
	414	A (No. 12), ?autumn; wind ad lib
	386	'Rondeaux' in A, 19 Oct; ?connected to K. 414; separate cello line
1783	413	F (No. 11), ?late 1782, ?perf. 11 Jan; wind ad lib
	415	C (No. 13), perf. 23 Mar; wind ad lib
1784	449	E♭ (No. 14), 9 Feb, for Ployer; wind ad lib
	450	B♭ (No. 15), 15 Mar, perf. 24 Mar; + fl, finale only
	451	D (No. 16), 22 Mar, perf. 31 Mar; + fl, tpts, timp
	453	G (No. 17), G, 12 Apr, for Ployer, perf. by her, Döbling, 13 Jun; +fl
	456	B♭ (No. 18), 30 Sep, ?for Paradis, perf. by her, Paris, Oct; + fl
	459	F (No. 19), 11 Dec; +fl, ?tpts, timp parts lost
1785	466	d (No. 20), 10 Feb, perf. 11 Feb; +fl, tpts, timp
	467	C (No. 21), Feb, perf. 10 Mar; +fl, tpts, timp
	482	E♭ (No. 22), 16 Dec, ?perf. 23 Dec; cls, no obs; +fl, tpts, timp
1786	488	A (No. 23), 2 Mar; cls, no obs; +fl; begun 1784
	491	c (No. 24), 24 Mar, ?perf. 7 Apr; + fl, cls., tpts, timp
	503	C (No. 25), 4 Dec, perf. 5 Dec; + fl, tpts, timp
1788	537	D (No. 26), 24 Feb, perf. Dresden 14 Apr 1789 and Frankfurt 15 Oct 1790; + fl, tpts, timp; 'Coronation'

| 1791 | 595 | B♭ (No. 27), 5 Jan, perf. 4 Mar. at Beer's concert; + fl; begun 1788 |

4.2b String concertos, comp Salzburg unless otherwise indicated

1773	207	Violin, B♭ (No. 1), 14 Apr
1774	190=186e	C, 2 vn, ob, cello, 31 May; + tpts [timp]; Concertone
1775	211	vn, D (No. 2), 14 Jun
	216	vn, G (No. 3), 12 Sep; fls for obs in slow mvt
	218	vn, D (No. 4), Oct[20]
	219	vn., A (No. 5 Turkish), 20 Dec
1776	261	Adagio, vn, E, ?to replace 2nd mvt K. 219
1777	269	'Rondeaux', vn, B♭, ?1775; ?replacement finale K. 207
1779	364	Sinfonia concertante, vn, va. E♭, ?late summer[21]
1781	373	Rondo, vn, C (Vienna, 2 Apr), perf. Antonio Brunetti 8 Apr

4.2c Wind concertos

1774	191	Bassoon, B♭, Salzburg, 4 Jun[22]
1777	314=271k	Oboe, C, Salzburg, mid-year; for Giuseppe Ferlendis
1778	313=285c	Flute, G, Mannheim, Jan–Feb; + 2 fl 2nd mvt; for Ferdinand Dejean
	314=285d	Flute, D, as K. 313; transcription of oboe concerto
	315=285e	Andante, fl, C (as K. 313, ?alternative 2nd mvt)
	299=297c	Flute and harp, C, Paris, Apr; for Comte and Mlle de Guines
1783	417	Horn, E♭, Vienna, 27 May; for Leutgeb
1786	495	Horn, E♭, Vienna, 26 Jun; for Leutgeb
1787	447	Horn, E♭, Vienna, undated; cls, no obs; for Leutgeb
1791	622	Clarinet (originally basset clarinet), A (Vienna, Oct); for Stadler[23]
	412=386b	Horn, D (Vienna, unfinished): 1st mvt, draft of rondo finale; for Leutgeb

[20] K. 218 may be the Strasburg concerto referred to by Mozart in letters, but K. 216 is also possible.

[21] K. 364 is sometimes thought to have been for Mozart to play with his father but more likely soloists were Brunetti and Joseph Hafeneder.

[22] Bassoon concerto: no dedication, probably not one of three allegedly comp for Baron von Dürnitz.

[23] First draft probably 1787: incomplete first movement with solo b-hn in G; before end of the draft the string parts are written a tone too high, suggesting that Mozart had mentally changed key to A.

4.3 Other orchestral

4.3a Serenades, Divertimenti, and miscellaneous orchestral music

1766	32	Galimathias musicum, Den Haag
1769	100=62a	Serenade in D, Salzburg, ?Aug;[24] + fls, tpts [timp]
	63	Cassation in G, Salzburg, ?Aug
	99=63a	Cassation in B♭, Salzburg
1771	113	Divertimento in E♭, Milan, Nov; standard orch, but a 2nd version + cls, c.a., bns
1772	136-3	Three divertimenti in four parts (?solo quartets)
	131	Divertimento in D, Salzburg, Jun; + fl, 4 hns[25]
1773	205=167A	Divertimento in D, Salzburg, ?Jul; hns, bn, str poss. with March, K. 290=167AB; hns, str
	185=167a	Serenade (Finalmusik) in D, Salzburg=Vienna, Aug; + fls, tpts, [timp], with March, K. 189=167b
1774	203=189b	Serenade (Finalmusik) in D, Salzburg, ?Aug; + bn, tpts, [timp]; March K. 237=189c
1775	204=213a	Serenade (Finalmusik) in D, Salzburg, 5 Aug; + fl, bn, tpts, [timp]; March K. 215=213b
	214	March in C, Salzburg, 20 Aug; + tpts [timp]
1776	239	Serenade in D (Serenata notturna), Salzburg, Jan; str and timp
	247	Serenade in F, Salzburg, Jun; hns, str; March K. 250=248b, Jul; + bns, tpts; March. K. 248, hns, str
	250=248b	Serenade in D (Haffner), Salzburg, perf. 21 Jul; + fl, bns, tpts, [timp]; March K. 249, 20 Jul, same orch
	251	Divertimento in D, Salzburg, ?26 Jul
	286=269a	Notturno in D, Salzburg, ?Dec (Jan 1777) for four orchestras (each hns, str)
1777	287=271H	Divertimento in B♭, Salzburg, perf. 16 Jun, for Countess Lodron; hns, str
1779	320	Serenade (Finalmusik) in D ('Posthorn'), Salzburg, 3 Aug; + fls, bns, tpts, posthorn, timp; two marches K. 335=320a
1780	334=320b	Divertimento in D, Salzburg (or ?1779), ?for Robinig family; hns, str; March K. 445=320c

---

[24] It is possible that some or all the 1769 pieces, and the D major March K. 62 which is reused in *Mitridate*, were intended as 'Finalmusik' for 6 or 8 Aug, but there is no direct evidence.

[25] Possibly 'Finalmusik', but unusually without trumpets and an associated march.

1782	408 (1, 3) =383e, F	Two Marches in C, probably Vienna
	409=383f	Minuet in C, Vienna; + fls, bns, tpts, timp
	408 (2)=385a	March in D, Vienna, Aug; + bns, tpts, timp; for use with 'Haffner' Symphony in Salzburg
1785	477=479a	*Mauerische Trauermusik* in c, Vienna, Nov, for memorial to Count Esterházy von Galantha and Duke of Mecklenburg-Strelitz; obs, cl, 3 b-hn, dbn, hns, strings
1787	522	*Ein musikalischer Spass* [A Musical Joke], Vienna, 14 Jun; hns, strings
	525	*Eine kleine Nachtmusik* (Serenade in G), Vienna, 10 Aug; strings
1788	546	Adagio and Fugue, c, Vienna, 26 Jun; strings arr. of K. 426 for two pianos

4.3b Social dances

1769	[deest]=61b	7 minuets (str), Salzburg
1770	[deest]=61g	2 minuets (fls, str), early in the year, Italy
	122=73t	Minuet in E♭ (obs, hns, str), possibly inauthentic, Bologna, Mar
	123=73g	Contredanse in B♭ (obs, hns, str), Rome, Apr
	104=61e	8 minuets (pic, obs, hns/tpts, str) autumn
1772	164=130a	6 minuets (fl, obs, hns/tpts, str), Salzburg, Jun
1772	103=61d	19 minuets (obs (fls), hns (tpts), str), Salzburg, summer (originally 20: later recast as 12)
1773	176	16 minuets (obs/fls, bn, hns/tpts, str), Salzburg, Dec
?1776	101=250a	4 'contredanses' (obs/fls, bn, hns, str), Salzburg; 1 and 4 are gavottes, 2 and 3 marked Andantino and Presto
1777	267=271c	4 contredanses (obs/fls, bn, hns/tpts, str), Salzburg
1783	363	3 minuets (obs, bns, hns, tpts, str), ?Salzburg, summer
	462=448b	6 contredanses (obs, hns, str), probably Salzburg, summer
	463=448c	2minuets (obs, hns, str), ?Salzburg, summer[26]
1784	461	6minuets (obs/fls, bns, hns, str), Vienna ?Carnival; No. 6 incomplete
1787	509	6 German dances (pic, fls, obs, cls, bns, hns, tpts, timp, str), Prague, 6 Feb

[26] The autograph of the contredanses K. 462 is dated 1784, but not in Mozart's hand; there is a musical link to K. 363, and some of the paper of K. 463 is the same, suggesting a close date of composition.

1788[27]	534, 535, 535a	2 contredanses, in D (pic, obs, hns, side drum, str), Vienna, 14 Jan, and in C, 'La Battaille' (pic, cls, bn, tpt, side drum, str), Vienna, 23 Jan; K. 535a, 3 contredanses orchestration lost, exist only in keyboard version
	536	6 German dances (pic, fls, obs/cls, bns, hns/tpts, timp, str), Vienna, 27 Jan
	567	6 German dances (pic, fls, obs/cls, bns, hns, tpts, timp, str), Vienna, 6 Dec
	568	12 minuets (fls/pics, obs/cls, bns, hns, tpts, timp, str), Vienna, 24 Dec
1789	571	6 German dances (fls/pics, obs/cls, bns, hns/tpts, timp, Turkish perc. (No.6), str), Vienna, 21 Feb
1789	585	12 minuets (fls/pics, obs/cls, bns, hns, tpts, timp, str), Vienna, Dec
	586	12 German dances
	587	Contredanse in C 'Die Sieg vom Helden Coburg'
?1790	106=588a	3 contredanses perhaps not for Redoutensaal, doubtful
1791	599	6 minuets, Vienna, 23 Jan
	600	6 German dances, Vienna, 29 Jan
	601	4 minuets (hurdy-gurdy), Vienna, 5 Feb
	602	4 German dances (hurdy-gurdy), Vienna, 5 Feb
	603	2 contredanses, Vienna, 5 Feb
	604	2 minuets, Vienna, 12 Feb
	605	3 German dances (with sleighbells in Trio of No. 3), Vienna, 12 Feb
	607=605a	Contredanse in E♭ 'Il trionfo delle donne', Vienna, 28 Feb
	606	6 German dances, Vienna, 28 Feb
	609	5 contredanses (fl, side drum, str), possibly earlier, end of 1787–88 if for Redoutensaal
	610	Contredanse in G, ?Salzburg summer 1783; *Les filles malicieuses*,[28] entered in Mozart's catalogue 6 March 1791
	611	German dance in C, Vienna, 6 March

4.3c Instrumental music for the liturgy (Epistle sonatas)

1772	67, 68–69	Three sonatas in E♭, B♭, D
1773	144	Two sonatas in D, F

---

[27] From January 1788, the dances were all, or nearly all, composed for the Redoutensaal in Vienna, and were required of Mozart in his role as Imperial Kammermusikus.

[28] The paper appears wrong for 1791. Tyson, 'New dates', 225.

1774	212	Sonata in B♭
1775	212	Sonatas in B♭
1776	241, 244, 245, 263	Four sonatas in G, F, D, C
1777	274, 278	2 sonatas in G, C
1779	329, 328	2 sonatas in C, C
1780	224, 225, 336	3 sonatas in F, A, C

5 Chamber music (publication details: unless indicated, year of publication = year of composition and place of publication is Vienna)

5.1 Chamber music with piano[29]

5.1a Works including wind instruments

1784	452	Quintet in E♭, Vienna, Mar; ob, cl, hn, bn, piano
1786	498	Trio in E♭ ('Kegelstatt'), Vienna, Aug; cl, va, piano
1791	617	Adagio and Rondo in C, Vienna, 23 May; fl, ob, va, cello, glass harmonica, for Kirchgässner, perf 19 Aug[30]

5.1b Chamber music for strings and piano

1764	10–15	6 trios in B♭, G, A, F, C, B♭, London; pub. 1765 as op. 3; vn or fl, cello, keyboard
1776	254	Trio (divertimento a 3) in B♭, Salzburg, Aug; pub. Paris ca.1782 as op. 3
1785	478	Quartet in g, Vienna, Oct; pub. Hoffmeister, ?1786; vn, va, cello, piano
1786	493	Quartet in E♭, Vienna, Jun; pub. Artaria, 1787 as op. 13; vn, va, cello, piano
	496	Trio in G, Vienna, Jul; pub. Hoffmeister, 1786; vn, cello, piano
	502	Trio in B♭, Vienna, Nov; pub. Artaria, 1788 as op. 15 no. 1; vn, cello, piano
1788	542	Trio in E, Vienna, Jun; pub. as op. 15 no. 2; vn, cello, piano
	548	Trio in C, Vienna, Jul; pub. as op. 15 no. 3; vn, cello, piano
	564	Trio in G, Vienna, Oct; pub. London, 1789; vn, cello, piano

[29] Piano is used throughout but in earlier works harpsichord is probable; Mozart usually writes 'clavier'.

[30] The performance date has been claimed as 10 Jun when Kirchgässner gave a concert in the Burgtheater. If Mozart's *Verzeichnüss* is to be trusted, the piece would have been ready, but documentary evidence exists only for the Aug performance in the Kärntnertor theatre.

5.1c For keyboard and violin

1762–4	6, 7	Two sonatas in C, D; pub. Paris, 1764 as op. 1
1763–4	8, 9	Two sonatas in B♭, G; pub. Paris, 1764 as op. 2
1766	26–31	Six sonatas in E♭, G, C, D, F, B♭, The Hague, Feb; published Amsterdam, 1766 as op. 4
1778	296	C, Mannheim, Mar c,; No. 2 of six sonatas, pub. Vienna: Artaria, 1781, in op. 2
	301 = 293a	Sonata in G, Mannheim, early 1778; first of six sonatas (K. 301–306) dedicated to electress of the Palatinate, pub. Paris, 1778 as op. 1
	302 = 293b	Sonata in E♭, as K. 301
	303 = 293c	Sonata in C, as K. 301
	304 = 300c	Sonata in e, Mannheim and Paris, spring
	305 = 293d	Sonata in A, Paris, summer 1778
	306 = 300l	Sonata in D, as K. 305
1780	378 = 317d	Sonata in B♭, ?Salzburg or Munich, early 1781; pub. with K. 296 as op. 2 no. 4
1781	359 = 374a	Variations in G on *La bergère Célimène'*, Vienna, ?May–Jun, pub. Artaria, 1786
	360 = 374b	Variations in g on *Au bord d'une fontaine* ('Hélas! J'ai perdu mon amant'), Vienna, Jun, pub. Artaria, 1786
	379 = 373a	Sonata in G, Vienna, Apr and early summer, pub. Artaria, 1781, as op. 2 (No. 5)
	376 = 374d	Sonata in F, as K. 379 (op. 2 no. 1)
	377 = 374e	Sonata in F, as K. 379 (op. 2 no. 3)
	380 = 374f	Sonata in E♭, as K. 379 (op. 2 no. 6)
?1782–3	396 = 385f	Fantasia (sonata mvt) in c, completed for posthumous publication as piano solo
1784	454	B♭, Vienna, Apr; pub. Torricella, 1784, as op. 7 no. 3
1785	481	E♭, Vienna, Dec; pub. Hoffmeister, 1786)
1787	526	A, Vienna, Aug; pub. Hoffmeister, 1787
1788	547	F, Vienna, Jul; 'for beginners'

5.2 Ensemble and chamber music without piano

5.2a Wind ensemble

1773	186 = 159b	Divertimento in B♭ (obs, cls, c.as, hns, bns), Milan or Salzburg, ?Mar
	166 = 159d	Divertimento in E♭ (obs, cls, c.as, hns, bns), Salzburg, Mar
	188 = 240b	Divertimento in C (fls, 5 tpts, 4 timp), Salzburg, middle of the year
1775	213	Divertimento in F (obs, hns, bns), Salzburg, Jul
1776	240	Divertimento in B♭ (obs, hns, bns), Salzburg, Jan

	252=240a	Divertimento in E♭ (obs, hns, bns), ?by Aug
	253	Divertimento in F (obs, hns, bns), Aug
1777	270	Divertimento in B♭ (obs, hns, bns), Jan
1781, 1782	375	Serenade in E♭ (obs, cls, hns, bns), first version (without oboes), Vienna, before mid-Oct; second version probably 1782, Jul
1782	388=384a	Parthia (Serenade) in c (obs, cls, hns, bns), Vienna; later arr. as string quintet K. 406
1781-2	361=370a	Serenade ('gran Partitta') in B♭ (obs, cls, b-hns, 4 hns, bns, string bass), uncertain date
1782?	410=440d	Adagio in F (b-hns, bn), Vienna
1782-3?	411=484a	Adagio in B♭ (cls, 3 b-hns), Vienna
1782-5?	Anh.229= 439b	5 divertimentos (3 b-hns), Vienna, pub. as for cls, bn; b-hns, bn, etc.
1782	[384]	Transcription of *Die Entführung* (obs, cls, hns, bns), Jul
1786	487=496a	12 duets (hns), Vienna, Jul; each in one mvt

5.2b Wind and strings

1775	292=196c	Sonata in B♭ (bn, vc), Munich, early in the year[31]
1777	285	Flute quartet in D (fl, vn, va, cello), Mannheim, Dec; for Dejean)
1778	285a	Flute quartet in G, Mannheim, by Feb; as K. 285
1781	370=368b	Oboe quartet in F (ob, vn, va, cello), Munich; for Ramm
1782	Anh.171= 285b	Flute quartet in C (Vienna; second mvt arr. from K. 361)
	407	Horn quintet in E♭ (hn, vn, 2 va, cello), Vienna, ?late 1782; for Leutgeb
1786	298	Flute quartet in A, Vienna, ?early 1787; ?for Jacquin
1789	581	Clarinet quintet in A (cl, 2 vn, va, cello), Vienna, Sep; for Anton Stadler

5.2c Strings only (quartets 2 vn, va, cello; quintets 2 vn, 2 va, cello)

1768	46d–e	Duets (vn, bass), Vienna, Sep
1770	80	Quartet, G, Lodi, Mar; Rondeau added, ?1773–74
1772	136–138 =125a-c	3 divertimenti (string quartet), D, B♭, F, Salzburg, early in the year; poss. for orchestral performance[32]

[31] If authentic, possibly a work for two bns, but earliest source as given here (Berlin: Hummel, ca.1800).

[32] The title 'Divertimento' often refers to music performed one to a part.

1772-3	155–60 = 134a,b, 157–59, 159a	6 quartets, D, G, C, F, B♭, E♭, Bolzano, Verona, Milan, Oct–early 1773
1773	168–73	6 quartets, F[33], A, C, E♭, B♭, d, Vienna, Aug–Sep
	174	Quintet in B♭, Salzburg, Dec
1777	266	Trio (2 vn, bass) in B♭, Salzburg
1782	387	Quartet in G, Vienna, Dec; partly fugal finale; first of 6 'Haydn' quartets, pub. Artaria, 1785 as Op.10
1783	421 = 417b	Quartet in d, Jun; second 'Haydn' quartet
	428 = 421b	Quartet in E♭, Vienna-Salzburg, ?Jun–Jul; third 'Haydn' quartet
1783	423-4	Duets (vn, va) in G, B♭, Salzburg, Jul–Oct; comp to help Michael Haydn
1784	458	Quartet in B♭, Nov; 'Hunt', fourth Haydn quartet
1785	464	Quartet in A, Jan; fifth 'Haydn' quartet
	465	Quartet in C, Jan; 'Dissonance', sixth 'Haydn' quartet
1786	499	Quartet in D, Vienna, Aug; 'Hoffmeister' quartet
1787	515	Quintet in C, Vienna, Apr; pub. Artaria, 1789
	516	Quintet in g, Vienna, May; pub. Artaria, 1790
1788	406 = 516b	Quintet in c, Vienna; arr. from wind octet (K. 388)
	563	Trio (vn, va, cello) in E♭ ('Divertimento'), Vienna, Sep
1789	575	Quartet in D, Vienna, Jun; first 'Prussian' quartet
1790	589	Quartet in B♭, Vienna, May; second 'Prussian' quartet
	590	Quartet in F, Vienna, Jun; third 'Prussian' quartet
	593	Quintet in D, Vienna, Dec
1791	614	Quintet in E♭, Vienna, Apr

5.2d Arrangements of music by the Bachs, with original preludes

1782	[deest] = 404a	6 preludes and fugues in d, g, F, F, E♭, f (vn, va, cello), [one of the F originally F♯], the last by W. F. Bach, the rest by J. S. Bach; original preludes to the first three and the last; Vienna, for van Swieten
	405	Five fugues in c, E♭, e, d, D (string quartet), from J. S. Bach

---

[33] Additional Minuet, K.168a, ?1775.

6 Keyboard music

6.1 Duets for two pianos and piano duet (four hands on one keyboard)

1765	Deest=19d	Sonata in C, piano duet, London, summer
1772	381=123a	Sonata in D, piano duet, Salzburg
1773–74	358=186c	Sonata in B♭, piano duet, Salzburg
1781	448=375a	Sonata in D, two pianos, Vienna, Nov, perf. with Josepha Auernhammer
1783	426	Fugue in c, two pianos, Vienna; arr. for strings, 1788, see K. 546
1786	497	Sonata in F, piano duet, Vienna, 1 Aug
	501	Andante with variations in G, piano duet, Vienna, 4 Nov
1787	521	Sonata in C, piano duet, Vienna, 29 May, for Francesca von Jacquin

6.2 Solo piano:

6.2a Sonatas

1775	279–84 = 189d, e, f, g, h, 205b	Six sonatas in C, F, B♭, E♭, G, D, Munich, early in the year; K. 284 for Baron Thaddäus von Dörnitz, pub. Vienna: Torricella, 1784, as op. 7 no. 2
1777	309=284b	Sonata in C, Mannheim, late 1777; for Rosa Cannabich
	311=284c	Sonata in D
1778	310=300d	Sonata in a, Paris, summer
1783	330–32 = 300h,i,k	Three sonatas in C, A, F, ?Salzburg, Jul–Oct; K. 331 in A with finale alla turca
	333=315c	Sonata in B♭, ?Linz; pub. Vienna: Torricella, 1784 as op. 7 no. 1
1784	457	Sonata in c, Vienna, 14 Oct; pub. with Fantasia K. 475
1786–88	533 and 494	Sonata in F, Vienna; Rondo K. 492 Vienna, 1786; mvts 1 and 2, 1788; pub. Vienna, 1788
1788	545	Sonata in C, Vienna; 'for beginners'
1789	570	Sonata in B♭, Vienna, Feb; pub. 1796 with spurious violin part)
	576	Sonata in D, Vienna, Jul

6.2b Variations, fantasias, and other pieces for solo keyboard

| 1761 | [deest]=1a-f[34] | Andante in C, 2 Allegros in C, F, 3 Minuets in F, G (K. 1), C |

[34] K1 in the first edition is the Minuet in G.

1762	2–5	3 Minuets in F, Allegro in B♭
	9a=5a	Allegro in C, summer
1766	Anh.208=24	Variations on 'Laat ons Juichen' (C. E. Graaf), The Hague, Jan; published The Hague, 1766
		Variations on 'Willem van Nassau', Amsterdam, Feb.
	deest=33B	Untitled piece in F, Zürich, Oct
1769	94=73h	Minuet in D, Salzburg
1770	deest=61gII	Minuet in C
1772	180=173c	Variations on 'Mio caro Adone' (Salieri, *La fiera di Venezia*)
1773	Deest=315g	8 Minuets arr. from lost orchestral version
1774	179=189a	Variations on a Minuet by Fischer, Salzburg, summer
1777	395=300g	Prelude (Capriccio) in C, Munich, Oct; for Nannerl
1778	354=299a	Variations on 'Je suis Lindor' (Baudron, for *Le Barbier de Séville*), Paris, early summer
	264=315d	Variations on 'Lison dormait' (Dezède, *Julie*), Paris, late summer
1781	352=374c	Variations on 'Dieu d'amour' (Grétry, *Les Mariages samnites*)
1781–2	265=300e	Variations on 'Ah, vous dirai-je, Maman', Vienna; previously thought to have been comp in Paris
	353=300f	Variations on 'La belle Françoise'
1782	394=383a	Prelude and fugue in C, Vienna, Apr
?1782	397=385g	Fantasia in d, unf.; completed for publication, 1804
	399=385i	Suite (Overture, Allemande, Courante, unf. Sarabande)
1783	398=416e	Variations on 'Salve tu, Domine' (Paisiello, *I filosofi immaginarii*)
1784	453a	Marche funebre del Sigr Maestro Contrapunto
	455	Variations on 'Unser dummer Pöbel meint' (Gluck, *Die Pilgrimme von Mekka*), Vienna, 25 Aug
1785	475	Fantasia in c, Vienna, 20 May; published with Sonata K. 457
1786	485	'Rondo' (sonata mvt) in D, 10 Jan
	500	Variations in B♭, ?on original theme, Vienna, 12 Sep
1787	511	Rondo in a, Vienna, 11 Mar
1788	540	Adagio (sonata mvt) in b, Vienna, 19 Mar
	54=547a-b	Variations in F, ?on original theme, Vienna, Jul
1789	573	Variations on Minuet (Duport, cello sonata), Potsdam, 29 Apr
	574	'Eine kleine Gigue' in G, Leipzig, 16 May
	355=576b	Minuet in D, Vienna, date uncertain
?1790	236=588b	Theme by Gluck in E♭ intended for variations?

| 1791 | 613 | Variations on 'Ein Weib ist das herrlichste Ding' (Schack or Gerl, from *Der dumme Gärtner*), Vienna, Mar |

6.2c Works for other instruments

1790	594	Adagio and Allegro, f, for mechanical organ, Vienna, Oct–Dec
1791	356=617a	Adagio, C, for glass harmonica, Vienna ?May
	608	Fantasia, f, for mechanical organ, Vienna, 3 Mar
	616	Andante in F, for mechanical organ, Vienna, 4 May

Personalia

Those listed are Austrian or German unless otherwise stated.

Adamberger, Johann Valentin (1740–1804), tenor, the first Belmonte, principal tenor with the Nationalsingspiel from 1780. His teacher was Valesi (q.v.). He and Mozart became friends. Mozart wrote him the arias K. 420 and 431, and one in *Davidde penitente*. He took part in *Der Schauspieldirektor* (his wife, Maria Anna, had a speaking role), and as a Mason, he performed some of Mozart's Masonic music.

Adlgasser, Anton Cajetan (1729–77), Salzburg composer, court and cathedral organist and friend of the Mozarts. He composed part of *Die Schuldigkeit des ersten Gebots* with Mozart and Michael Haydn. In 1779 Mozart succeeded him as organist.

Albertarelli, Francesco (?), Italian baritone, title-role in the Vienna production of *Don Giovanni* (1788). Mozart wrote him the aria K. 541. He left for London in 1790.

Albrechtsberger, Johann Georg (1736–1809), composer, theorist, and teacher esteemed by Mozart. He moved to Vienna in 1767. He became organist at St Stephan's in 1793, the post Mozart would have inherited. He instructed Beethoven in counterpoint, and taught Eybler (q.v.), Hummel (q.v.), and Mozart's younger son.

Amicis, Anna Lucia de (1733–1816), Italian soprano, Giunia in *Lucio Silla*. She had met Mozart in 1763, at Mainz, impressed him in Naples in 1770, and was an important factor in the success of Mozart's opera.

André, Johann Anton (1775–1842), publisher (also composer), who after Mozart's death purchased several manuscripts and published many of them.

Arco, Counts Johann George (1705–92) and his son Karl Joseph (1743–1810), court officials in Salzburg. The father supported Mozart; the son tried to persuade Mozart, in 1781, to remain in the archbishop's employment, before kicking him out.

Artaria, family of Italian origin, in Vienna from 1766, dealing in art and publishing music, including Mozart's sonatas (1781), keyboard music, songs, the quartets dedicated to Haydn, and the quintets K. 515 and 516. Artaria continued publishing Mozart's works into the nineteenth century.

Attwood, Thomas (1765–1838), English composer. The Prince of Wales (later George IV) sponsored his visit to Italy and Vienna; in 1785–86 he studied harmony, counterpoint, and composition with Mozart before returning home with the Storaces (q.v.). During his long career as organist and composer, he promoted Mozart in England and later befriended Mendelssohn.

Auernhammer, Josepha (1758–1820), pianist and composer. Her father Johann Michael (d. 1782) helped Mozart on his arrival in Vienna. Mozart taught Josepha, and respected her musicianship sufficiently to perform with her the two-piano sonata K. 448; he dedicated his first Vienna publication to her.

Auersperg, noble Viennese family, whose private theatre presented many productions using amateur singers, including the 1786 revival of *Idomeneo*.

Bach, Johann Christian (1735–82), composer, youngest son of J. S. and Anna Magdalena Bach. He studied with his half-brother Carl Philip Emanuel, then with Padre Martini, before settling in England in 1762, becoming known as 'the London Bach' and befriending the Mozarts there. His vocal and instrumental music had a profound effect on Mozart; they last met in Paris in 1778.

Baglioni, Antonio (?), Italian tenor, joined the Prague company in 1787 and was the first Don Ottavio; he created the role of Tito in 1791.

Barisani, Salzburg family of Italian origin, friends of the Mozarts. Silvestro (1719–1810) was the archbishop's doctor from 1766; his son Johann (1756–1826) was Leopold's doctor; Sigmund (1758–87) moved to Vienna and was Wolfgang's doctor; the composer was deeply affected by his early death.

Barrington, Daines (1727–1800), English lawyer of distinguished family, barrister, and Fellow of the Royal Society, to which he reported on the prodigies Mozart and Crotch.

Bassi, Luigi (1766–1825), Italian baritone, the first Don Giovanni. With the Prague opera company from 1784 to 1806, he previously sang the count in *Figaro*. His voice lay 'between tenor and bass'. He was considered an excellent actor; his singing received mixed reactions.

Bedini, Domenico (?), Italian castrato. He had been on the stage for at least twenty years when he created the role of Sesto in *La clemenza di Tito* (Prague, 1791).

Becke, Johann Baptist (?), flautist at Munich, friend of the Mozarts; he came to Salzburg for *Il re pastore* in 1775, corresponded with Leopold, comforted Mozart before his return to Salzburg in 1779, and wrote to Leopold in an attempt to turn away his wrath.

Beecke, Ignaz (1733–1803), pianist and composer who encountered Mozart in Paris (1764), then ten years later in Munich, where they played in competition at Franz Joseph Albert's inn *Zum schwarzen Adler*. There were further meetings in 1777 and 1790, when they played a concerto arrangement, probably in Mainz although, as with Clementi, Mozart was not complimentary about his 'rival'.

Benucci, Francesco (ca. 1745–1824), Italian bass, the first Figaro. He was *primo buffo* in Vienna from 1783 for ten years, creating roles by Salieri, including Axur, and Martín y Soler, including Titta (*Una cosa rara*), and Mozart (Figaro, Guglielmo in *Così*). An exceptional actor, with a wide vocal range, he immediately attracted Mozart's attention and Bocconio (*Lo sposo deluso*) was meant for him. He also sang Leporello in 1788. His last new role in Vienna was Count Robinson in Cimarosa's *Il matrimonio segreto* (1792).

Bernasconi, Antonia (1741–1803), German soprano (she took her stepfather's surname), the first Alceste in Gluck's opera (1767). Mozart intended her for Ninetta in *La finta semplice*, and she sang Aspasia (*Mitridate*) in Milan (1770). After a period in London she returned to Vienna about 1780, continuing to sing Gluck roles.

Böhm, Johann (?–1792), actor and theatre manager, who like Schikaneder performed and directed Singspiel. He took a troupe to Salzburg in 1779 and in 1780 produced a German version of *La finta giardiniera* in Augsburg. Mozart stayed with him in Frankfurt in 1790.

Bondini, Caterina (?), Italian soprano, married to Pasquale Bondini (?ca. 1737–89), singer and impresario. Pasquale managed the company in Prague when it gave *Figaro* in 1786, with Caterina as Susanna; in 1787 she created Zerlina in *Don Giovanni*.

Bonno, Giuseppe (1711–88), Italian composer, court composer in Vienna from 1739. By the time Mozart came to Vienna he was devoted mainly to teaching and administration. He was friendly, but the Mozarts vainly hoped his death might release a post for Wolfgang.

Born, Ignaz von (1742–91), mineralogist. From 1776 he had court appointments in Vienna, as museum curator and advisor on mining. Mozart wrote a cantata (K. 471) to honour his elevation to the nobility, performed at the Masonic lodge 'Zur wahren Eintracht', of which Born was master. In 1784 he published an article on Egyptian mysteries, but quitted the brotherhood. Nevertheless, he is sometimes assumed to be the model for Sarastro in *Die Zauberflöte*.

Breitkopf, music publishers in Leipzig whose large catalogue of symphonies included works by the Haydns and Mozarts. Leopold contacted them about his son to no effect, but in 1798 the firm, now Breitkopf & Härtel, announced a complete edition of Mozart's works. This project was never finished, although they later published the first complete edition (1877–83), Otto Jahn's biography, and Köchel's catalogue.

Bridi, Giuseppe (1763–1836), Italian banker and amateur musician who may have met Mozart in Italy. He came to Vienna in 1781 and in 1786 sang the title role in *Idomeneo*.

Brunetti, Antonio (1744–86), Salzburg court violinist, married to Maria Josepha Judith Lipp. He may have been the performer of Mozart's violin concertos; but during his stay in Vienna (1781) Mozart distrusted him.

Bullinger, Abbé Franz Joseph (1744–1810), Jesuit who became a teacher in the Arco family when his order was closed (1773). He befriended the Mozarts and helped with travel money in 1777; he supported the family when Mozart's mother died.

Burney, Charles (1726–1814), English musician and music historian who reported on Mozart as Wunderkind. They met again in Italy in 1770, but Burney did not visit Salzburg when in Austria (1772).

Bussani (née Sardi), Dorotea (1763–?after 1810), Italian soprano, married in 1786 to Francesco (1743–ca. 1810?), Italian bass in the Burgheater troupe from 1783. They created in *Figaro*, Cherubino and Bartolo (doubling Antonio), and in *Così*, Despina and Alfonso. In 1788 Francesco sang Masetto and the Commendatore in *Don Giovanni*, and Dorotea created Fidalma in *Il matrimonio segreto*. Francesco stage-managed *Der Schauspieldirektor*. They later sang in Italy, Lisbon, and London.

Calvesi, Vincenzo (?), Italian tenor, in the Burgtheater troupe in 1785–86 and ca. 1790; the first Ferrando in *Così*. He and Kelly were the Eufemio twins in Storace's *Gli equivoci*, and he sang in the two ensembles Mozart wrote for Bianchi's *La villanella rapita*.

Cannabich, Christian (1731–98), violinist, conductor, and composer, Konzertmeister in Mannheim until he removed to Munich. Cannabich met Mozart as a child, and welcomed him cordially in 1777. Mozart admired his musicianship and taught piano to his daughter Rosina ('Rosa', b. 1764); the slow movement of the sonata K. 309 was intended as her 'portrait'. Cannabich helped preparations for *Idomeneo* and probably directed the premiere with Mozart himself. He composed a commemorative ode with citations from Mozart's music.

Carl Theodor (1724–99), Elector Palatine from 1742 and Elector of Bavaria from 1777. His court in Mannheim was musically the most brilliant of the age, staffed by composers such as Johann Stamitz, Cannabich, and Holzbauer. He appreciated Mozart and admired *Idomeneo* but stopped well short of offering him an appointment.

Cavalieri (née Cavalier), Caterina (1755–1801), soprano, the first Konstanze. A pupil and favourite of Salieri (if not his mistress, as often stated), she transferred from the Nationalsingspiel to the Italian company at the Burgtheater in 1783. She sang Mlle Silberklang in *Der Schauspieldirektor*, as Elvira in the Vienna *Don Giovanni* she was given the aria 'Mi tradì'.

She also sang in *Davidde penitente* and was the Countess in the 1789 *Figaro*.

Ceccarelli, Francesco (1752–1814), Italian castrato employed at Salzburg from 1777. He was friendly with the Mozarts and is often mentioned in the letters, particularly in Vienna in 1781. Mozart composed a scena (K. 374) for him, and in letters praised him above other singers.

Cigna-Santi, Vittorio Amadeo (ca. 1730–?95), librettist of *Mitridate, re di Ponto*, adapted from Parini's translation of Racine and set by Gasparini in Turin and Mozart in Milan (1770).

Clementi, Muzio (1752–1832), Italian composer and keyboard virtuoso, who spent much of his adult life in England. He encountered Mozart at the end of 1781 when Joseph II arranged a keyboard 'duel'; his admiration for Mozart was not reciprocated. Clementi is a major figure in the development of keyboard music, not only in Britain.

Colloredo, Count Hieronymus (1732–1812), the last Prince-Archbishop of Salzburg. He was elected in 1772, and left before French troops arrived in 1800. His difficulties with the Mozarts are symptomatic of an autocratic manner which was combined with Enlightenment ideas paralleling those of Joseph II.

Coltellini, Celeste (1760–1829), Italian soprano and artist, daughter of Marco (1719–77). Marco produced librettos for Gluck, Gassmann, and Mozart (*La finta semplice*) in Vienna and reformist works for Traetta. Celeste was in the buffo troupe at the Burgtheater in 1785 and sang in the ensembles Mozart composed for Bianchi's *La villanella rapita*.

Consoli, Tommaso (ca. 1753–after 1811), Italian alto castrato, employed in Munich and probably the first Ramiro in *La finta giardiniera* in 1775; he visited Salzburg to sing Aminta in *Il re pastore*. He ended his career in the Sistine Chapel choir.

Dal Prato, Vincenzo (1756–ca. 1828), Italian soprano castrato, the first Idamante in *Idomeneo*. Although he had several years' experience, he appeared to Mozart under-trained, a poor actor, and a slow learner.

Da Ponte, Abbé Lorenzo (né Emanuele Conegliano, 1749–1838), Italian librettist. A baptized Jew (his name taken from the bishop of Ceneda), he lived the life of a minor Casanova with a gift for satirical verse, and had to escape scandal in Venice. In Vienna he impressed Joseph II and became poet to the opera. He wrote librettos for Salieri, Storace, Martín y Soler, Righini, and, for Mozart, *Figaro*, *Don Giovanni*, and *Così fan tutte*. He may have contributed to *Lo sposo deluso*, adapted words for *Davidde penitente*, and provided texts for the 1786 *Idomeneo*. After Joseph's death he and his then mistress Ferrarese were dismissed. He later married an Englishwoman. He had scant success in London and emigrated to the United States in 1805, becoming professor of Italian at Columbia university. His memoirs are indispensable but unreliable, and different versions are inconsistent.

Dauer, Johann Ernst (1746–1812), German tenor at the Burgtheater, the first Pedrillo in *Die Entführung*. He continued to play in Singspiel at the Kärntnertortheater.

Dejean, Ferdinand (1731–97), businessman, doctor and flautist, who took lessons from Wendling at the time Mozart was in Mannheim (1777). Dejean commissioned sets of concertos and quartets, but Mozart fulfilled less than half the commission and received 96, rather than 200, gulden. They may have met again in Vienna in the early 1780s.

Dittersdorf, Carl Ditters von (1739–99), Viennese composer mainly of chamber music, symphonies, and Singspiel, who had worked with Gluck. According to Kelly he played second violin to Haydn in Mozart's quartets. His *Doktor und Apotheker* (1786) was one of the most successful Singspiels from the Kärntnertortheater repertoire.

Dušek (Duschek, née Hambacher), Josepha (1754–1824), Bohemian soprano, wife of Franz Xaver Dušek, a composer based in Prague. The couple visited Salzburg in 1777 and made friends with the Mozarts. Mozart stayed at their summerhouse, Villa Bertramka, in 1787, finishing *Don Giovanni*. Mozart wrote two arias for her (K. 272, 528) and she took part in performances on his North German tour of 1789.

Esterházy, noble Hungarian family. Mozart had no connection to its most famous member, Haydn's Prince Nicholas, but Count Johann Baptist Esterházy was a fellow mason and patron, and hosted several of Mozart's concert performances in Vienna.

Ettore, Guglielmo d' (ca. 1740–71), Italian tenor, sang the title-role in *Mitridate*, including an aria from the earlier setting by Gasparini and making Mozart rewrite his entrance aria.

Eybler, Joseph Leopold von (1765–1846), composer, student of Albrechtsberger, for whom Mozart wrote a warm testimonial in 1790. Eybler worked on the Requiem, but abandoned it to Süssmayr, whose completion Eybler directed in a memorial for Haydn. His contributions to the Requiem have been adopted in alternative completions.

Ferrarese del Bene, Adriana (1755–ca. 1800?), Italian soprano, the first Fiordiligi. A student of Sacchini, she came to Vienna after singing in London and Milan. In 1789, she sang Susanna, with two new arias. She became Da Ponte's mistress and Fiordiligi was written to exploit her wide range and virtuosity. She was dismissed by Leopold II and pursued her career in Poland and Italy.

Firmian, Count Karl Joseph (1718–82), diplomat, man of learning, and governor-general of Lombardy from 1759; nephew to Archbishop Firmian of Salzburg. Firmian was helpful to the Mozarts on the first Italian journey, when he was responsible for the commission for *Mitridate*.

Fischer, Ludwig (1745–1825), bass. Mozart was profoundly impressed by his ability, not just his low notes, and developed the role of Osmin for him. He planned to rewrite the role of Idomeneo for him, with a tenor Idamante, but no production was commanded. Mozart also wrote for Fischer the aria K. 432 (probably) and (certainly) his second setting of 'Alcandro lo confesso' (K. 512).

Freystädtler, Franz Jacob (1761–1841), composer. He came to Vienna from Salzburg, via Munich, in 1786, where he studied with Mozart; some of his exercises survive and are published in NMA with those of Ployer. Mozart referred to him as Gaulimauli. He was the first composer asked to complete the Requiem.

Gamerra, Giovanni de (1743–1803), Italian poet at the ducal theatre in Milan from 1770–4, when he wrote the libretto for *Lucio Silla*. He spent two periods in Vienna, in the 1770s and after Mozart's death, and translated *Die Zauberflöte* into Italian.

Gebler, Baron Tobias Philipp (1726–86), government official and playwright. Gebler was a freemason, master of a Viennese lodge from 1784. His *Thamos, König in Aegypten* (1773, based on Terrasson's novel *Sethos*) was provided with choruses by Mozart ca. 1773 and expanded to include melodrama, possibly for Böhm's company (ca. 1779).

Gerl, Barbara (née Reisinger, 1770–1806), soprano, married to Franz Xaver (1764–1827), erstwhile student of Leopold Mozart, bass singer and composer; members of Schikaneder's company, the first Papagena and Sarastro. Barbara played Lubanara in *Der Stein der Weisen* and was thus the cat in the duet contributed by Mozart; Franz Xaver composed part of that opera. Mozart wrote his last concert aria for him (K. 612). He sang other Mozart roles in German including Figaro.

Gieseke, Karl Ludwig (Metzler, Johann Georg, 1761–1833), actor, author, and scientist who emerged from obscurity as jobbing poet and actor with Schikaneder (his role in *Die Zauberflöte* was first slave) to become professor of mineralogy in Dublin. His claim to be the author of the libretto is impossible to test.

Gluck, Christoph Willibald (1714–87), Austrian composer and like Mozart a Papal Knight. Already eminent when Mozart first came to Vienna, Gluck was unfairly suspected of intriguing against the production of *La finta semplice*. In 1781, the production of *Die Entführung* was postponed because Gluck operas were revived, but Gluck later praised it. His death released funds some of which were diverted to appoint Mozart Imperial Kammermusikus in 1787.

Goldhahn, Joseph Odilo, Viennese Freemason and businessman who may have lent Mozart money and who witnessed the inventory of Mozart's estate; he is referred to in a number of letters including that of 8–9 October 1791.

Gottlieb, Anna (1774–1856), actress and soprano. Her parents were actors in the Burgtheater, where, aged twelve, she created Barbarina in *Figaro*. She joined Schikaneder's company in 1789, and created Pamina in *Die Zauberflöte*.

Grimm, Baron Friedrich Melchior (1723–1807), diplomat and man of letters. Resident in Paris from 1749, he mixed with the philosophes and contributed to the controversy over the Italian buffo company in 1752–53. He compiled *Correspondance littéraire* (1753–73), a manuscript bulletin on French culture widely distributed to European courts. On their first visits to Paris the Mozarts benefited from his contacts and his favourable accounts of them; they expected as much in 1778 and were disillusioned. Although Grimm offered hospitality to Mozart, he told Leopold that there was no future for him in Paris.

Guardasoni, Domenico (ca. 1731–1806), Italian impresario in Prague, deputy to Bondini at the time of *Don Giovanni*. When Salieri declined, he passed the commission for *La clemenza di Tito* on to Mozart.

Gyrowetz, Adalbert (1763–1850), Bohemian composer, whom Mozart assisted by performing a symphony at a subscription concert in Vienna. Much travelled in his early career, he found another of his symphonies published in Paris as Haydn's; he eventually settled in Vienna.

Haffner, Salzburg merchant family, friendly to the Mozarts. They are immortalized in the names given to the serenade K. 250 and the symphony K. 385.

Hagenauer, Johann Lorenz (1712–92), Salzburg merchant, friend and landlord of the Mozarts from 1747–73. Hagenauer helped Leopold with financial arrangements and received over sixty letters forming a diary of the family's travels in the 1760s. Mozart composed a Mass (K. 66) when Hagenauer's son Kajetan entered the priesthood.

Haibel, Sophie (née Weber, 1763–1846, married 1807), Mozart's sister-in-law, youngest of the Webers, she left an account of his death; following that of her own husband, she lived with Constanze in Salzburg.

Hasse, Johann Adolf (1699–1783), the leading opera seria composer of his generation and a favourite of the Imperial court poet Metastasio. He recognised Mozart's genius; he may have tried to persuade the authorities to accept *La finta semplice*; in 1771, his last opera *Ruggiero* was overshadowed by *Ascanio in Alba*.

Hässler, Johann Wilhelm (1747–1822), composer and keyboard player, whom Mozart disparaged; they met in Dresden in 1789 for musical 'duels', but Mozart found him no better than Albrechtsberger on the organ and Josepha Auernhammer on piano.

Hatzfeld, Count August Clemens von (1754–87), priest and amateur violinist, student of Vachon. In Vienna, he befriended Mozart and played his quartets. For the performance of *Idomeneo* in 1786, Mozart composed a new aria (K. 490) with violin obbligato for Hatzfeld, and he was deeply unhappy at his death.

Hatzfeld, Countess Hortensia (1750–1813), Viennese patron of music and amateur singer and pianist, sister-in-law of the above. She was part of the brilliant circle in which Mozart moved in the early 1780s, their connection culminating in the performance of *Idomeneo*, in which she sang Elektra. Through Rhineland connections (she was the niece of the Elector and Archbishop of Köln), she became a patron of Beethoven.

Haydn, Franz Joseph (1732–1809), composer. Distinguished like Mozart in every principal genre, his European reputation rested on his symphonies and chamber music, at least until the composition of *Die Schöpfung* (The Creation). His operas were mainly confined to the Eszterháza theatre. While visiting Vienna, he played the quartets dedicated to him, and praised Mozart to Leopold.

Haydn, Johann Michael (1737–1806), composer, brother of the above, spent most of his life (from 1763) in Salzburg as Konzertmeister, composing sacred and secular music. The Mozarts' view of him was ambivalent, but Wolfgang helped him by composing violin and viola duets in 1783. He performed a symphony of Haydn in Vienna with his own slow introduction (the work once assumed to Mozart's and published as No. 37). Mozart was probably influenced by Haydn in his sacred music and symphonies.

Heina, Franz Joseph (1729–90), French horn player and publisher who befriended the Mozarts in 1763 and supported Wolfgang in Paris in 1778, obtaining a German doctor and priest for his mother.

Henneberg, Johann Baptist (1768–1822), composer, from 1790 Kapellmeister in Schikaneder's company at the Theater auf der Wieden. He wrote much of the music for *Der Stein der Weisen* (1790), some of it very good, and directed rehearsals for *Die Zauberflöte*, conducting it after the third performance.

Heufeld, Franz Reinhard von (1731–95), author and theatre administrator in Vienna. In 1778 he suggested Mozart write an opera for the Nationalsingspiel: Mozart dismissed the idea (letter of 4 February 1778), but followed this advice a year later, writing *Zaide*.

Hofdemel, Franz (ca. 1755–91), Viennese lawyer whose wife Maria Magdalena had piano lessons with Mozart. A fellow-mason, he loaned money to Mozart in 1789. On 6 December 1791 he attacked his pregnant wife, then killed himself. She survived, was granted a pension by Leopold II, and bore a posthumous son. The attack occurred the day after Mozart's death, leading to an unfounded rumour that he and Maria Magdalena had been having an affair, and that Hofdemel had poisoned Mozart.

Hofer, Josepha (née Weber? 1759–1819), soprano, the first Queen of Night; Franz de Paula (1755–96), violinist. Josepha, eldest child of Fridolin and Caecilia Weber, married Hofer, a friend of the Mozarts, in 1788. Mozart wrote slightingly of her to highlight the virtues of Constanze. Josepha was in Schikaneder's company from its inception, but because of pregnancy did not sing in *Der Stein der Weisen*. Mozart composed an aria for her for a Paisiello opera (K. 580). Franz Hofer travelled with Mozart to Frankfurt in 1790.

Hoffmeister, Franz Anton (1754–1812), Viennese composer and music publisher. He published some first editions of Mozart's chamber works including the piano quartet K. 478, the Trio K. 496, two violin sonatas, and the string quartet K. 499, which bears his name. He helped Mozart financially, but he sold his rights in the music to Artaria after Mozart's death.

Holzbauer, Ignaz (1711–83), composer who became a Kapellmeister in Mannheim from 1753–78. Mozart admired his *Günther von Schwarzburg* (1777), and some of his sacred music; in Paris he supplied additional music to Holzbauer's 'Miserere' for the Concert Spirituel.

Hummel, Johann Nepomuk (1778–1837), composer and pianist, born in Bratislava and later Kapellmeister for the Esterházy family and in Weimar. Hummel resided in Mozart's house as his student in ca. 1786–87 before being toured as a prodigy.

Ippold (or Yppold), Franz Armand d' (ca. 1730–90), teacher and military councillor in Salzburg. A friend of the Mozarts, he wanted to marry Nannerl, and she, though much younger, reciprocated his feelings; writing from Vienna, Mozart urged them to come there as a couple.

Jacquin, Gottfried von (1767–92), Viennese civil servant and amateur musician, and an admiring friend and pupil of Mozart. He was the recipient of effusive letters about *Figaro* and *Don Giovanni* in Prague. He may have composed music later published as Mozart's; in turn, Mozart wrote him an aria (K. 513), and composed two songs (K. 529, 530) for him, the latter published as Jacquin's.

Jenamy, Victoire (?), French pianist, daughter of Jean-Georges Noverre. She came to Salzburg in 1777, and Mozart wrote the concerto K. 271 for her. A misreading of her name led to her being known until recently as Mlle 'Jeunehomme'.

Kelly (O'Kelly), Michael (1762–1826), Irish tenor, the first Basilio and Curzio in *Figaro*. He studied in Italy and joined the opera buffa company in Vienna in 1783, creating numerous roles including one of the twins in Storace's *Gli equivoci* (1786), a few months after *Figaro*. He returned to London, and had long career as singer and impresario. In 1826 he published *Reminiscences* including anecdotes about Mozart.

Kirchgässner, Maria Anna (1769–1808), performer on the glass harmonica, blind from childhood. In 1791 Mozart composed two pieces for her (Adagio K.356=617a, Adagio and Rondo K. 617).

Kozeluch, Leopold (1747–1818), Bohemian composer, pianist, teacher, and publisher, resident in Vienna from 1778. He declined to replace Mozart in Salzburg in 1781. Mozart told Puchberg in July 1789 that Kozeluch would publish the 'Prussian' quartets. Kozeluch has been branded as one who intrigued against Mozart, but the evidence is tenuous.

Lange (née Weber), Aloysia (ca. 1760–1839), soprano, Mozart's sister-in-law, and Joseph (1751–1831), actor and painter. Aloysia, second of the Weber sisters, attracted Mozart in Mannheim in 1777; he proposed to promote her, and composed two arias for her. She snubbed him on his return journey. In Vienna she became a highly paid singer at the Burgtheater and married Lange. Mozart continued to compose difficult arias for her; in 1785 Leopold commented on the discrepancy between her loud held notes and soft ornamental singing and high notes. She sang Konstanze in revivals of *Die Entführung*, Mme Herz in *Der Schauspieldirektor*, and Anna in the Vienna *Don Giovanni*.

Laschi, Luisa (ca. 1760–ca. 90?), also Mombelli (m. late 1786), Italian soprano. She joined the buffo troupe at the Burgtheater in 1784 and again in 1786, creating the Countess in *Figaro*, and sang Zerlina in the Vienna *Don Giovanni*.

Legros, Joseph (1739–91), French tenor. He had a long career at the Paris Opéra, and directed the Concert Spirituel from 1777. He was hospitable to Mozart in 1778, but neglected to programme the wind sinfonia concertante. He commissioned the additional choruses to Holzbauer's Miserere, and the symphony now known as the 'Paris' (K.297), persuading Mozart to write a new slow movement.

Leutgeb, Joseph (1732–1811), horn player. Based in Salzburg, he was internationally known as a virtuoso by the 1760s. He moved to Vienna in 1777 and adopted his father-in-law's occupation of cheese-monger. In the 1780s Mozart composed a quintet and three concertos, central to the horn-player's repertory, which mark considerable esteem for his playing (though Leutgeb was the victim of his banter). A fourth concerto was unfinished.

Lichnowsky, Count, later Prince, Karl (1761–1841), patron to whom Mozart may have given lessons. He accompanied Mozart to North Germany in 1789 and sued him in 1791 for a large debt. There is no record of it being repaid, and he may have let the matter drop after Mozart's death. He became a patron of Beethoven.

Linley, Thomas (1756–78), English composer, son of Thomas Linley senior (1733–95). A prodigy on the violin, he became friends with Mozart in Florence in 1770. His promising career as a composer, mainly of theatre music, was ended by a boating accident.

Lodron (née Arco), Countess Antonia (1738–80), sister of Karl Joseph Arco (q.v.). Herself a pianist, she had her daughters taught by Leopold and Nannerl. Mozart composed a pair of divertimenti (K. 247, 287) for her, and the concerto for three pianos (K. 242).

Mandini, family of singers: Maria (née Soleri de Vesian), French soprano, wife of Stefano Mandini (1750–ca. 1810), Italian baritone. They were in the Burgtheater buffo troupe from 1783. Stefano played Count Almaviva in Paisiello's *Il barbiere di Siviglia* and in *Figaro*; Maria played Marcellina. They left for Naples before the Vienna production of *Don Giovanni*, a role for which Mandini, an excellent actor, was obviously suited. Paolo Mandini (1757–1842), Stefano's brother, appeared in Vienna during the 1780s but apparently not in Mozart's operas.

Manzuoli, Giovanni (ca. 1720–82), Italian castrato who taught singing to Mozart in London, and appeared in the title-role of *Ascanio in Alba* (Milan, 1771).

Marchand, Heinrich (1769–?1812 or after), German violinist and pianist, and his sister Maria Margarethe ('Gretl', 1768–1800), a singer, lived and studied with Leopold Mozart from 1781–84. Heinrich was employed in Salzburg where he played Mozart's concerto K.466 in 1786.

Marchetti-Fantozzi, Maria (1767–after 1897), Italian soprano, the first Vitellia in *La clemenza di Tito*, where Mozart exploits her exceptional range.

Martini, Giovanni Battista ('Padre' Martini, 1706–84), Italian composer, theorist and the most famous music teacher and music historian of his age. Mozart learned from him in 1770 and continued to esteem him highly, keeping in touch for several years and sending him music and a portrait.

Martín y Soler, Vicente (1754–1806), Spanish composer who composed three operas for Vienna with libretti by Da Ponte. He was on good terms with Mozart, who wrote a rude canon about him, and used one of his tunes in the supper scene of *Don Giovanni*. He subsequently worked in St Petersburg.

Mazzolà, Caterino (?1745–1806), Italian librettist. He befriended Da Ponte on his exile from Venice, and briefly succeeded him as court poet in Vienna in 1791, turning Metastasio's *La clemenza di Tito* into a 'real opera' for Mozart.

Mesmer, Franz Anton (1734–1815), Austrian doctor who lived in Vienna and possessed a theatre in which *Bastien und Bastienne* was performed in 1768. He later developed the healing method of 'animal magnetism' made fun of when Despina appears as a doctor in *Così fan tutte*.

Morella, Francesco (?), Italian tenor, Ottavio in the Vienna production of *Don Giovanni*, for whom Mozart composed 'Dalla sua pace'.

Mysliveček, Joseph (1737–81), Bohemian composer who studied in Italy and worked there for much of his career, composing operas and orchestral and chamber music. He met the Mozarts in Bologna (1770), then in Milan; Mozart visited him in hospital in Munich (1777) where he was suffering the effects of venereal disease.

Noverre, Jean-Georges (1727–1810), ballet master in Vienna and Paris, with Gasparo Angiolini responsible for the revolution in dramatic ballet. He choreographed *Les petits riens*, for which Mozart wrote most of the music; father of Victoire Jenamy.

Paisiello, Giovanni (1740–1816), Italian composer, greatly admired by Joseph II and later by Napoleon. His *Il barbiere di Siviglia*, premiered in St Petersburg and produced in Vienna in 1783, stimulated the composition of *Figaro*. *Il re Teodoro in Venezia* was commissioned for Vienna (1784). He expressed considerable admiration for Mozart.

Panzachi, Domenico (1733-after 1805), Italian tenor, in Munich from 1762 and the first Arbace in *Idomeneo*; Mozart inserted a new recitative ('Sventurata Sidon') to exploit his acting talent.

Paradis (Paradies), Maria Theresia (1759–1824), pianist and composer, blind from an early age; a patient of Mesmer. She visited Salzburg in 1783 and Mozart wrote a concerto for her, probably K. 456.

Parini, Giuseppe (1729–99), Italian poet, librettist of *Ascanio in Alba*.

Pichler, Karoline (née Greiner, 1769–1843), poet and musician, whose family knew Mozart, of whom she left reminiscences. Some of her verses were set by Schubert.

Ployer, Maria Anna Barbara von ('Babette') (1765–ca. 1810), pianist who studied piano and composition with Mozart; he wrote two piano concertos for her (K. 449, 453).

Ponziani, Felice (?) the first Leporello in *Don Giovanni*.

Puchberg, Johann Michael (1741–1822), Viennese merchant, a freemason, who loaned Mozart several small sums; dedicatee of the string trio K.563.

Pufendorf, Anna von (ca. 1757–1843), amateur soprano and promoter of domestic concerts. She sang Ilia in *Idomeneo* at the Auersperg theatre in 1786.

Pulini, Antonio (?), tenor, mentioned by Leopold on 30 January 1768 (with *La finta semplice* in mind); he sang Idamante in *Idomeneo* at the Auersperg theatre in 1786, with the new aria K. 490, and rewritten versions of the trio and quartet.

Punto, Giovanni (Stich, Jan Václav, 1746–1803), horn player from Bohemia who also played violin and composed; Mozart met him in Paris and he would have played in the lost wind Sinfonia concertante.

Raab, Maria Anna ('Mitzerl', 1710–88), friend of the Mozarts in Salzburg, their landlord in the 'Tanzmeisterhaus' from 1773.

Raaff, Anton (1714–97), tenor, the first Idomeneo. He was in the service of Carl Theodor in Mannheim from 1770. He befriended Mozart in Mannheim and Paris and despite reservations about his age, and his singing and acting, Mozart wrote him the aria K. 295, and worked closely with him on the title-role of *Idomeneo*.

Ramm, Friedrich (1744–1811), oboist at Mannheim, then Munich, one of those for whom the lost sinfonia concertante was written for Paris. He played Mozart's concerto and the oboe quartet (K. 370) was written for him, as was the oboe part of *Idomeneo*.

Rauzzini, Venanzio (1746–1810), Italian castrato soprano and composer, the first Cecilio in *Lucio Silla*. Mozart wrote for him the solo motet *Exsultate jubilate*. He went to England in 1774, and taught Nancy Storace; he later composed a Requiem performed in London shortly after the British premiere of Mozart's.

Righini, Vincenzo (1756–1812), Italian composer and singing teacher. His first opera, *Don Giovanni* (Prague, 1776) was given in Vienna in 1777, in German. He worked in Vienna from 1780, teaching singing to Princess Elisabeth of Württemburg, and had three operas performed at the Burgtheater: *Armida* (1782), *L'incontro aspettato* (1785), and *Il Demogorgone* (text by Da Ponte, 1786). He left Vienna for Mainz in 1787.

Ritter, Georg Wenzel (1748–1808), bassoonist known to Mozart at Mannheim, Paris, and Munich (see Ramm).

Rodolphe, Jean-Joseph (1730–1812), Strasbourg violinist and composer, in Paris from 1767; he befriended Mozart in 1778 and gained him the offer of an organist's post at Versailles.

Rosenberg-Orsini, Count Franz Xaver Wolf (1723–96), diplomat and administrator, director of court theatres in Vienna from 1776–91. The Mozarts first met him in the service of the Grand Duke of Tuscany (1770) and with Archduke Maximilian in Salzburg (1775). In Vienna, he encouraged Mozart in connection with *Die Entführung*, and with opera buffa, but he disliked Da Ponte (preferring the poet Giambattista Casti).

Salieri, Antonio (1750–1825), Italian composer brought to Vienna by Gassmann, and succeeding him as court composer and conductor of Italian opera (mainly opera buffa) in 1774. His connection with Gluck led to the composition of three French operas for Paris; the last, *Tarare*, was converted into the Italian *Axur* by Da Ponte (Vienna, 1788). Other important premieres in Mozart's time included *Prima la musica*, *La grotta di Trofonio*, and *La cifra*. He declined the libretto which became *Così fan tutte* and the commission for the coronation opera in 1791; he used Mozart's music for the coronation ceremonies of 1790–91 and conducted one of the late symphonies. He later taught Beethoven and Schubert.

Saporiti, Teresa (1763–1869), Italian soprano, the first Donna Anna. She was in the Prague company from 1782 to 1788 and was possibly related by marriage to the impresario Bondini. Little is known of the remainder of her career. Her name was punned on in the supper scene ('O che piatto saporito'/'what a tasty dish').

Schachtner, Johann Andreas (1731–95), trumpeter, violinist, and writer, active in Salzburg from 1754. He helped adapt the librettos of *Bastien und Bastienne* and *Zaide*, contributed additional text to Gebler's *Thamos*, and made a translation of *Idomeneo*. His reminiscences of Mozart's childhood, sent to Nannerl after Wolfgang died, are a unique anecdotal source.

Schack, Benedikt (1758–1826), tenor and composer, the first Tamino. After working as a Kapellmeister in Silesia, he joined Schikaneder's company in 1786. With Gerl and Henneberg, he contributed music to *Der Stein der Weisen*. His wife Elisabeth sang Third Lady. A good friend of Mozart, he is one of those alleged to have sung parts of the Requiem round his deathbed.

Schikaneder, Emanuel (1751–1812), impresario, actor and writer. He was directing a troupe from 1778 and visited Salzburg in 1780. He rented the Freihaustheater (Theater auf der Wieden) in Vienna, writing and producing Singspiel, and taking leading comic roles (Lubano in *Der Stein der Weisen*, Papageno in *Die Zauberflöte*). His brother and wife were also in the troupe. Frequently in financial trouble, he kept bouncing back, and in 1801 opened the Theater an der Wien, but his life ended in financial disaster and madness.

Schrattenbach, Sigismond Christoph (1698–1771), Dean of Salzburg from 1750 and Prince Archbishop of Salzburg from 1753 to his death; Mozart's first employer.

Seeau, Count Joseph Anton (1713–99), theatre intendant in Munich, who remained in post after Carl Theodor became Elector of Bavaria. Seeau was involved with the commissions for *La finta giardiniera* and *Idomeneo*, but Mozart distrusted him.

Stadler, Anton (1753–1812), clarinettist who inspired Mozart. The Serenade K. 361 was performed at his benefit concert in 1784. He also played the basset-horn, alongside his brother Johann, and had a modified clarinet that descended a third lower (now called 'basset-clarinet') for which Mozart composed his quintet and concerto, and an obbligato in *La clemenza di Tito*.

Stadler, Abbé Maximilian (1748–1833), cleric, musician, and music historian. He trained as a priest at Melk and was later at other monasteries including Kremsmünster. He heard Mozart play at Melk in 1767 and met him in Vienna. At the request of Constanze, he reviewed Mozart's surviving manuscripts, prepared a catalogue, and completed fragments for publication. In the 1820s he participated in the controversy concerning the authenticity of the Requiem.

Stein, Johann Andreas (1728–92), piano and organ builder resident in Augsburg. Mozart particularly liked his pianos and played one in his contest with Clementi (but his own was by Walter). Stein's business was carried on in Vienna by his daughter Nanette Streicher.

Stephanie, Johann Gottlieb (1741–1800, 'the Younger' to distinguish him from his half-brother Christian Gottlob), actor and dramatist. He met the Mozarts no later than 1773, and in 1781, in charge of the German opera company in Vienna, he gained Mozart the commission and adapted the libretto for *Die Entführung*. He also wrote *Der Schauspieldirektor*.

Stoll, Anton (1747–1805), choirmaster at Baden near Vienna, for whom Mozart composed *Ave verum corpus* (K. 618).

Storace, Ann Selina ('Nancy', 1765–1817), English soprano, the first Susanna. She studied with Rauzzini before visiting Italy where she made her stage début aged fourteen. She sang at the Burgtheater from 1783, and Mozart intended her for Eugenia (*Lo sposo deluso*). She sang Rosina in *Il barbiere di Siviglia* but Susanna in *Figaro*. She created roles by Salieri (*La grotta di Trofonio*, *Prima la musica*), Martín y Soler (*Una cosa rara*), and her brother Stephen. For her farewell concert Mozart composed the scena with piano obbligato (K. 505). She travelled home with her brother, Attwood, and Kelly, and made a career in Italian and English opera in London.

Storace, Stephen (1762–96), English composer, brother of Ann Selina. Two of his operas were produced at the Burgtheater: *Gli sposi malcontenti* (1785), during the first performance of which (1 June) Nancy lost her voice, and *Gli equivoci* (1786). A promising career in London opera was cut short by his premature death.

Süssmayr, Franz Xaver (1766–1803), composer, in Vienna from 1788, where he studied with Salieri. From about 1790 he became attached to Mozart and may have assisted him by writing recitatives for *La clemenza di Tito*. He completed the Requiem and part of the D major horn concerto (K. 412).

Swieten, Baron Gottfried van (1733–1803), Imperial official (librarian and censor), amateur composer, and enthusiast for older music. At his Sunday salon from 1781 Mozart played, studied, and arranged works by Handel and Bach. Swieten assisted Constanze at the time of Mozart's death and funeral despite having just been dismissed by Leopold II.

Teyber, Therese (1760–1830), Austrian soprano, the first Blonde. She was a member of a family of Viennese musicians involved in court music, in the Nationalsingspiel, and in Schikaneder's company; she took over the role of Zerlina from Laschi. Anton Teyber (1756–1816) succeeded Mozart as Imperial Kammermusikus.

Thun (Thun-Hohenstein), Countess Wilhelmine (1744–1800), wife of Count Franz (1734–1801) met Mozart in childhood and became one his most important patrons in the 1780s; he frequently visited her house and she subscribed to his concerts. Her father-in-law Count Johann (1711–88) was Mozart's host in Linz and Prague.

Trattner, Johann Thomas von (1717–98), Viennese businessman, owner of the Trattnerhof where Mozart lived and gave concerts in 1784–85; he and his wife Maria Theresia (a pupil of Mozart) stood as godparents to his children, and she received the dedication of the Fantasia and Sonata in C minor (K. 475/457).

Valesi, Giovanni (1735–1816), German tenor, teacher of Adamberger; he sang the High Priest in *Idomeneo*.

Vanhal, Johann Baptist (1739–1813), Bohemian composer in Vienna from 1761 and again from 1780. He was a prolific composer of symphonies and chamber music. According to Kelly he played in string quartets with Mozart, Haydn, and Dittersdorf.

Varesco, Abbate Gianbattista (1735–1805), chaplain to the Archbishop of Salzburg and librettist of *Idomeneo* and *L'oca del Cairo*.

Villeneuve, Luisa (?–?), soprano, the first Dorabella in *Così*. She joined the Vienna troupe in 1789, and Mozart wrote her three substitute arias (K. 578, 582, 583) for operas by Cimarosa and Martín y Soler.

Vogler, Abbé Georg Joseph (1749–1814), composer and chaplain, later vice-Kapellmeister in Mannheim, despised by Mozart as an 'incompetent' and 'jester'; later the teacher of Mozart's younger son.

Waldstätten, Baroness Martha Elisabeth was hospitable to Mozart in the early Vienna period. Leopold was anxious to meet this 'woman of my heart, since I, *invisus*, have been the man of her heart' (letter to Nannerl, 16 Apr 1785, referring to correspondence of 1781–82).

Walsegg-Stuppach, Count Franz (1763–1827), musical patron. He owned an estate outside Vienna, and property in the city where Michael Puchberg lived. He organised regular chamber-music sessions and commissioned music through an agent, which he then presented as his own. This harmless absurdity (which deceived nobody) took on a sinister aspect when he commissioned Mozart's Requiem as a memorial to his wife, his agent becoming the 'grey stranger' of legend.

Walter, Anton (1752–1826), Viennese piano and organ builder. Mozart possessed a Walter piano and used it in his subscription concerts. The instrument passed from Constanze to her son Carl Thomas, who gave it in 1856 to the Salzburg Mozarteum.

Weber, Caecilia, Mozart's mother-in-law, married to Fridolin; their daughters were Josepha (see Hofer), Aloysia (see Lange), Constanze Mozart, and Sophie (see Haibel). They met Mozart in Mannheim; Fridolin died soon after moving to Vienna. Mozart was her lodger in 1781; relations became strained in connection with Constanze but recovered after their marriage.

Weigl, Joseph (1766–1846), Austrian composer, godson of Joseph Haydn and pupil of Salieri. He attended Swieten's Sunday afternoons and admired Mozart; he played in the Burgtheater orchestra from 1785. He wrote over thirty operas, his greatest success being *Die Schweizerfamilie* (1809).

Wendling, German family of musicians based in Mannheim, then Munich. Johann Baptist (1723–97) played flute and would have played the lost sinfonia concertante in Paris. His wife Dorothea (née Spurni, 1736–1811) was the first Ilia in *Idomeneo*; Mozart had written her the aria K. 295a. Mozart enjoyed their company and that of their children. Their daughter Elisabeth (1752–94), a mistress of Carl Theodor, was a singer for whom Mozart composed two French songs (K. 307–8=284d, 295b). Franz

Anton (1729–86), brother of Johann, was a violinist, also married to a singer, Elisabeth (née Sarselli, 1746–86), the first Elektra in *Idomeneo*.

Wetzlar von Plankenstern, Baron Raimund (1752–1810), the Mozarts' landlord in Vienna early in their marriage, a supporter of the subscription concerts, and godfather to their first child.

Winter, Peter von (1754–1825), German composer. From Vienna he passed information unfavourable to Mozart's character to Leopold. He later had several operas performed by Schikaneder's troupe.

Winter, Sebastian (1743–1815), manservant of the Mozarts on their travels to Paris; in 1784 Leopold arranged through Winter that his current employer Prince Fürstenberg should buy some of Mozart's works, but they failed to negotiate a regular income.

Zinzendorf, Count Johann Karl (1739–1813), government official and diarist. His incessant attendance at the opera is recorded in his immense diary, written in French; there are many comments on singers and a few on Mozart. The information gained (including the state of the weather on the day of Mozart's funeral) is useful, but it would be a mistake to regard him as a guide to general opinion.

Select Bibliography

Abert, H. *W. A. Mozart: neu bearbeitete und erweiterte Ausgabe von Otto Jahns 'Mozart'*. Leipzig, 1919–21.

Allanbrook, W. J. *Rhythmic Gesture in Mozart: Le nozze di Figaro and Don Giovanni*. Chicago, 1983.

Anderson, E., trans. and ed. *The Letters of Mozart and his Family*. 3rd ed. Basingstoke, 1985.

Angermüller, R. *Mozart—Die Opern von der Uraufführung bis heute*. Fribourg, 1988. Translated by S. Spencer as *Mozart's Operas*. New York, 1988.

Angermüller, R., and O. Schneider. *Mozart Bibliographie*. Mozart-Jahrbuch, 1975 and supplements.

Bauer, W. A., O. E. Deutsch, and J. H. Eibl. *Mozart: Briefe und Aufzeichnungen*. Kassel, 1962–75.

Bauman, T. *W. A. Mozart: Die Entführung aus dem Serail*. Cambridge, 1987.

Brandenburg, S., ed. *Haydn, Mozart and Beethoven. Studies in the Music of the Classical Period. Essays in honour of Alan Tyson*. Oxford, 1998.

Branscombe, P. *W. A. Mozart: Die Zauberflöte*. Cambridge, 1991.

Braunbehrens, V. *Mozart in Wien*. Munich, 1986. Translated by T. Bell as *Mozart in Vienna, 1781–1791*. London, 1990.

Broder, N., ed. *Mozart Symphony in G minor*. New York, 1967.

Brown, B. A. *W. A. Mozart: Così fan tutte*. Cambridge, 1995.

Burney, C. *The Present State of Music in France and Italy*. 1771; *The Present State of Music in Germany and the Netherlands*. 1773. See Percy A. Scholes, *Dr Burney's Musical Tours in Europe*. 2 vols. London, 1959.

Carter, T. *W. A. Mozart: Le nozze di Figaro*. Cambridge, 1987.

Clive, P. *Mozart and his Circle*. New Haven and London, 1993.

Dent, E. J. *Mozart's Operas, a Critical Study*. London, 1913. Rev. 2nd ed., 1947.

Deutsch, O. E. *Mozart: die Dokumente seines Lebens, gesammelt und erläutert*. Kassel, 1961. Translated by E. Blom, P. Branscombe, and J. Noble as *Mozart: a Documentary Biography*. London, 1965.

Edge, D. 'Mozart's Fee for *Così fan tutte*'. *Journal of the Royal Musical Association* 116 (1991), 211–35.

Einstein, A. *Mozart. His Character, his Work*. Translated by Arthur Mendel and Nathan Broder. London, 1946.

Eisen, C., ed. *Mozart Studies*. Oxford, 1991.

———, ed. *New Mozart Documents. A Supplement to O. E. Deutsch's Documentary Biography*. London, 1991.

Gianturco, C. *Mozart's Early Operas*. London, 1981.

Goehring, E. J. *Three Modes of Perception in Mozart. The Philosophical, Pastoral, and Comic in* Così fan tutte. Cambridge, 2004.

Grayson, D., *Mozart: Piano Concertos Nos. 20 and 21.* Cambridge, 1998

Gutman, R. W., *Mozart. A Cultural Biography.* New York and London, 1999

Haberkamp, G. *Die Erstdrück der Werke von Wolfgang Amadeus Mozart.* Tutzing, 1986.

Halliwell, R. *The Mozart Family.* Oxford, 1998.

Head, M. *Orientalism, Masquerade and Mozart's Turkish Music.* London, 2000.

Heartz, D. *Haydn, Mozart, and the Viennese School. 1740–1780.* New York, 1995.

———. *Music in European Capitals. The Galant Style, 1720–1780.* New York, 2003.

———. *Mozart's Operas.* Edited, with contributing essays by T. Bauman. Berkeley and Los Angeles, 1990.

Hildesheimer, W. *Mozart.* Frankfurt am Main, 1977. Translated by M. Faber as *Mozart.* London, 1983.

Honolka, K. *Papageno.* Salzburg and Vienna, 1984. Translated by M. J. Wilde as *Papageno: Emanuel Schikaneder. Man of the Theater in Mozart's Time.* Portland, OR, 1984.

Hunter, M. *The Culture of Opera Buffa in Mozart's Vienna. A Poetics of Entertainment.* Princeton, 1999.

Hunter, M., and J. Webster, eds. *Opera Buffa in Mozart's Vienna.* Cambridge University Press, 1997.

Irving, J. *Mozart: the Haydn quartets.* Cambridge, 1998.

———. *Mozart's Piano concertos.* Aldershot, 2003.

———. *Mozart's Piano sonatas.* Cambridge, 1997.

Jahn, O. *W. A. Mozart.* Leipzig, 1856.

Keefe, S. P. *The Cambridge Companion to Mozart.* Cambridge, 2002.

———, ed. *Mozart's Piano Concertos: Dramatic Dialogue in the Age of Enlightenment.* Woodbridge and Rochester NY, 2001.

———, ed., *Mozart Studies.* Cambridge, 2006.

Kelly, M. *Reminiscences.* London, 1826. Repr. as *Solo Recital.* London, 1972.

Kerman, J., ed. *Mozart: Piano Concerto in C major, K. 503.* New York, 1970.

———. *Opera as Drama.* 2nd ed. London, 1988.

King, A. H. *A Mozart Legacy.* London, 1984.

Köchel, L. von. *Chronologisch-thematisches Verzeichnis sämtlicher Tonwerke* Wolfgang Amade Mozarts. Leipzig, 1862. 3rd ed. Edited by Alfred Einstein. Leipzig, 1937. 6th ed. Edited by F. Giegling, A. Weinmann, and G. Sievers. Leipzig, 1964.

Kunze, S. *Mozarts Opern.* Stuttgart, 1984.

Landon, H. C. R., ed. *The Mozart Compendium. A Guide to Mozart's Life and Music.* London, 1990.

———. *Mozart. The Golden Years, 1781–1791.* London, 1989.

———. *Mozart and Vienna.* New York, 1991.

———. *1791. Mozart's Last Year.* London, 1988.

Landon, H. C. R., and D. Mitchell, eds. *The Mozart Companion.* London, 1956.

Lawson, C. *Mozart: Clarinet Concerto.* Cambridge, 1996.

Link, D., ed. *Arias for Nancy Storace, Mozart's First Susanna.* Middleton, WI, 2002.

———, *Arias for Francesco Benucci, Mozart's First Figaro.* Middleton, WI, 2004.

———. *The National Court Theatre in Mozart's Vienna.* Oxford, 1998.

———, ed., with Judith Nagley. *Words About Mozart: Essays in Honour of Stanley Sadie.* Woodbridge, 2005.

Maunder, R. *Mozart's Requiem. On Preparing a New Edition.* Oxford, 1988.

Medici, N., and R. Hughes, eds. *A Mozart Pilgrimage. The Travel Diaries of Vincent and Mary Novello.* London, 1955.

Morris, J. M. ed. *On Mozart.* Woodrow Wilson Center and Cambridge, 1994.

Morrow, M. S. *Concert Life in Haydn's Vienna: Aspects of a Developing Musical and Social Institution.* Stuyvesant, NY, 1988.

Mozart, W. A. *Verzeichnüss aller meine Werke.* Manuscript list kept by Mozart from February 1784 as *Mozart's Thematic Catalogue. A Facsimile.* Edited by Albi Rosenthal and Alan Tyson. London, 1991.

Ratner, L. G. *Classic Music. Expression, Form and Style.* New York, 1980.

Rice, J. A. *Antonio Salieri and Viennese Opera.* Chicago, 1998.

———. *W. A. Mozart: La clemenza di Tito.* Cambridge, 1991.

Rosen, C. *The Classical Style. Haydn, Mozart, Beethoven.* London, 1971.

———. *Sonata Forms.* New York, 1980.

Rushton, J. *W. A. Mozart: Don Giovanni.* Cambridge, 1981.

———. *W. A. Mozart: Idomeneo.* Cambridge, 1993.

Sadie, S. *The New Grove Mozart.* Basingstoke, 1982.

———, ed. *Mozart and his Operas.* London, 2000.

———, ed. *Wolfgang Amadè Mozart. Essays on his Life and Music.* Oxford, 1996.

Schneider, O., and A. Algatzy. *Mozart-Handbuch. Chronik—Werk—Bibliographie.* Vienna, 1962.

Schroeder, D. *Mozart in Revolt. Strategies of Resistance, Mischief and Deception.* New Haven, 1999.

Sisman, E. *Mozart: 'Jupiter' Symphony.* Cambridge, 1993.

Solomon, M. *Mozart. A Life.* London, 1995.

Spaethling, R. *Mozart's Letters, Mozart's Life.* New York and London, 2000.

Stafford, W. *Mozart's Death.* London, 1991. Published in the United States as *The Mozart Legends.*

Steptoe, A. *The Mozart-Da Ponte Operas.* Oxford, 1988.

Till, N. *Mozart and the Enlightenment.* London, 1992.

Todd, R. L., and P. Williams. eds. *Mozart in Performance.* Cambridge, 1991.

Tyson, A. *Mozart: Studies of the Autograph Scores.* Cambridge, MA, 1987.

Wolff, C. *Mozart's Requiem: Historical and Analytical Studies.* Berkeley and Los Angeles, 1994.

Wyzewa, T. de, and G. de Saint Foix. *W.-A. Mozart: sa vie musical et son oeuvre.* Paris, 1936. Reprint, New York, 1980.

Zaslaw, N. *Mozart's Piano Concertos. Text, Context, Interpretation.* Ann Arbor, 1996.

———, ed. *Mozart's Symphonies: Context, Performance Practice, Reception.* Oxford, 1989.

Zenger, M., and O. E. Deutsch. *Mozart und seine Welt in zeitgenössischen Bildern/Mozart and his World in Contemporary Pictures.* Kassel, 1961.

Index